Richelieu and Mazarin

European History in Perspective
General Editor: Jeremy Black

Benjamin Arnold *Medieval Germany, 500–1300*
Ronald Asch *The Thirty Years' War*
Christopher Bartlett *Peace, War and the European Powers, 1814–1914*
Robert Bireley *The Refashioning of Catholicism, 1450–1700*
Donna Bohanan *Crown and Nobility in Early Modern France*
Arden Bucholz *Moltke and the German Wars, 1864–1871*
Patricia Clavin *The Great Depression, 1929–1939*
Paula Sutter Fichtner *The Habsburg Monarchy, 1490–1848*
Mark Galeotti *Gorbachev and his Revolution*
David Gates *Warfare in the Nineteenth Century*
Alexander Grab *Napoleon and the Transformation of Europe*
Martin P. Johnson *The Dreyfus Affair*
Peter Musgrave *The Early Modern European Economy*
J. L. Price *The Dutch Republic in the Seventeenth Century*
A. W. Purdue *The Second World War*
Christopher Read *The Making and Breaking of the Soviet System*
Francisco J. Romero-Salvado *Twentieth-Century Spain*
Matthew S. Seligmann and Roderick R. McLean
Germany from Reich to Republic, 1871–1918
Brendan Simms *The Struggle for Mastery in Germany, 1779–1850*
David J. Sturdy *Louis XIV*
David J. Sturdy *Richelieu and Mazarin*
Hunt Tooley *The Western Front*
Peter Waldron *The End of Imperial Russia, 1855–1917*
Peter G. Wallace *The Long European Reformation*
James D. White *Lenin*
Patrick Williams *Philip II*

European History in Perspective
Series Standing Order
ISBN 0–333–71694–9 hardcover
ISBN 0–333–69336–1 paperback
(*outside North America only*)

You can receive future titles in this series as they are published by placing a standing order. Please contact your bookseller or, in case of difficulty, write to us at the address below with your name and address, the title of the series and the ISBN quoted above.

Customer Services Department, Palgrave Ltd
Houndmills, Basingstoke, Hampshire RG21 6XS, England

Richelieu and Mazarin
A Study in Statesmanship

DAVID J. STURDY

First published 2004 by
PALGRAVE MACMILLAN
Houndmills, Basingstoke, Hampshire RG21 6XS and
175 Fifth Avenue, New York, N.Y. 10010
Companies and representatives throughout the world

PALGRAVE MACMILLAN is the global academic imprint of the Palgrave
Macmillan division of St. Martin's Press, LLC and of Palgrave Macmillan Ltd.
Macmillan® is a registered trademark in the United States, United Kingdom
and other countries. Palgrave is a registered trademark in the European
Union and other countries.

ISBN 0–333–75399–2 hardback
ISBN 0–333–75400–X paperback

This book is printed on paper suitable for recycling and made from fully
managed and sustained forest sources.

A catalogue record for this book is available from the British Library.

Library of Congress Cataloging-in-Publication Data
Sturdy, D. J. (David J.)
    Richelieu and Mazarin : a study in statemanship / David J. Sturdy.
        p.   cm. — (European history in perspective)
    Includes bibliographical references and index.
    ISBN 0–333–75399–2 (cloth) — ISBN 0–333–75400–X (pbk.)
    1. Richelieu, Armand Jean du Plessis, duc de, 1585–1642—Influence.
    2. Mazarin, Jules, 1602–1661—Influence.   3. Statesmen—France—
    Biography.   4. Cardinals—France—Biography.   5. France—Politics
    and government—1610–1643.   6. France—Politics and government—
    1643–1715.   I. Title.   II. Series.

    DC123.9.R5S78 2003
    944'.033'0922—dc21   2003051975

10   9   8   7   6   5   4   3   2   1
13 12 11 10 09 08 07 06 05 04

Printed in China

To Peggy and Joyce Allbutt

Contents

Preface

In the minds of generations of students, the names of Richelieu and Mazarin are linked in political partnership even though they collaborated directly only for a few years. Mazarin is commonly seen as the natural successor to Richelieu, as somebody who persisted with Richelieu's policies in spirit if not invariably to the letter. If this view may be expressed through an architectural metaphor, Richelieu was the designer and first master builder, while Mazarin completed what his mentor had begun, perhaps adding a few personal flourishes here and there. Other continuities and parallels can readily be identified. Both men were entangled in complicated triangular relationships with monarchy: Richelieu with Queen Marie de' Medici and her son Louis XIII, and Mazarin with Queen Anne and her son Louis XIV. Both ministers were cardinals (although Mazarin, unlike Richelieu, was never ordained a priest); they each rose to political heights from unlikely social backgrounds, especially Mazarin, who was born and brought up in Italy; they unashamedly exploited their political eminence to enrich themselves and their families; and from their own times to the present day, they have proved to be a subject of abiding interest to memoirists, historians, novelists, and film and television producers. On such grounds alone it makes sense to write a study which takes Richelieu and Mazarin as its subject and seeks to assess their combined, as well as individual, significance for the political evolution of France from the early 1620s to the 1660s, and perhaps even beyond.

There are other grounds for treating them in tandem. In recent years, separate studies of Richelieu and Mazarin have been published, some providing a comprehensive analysis of their lives and careers, others dealing with particular facets of their policies or with more personal topics, such as the strategies through which they amassed their fortunes. Such works have considerably expanded our understanding of Richelieu and Mazarin, but it is also of value to take stock of recent research and integrate it into an assessment of their combined contribution to the evolution of French history in the seventeenth century.

The question then arises of the most appropriate method to adopt. This book is aimed chiefly at undergraduates and other students, but it also hopes to appeal to a more general readership which might have an interest in the history of France during this period but claims no expertise. At first my instinct was to adopt a wholly comparative approach and organise the text around themes through which Richelieu and Mazarin might be compared and contrasted from start to finish; but having taken advice from others I decided on a different approach: to plan the book around the individual ministries of Richelieu and Mazarin, but treat similar themes in both cases. This structure means that the comparative element is woven into a chronologically arranged text, but is taken up explicitly in the concluding discussion. Such a structure is probably more helpful to the reader who does not already possess a deep knowledge of the subject and would welcome guidance through the struggles and triumphs of the public careers of these two men. It also permits discussion of some of the wider issues in the history of this period: the structure of politics, techniques of government and administration, questions of 'absolutism', problems of public finance, the nature and variety of resistance to the cardinals' policies (especially that great mid-century crisis, the Frondes), and problems of foreign policy and warfare.

Another aspect of method concerns selection. A book of some 60,000 words has to focus upon subjects which, in the opinion of the author, constitute a coherent discussion and can be defended as essential to our understanding both of Richelieu and Mazarin and of the major trends within French history during this period; other topics, which might be of interest and importance in their own terms but which are not central to a particular historical exercise, have to be merely alluded to; in the present book, for example, the ecclesiastical patronage exercised by Richelieu and Mazarin falls into this category. Nevertheless, although certain subjects might receive less emphasis than they would in a longer text, this is not to deny their historical significance; it is a feature determined by the nature of the exercise in hand.

The temptation in a short book is to become fixated on Richelieu and Mazarin themselves and thereby to slip into a 'great man' version of

history. Such an approach would not only be misleading, it would rest
on a grossly reductionist version of historical causation. Even the most
powerful of kings or ministers in the early modern period exercised
limited power beyond the immediate circle of court and government.
One of the purposes of the first chapter is to drive this point home as
emphatically as possible. The chapter describes aspects of government
and administration in France and emphasises the severe restrictions under
which any minister of the king worked. France was too big a country,
and seventeenth-century instruments of government were too clumsy,
for any one minister to impose his undiluted will. France contained
a plethora of provincial, municipal and even village institutions whose
sense of tradition and autonomy militated against any unquestioning
submission to policies emanating from the crown. France was a kingdom
wherein several languages were spoken, different legal systems operated
and provincial loyalties coexisted alongside loyalty to the king, and in
their own way these forces exerted a notable influence upon the movement of French history. The dynamics of history can never be limited to
the wills and actions of individuals, no matter how energetic and purpose-
ful those persons may have been; one of the aims of the present book is
to illustrate the extent to which Richelieu and Mazarin had to work
within a range of constraining factors that imposed limits upon what
they could hope to do or achieve.

   With regard to Richelieu, one of the most tenacious versions of his
career concerned the means whereby he achieved political power. He
himself encouraged the view that it was through sheer brilliance and dili-
gence that he had moved from provincial obscurity to national, indeed
international, prominence. There is no denying that Richelieu devoted
himself to unremitting hard work, and that he possessed a political mind
which had few equals in his own lifetime or since; but thanks to recent
research, we are now conscious of the role of accident and unforeseen
circumstance in his political ascension. His social origins cannot be
depicted simply as 'obscure' for, as Chapter 2 points out, his father
served and knew Henri III, and had influential connections in the high
aristocracy; moreover, Richelieu's entry into holy orders (a decision
which conditioned the rest of his career) was a result of family contin-
gency, not conscious intent; and it was because of his nomination to a
bishopric that the events bringing him to the attention of Marie de'
Medici unfolded. Even then, the fluctuating tenor of politics around
Marie de' Medici and her son Louis XIII was such that circumstance,
as well as design, played its part in bringing Richelieu into the king's

entourage; and once there, it was several years before he could be reasonably confident that the kinds of accidents that had raised him to royal service would not bring him down again.

There was an element of fortuity also in Mazarin's rise to political power in France, although this has always been recognised by historians and there is no novelty attaching to the proposition. What is at issue is the precise nature and sequence of the events which brought this Roman (Mazarin always considered himself as such, even though he was born outside the city) to the attention of Richelieu, and from there to the service of the king of France. There was nothing in his family origins to suggest that his life might adopt such a course; on the other hand, his association with the Barberini family (to which Pope Urban VIII belonged) brought him into papal diplomatic service at a time when France and Spain were locked in confrontation in northern Italy and were looking to Rome for possible mediation. Mazarin was one of those designated by the pope to attempt to resolve this dispute. It was from the particular concatenation of events and circumstances attending the Franco-Spanish problem that he came to the attention of Richelieu, and from there entered the service of Louis XIII and Louis XIV.

Similar comments may be made about all the themes with which this book deals. At every stage it is necessary to stress the interplay between those actions and achievements of Richelieu and Mazarin that they consciously conceived and executed, and the dictates of circumstance which frequently forced the ministers to adjust and respond. This is no sense diminishes their status as statesmen; on the contrary it enhances their reputations, for one of the tests of statesmanship is the ability to be flexible and cope with unexpected crises. By this measure both Richelieu and Mazarin were adept, although it does not follow that they were invariably successful. They each had their share of failure and had to face what, at times, was virulent criticism from within the social and political elites. They also had to confront much popular resistance, as riot and rebellion remained endemic throughout the decades of their ministries. Their policies imposed a heavy price on the subjects of Louis XIII and Louis XIV, and this too must count in any assessment of them as ministers of the crown.

This book arose from an earlier volume which I contributed to the *European History in Perspective* series: *Louis XIV* (1998). The general editor, Jeremy Black, proposed that the present companion volume be written, so that, taken together, the two would cover most of the seventeenth and early eighteenth centuries. I was pleased and flattered to be invited, and express my thanks to him, both as a friend and as an unstinting adviser. I am indebted also to others too numerous to mention; but as ever, my thanks go especially to my wife for her support and assistance as reader and textual critic.

DAVID J. STURDY

Coleraine

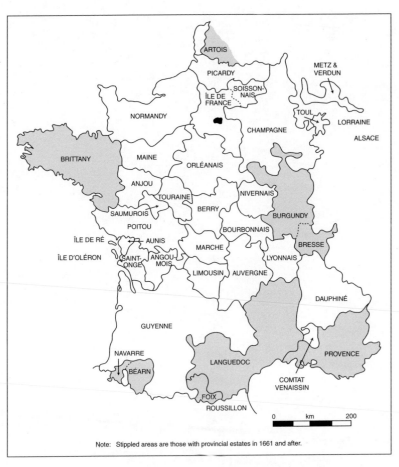

ARTOIS

PICARDY

METZ &
VERDUN

SOISSON-
NAIS

ÎLE DE
FRANCE

NORMANDY

TOUL

LORRAINE

CHAMPAGNE

ALSACE

BRITTANY

MAINE

ORLÉANAIS

ANJOU

TOURAINE

NIVERNAIS

SAUMUROIS

BERRY

BURGUNDY

POITOU

BOURBONNAIS

BRESSE

ÎLE DE RÉ

AUNIS

ÎLE D'OLÉRON

SAINT-
ONGE

ANGOU-
MOIS

MARCHE

LYONNAIS

LIMOUSIN

AUVERGNE

DAUPHINÉ

GUYENNE

NAVARRE

BÉARN

LANGUEDOC

PROVENCE

COMTAT
VENAISSIN

FOIX

ROUSSILLON

0   km   200

Note: Stippled areas are those with provincial estates in 1661 and after.

The provinces of France in the seventeenth century

Chapter 1:   The Government of France

King and Principal Minister

In 1610, Henri IV, the first Bourbon king of France, was assassinated; his son and heir, Louis XIII, was eight years old. Since a king of France did not reach his majority and rule directly until his thirteenth birthday, Louis's widowed mother Marie de' Medici served as Regent and governed in his name until he came of age on 27 September 1614. Louis's reign was not only long (it lasted until 1643), it covered some of the most tumultuous decades in the history of France before the Revolution. In the 1610s and 1620s, court intrigue, the manoeuvres of aristocratic factions, ministerial instability, extensive socio-economic distress, riot, rebellion, religious division and conflict and, further afield, the onset of the Thirty Years War, confronted the French state with such a prodigious array of problems that these and the following decades have often been dubbed France's 'age of crisis'.[1] Whilst some problems were of recent origin, others went back a century or more and related to questions of the long-term constitutional, political, social and economic development of France. Louis XIII was brought to the throne by an act of violence against his father, and violence in one form or another provided an abiding backdrop to his reign.

French monarchic tradition vested sovereignty exclusively in the king; but although he was thereby 'absolute' (that is, he did not share sovereignty with another person or an assembly), he took advice before formulating policy. The king could consult whomever he wished, but certain categories of people did anticipate being solicited for their views: members of the royal family and great aristocrats because of their elevated birth, commanders of the army (usually drawn from the

1

aristocracy), and leading prelates whose guidance was necessary on matters which raised theological or doctrinal questions. Whatever their expectations, however, such people did not, as of right, attend the king's inner council (*conseil d'état*[2]), wherein policy was discussed and decisions were taken; members of the council were admitted only by invitation from the king or, during the Regency, Marie de' Medici. During Louis XIII's mature years there were few occasions when princes of the blood or aristocrats sat on the council, for he preferred to exclude them from the central decision-making process. At any one time the *conseil d'état* comprised a mere handful of advisers; its powers knew few limits, but attendance was determined by faithful service to the crown.

Several ministers, secretaries of state and others who appeared in Louis XIII's and Louis XIV's *conseil d'état* will make an appearance in this book but, of course, the central figures are Armand-Jean du Plessis, Cardinal – eventually Duc de – Richelieu and Cardinal Jules Mazarin. They were symptomatic of a Europe-wide trend towards the emergence of principal ministers who exercised extensive political powers (to the point where critics accused them of usurping royal authority) and whose relationship with the monarch was based on mutual trust. In this context one can bring to mind such examples as Olivares in Spain, Oxenstierna in Sweden, Wentworth in Ireland, Nikon in Russia or the Köprölü Grand Vizirs in Turkey. Monarchs and principal ministers were mutually dependent. The former authorised the latter to execute policies which might be provocative, controversial, even of dubious legality, but which were deemed necessary for the good of the state. Ministers drew to themselves, and away from their masters or mistresses, the opprobrium which radical policies generated. Richelieu, Mazarin and their counterparts elsewhere served their respective rulers with utter fidelity, becoming the subject of conspiracies and other forms of resistance in the process. In return, monarchs bestowed titles and monetary rewards in abundance upon them – both Richelieu and Mazarin died extremely wealthy men – but contended that this was a price worth paying. Principal ministers upheld the authority of the monarch at considerable danger to themselves, and thereby merited generous rewards. The steps by which Richelieu and Mazarin became principal ministers will be discussed later, but they were not unique figures; they were characteristic of a wider phenomenon.

The appeal of a principal minister to the king of France was all the greater in that the prestige of monarchy had been undermined by the Wars of Religion, which lasted from the early 1560s to the end of the century. The last three Valois kings – Francis II, Charles IX and Henri III – had been brothers; they all died in tragic circumstances and left no male heirs. During their reigns, the kingdom at times came close to collapse under the impact of civil war, and when Henri III was assassinated in 1589 his successor was a cousin twenty-three times removed, Henri de Bourbon, who took the title Henri IV. Henri IV was a Huguenot, as French Protestants were known, and he faced strong resistance to his succession from his Catholic subjects. His conversion to Catholicism in 1593 was crucial to the diminution of that resistance, and when he afforded his Huguenot subjects legal recognition and formal status by the Edict of Nantes (1598), the civil wars ended. There was no disguising the fact that, since the outbreak of the Wars of Religion, the monarchy had been incapable of matching its claims to authority by its actions. For long periods, the conflict of rival religious groups and aristocratic factions, often aided and abetted from outside the country, had reduced the crown to impotence; and although Henri IV took steps to restore royal authority, his assassination further demonstrated how vulnerable was the king of France to sudden disaster. In a kingdom whose five most recent rulers had died either prematurely or violently,[3] the attraction of a principal minister was self-evident.

The relationship between king and principal minister was, above all, political, but could be complicated by the emergence of royal 'favourites': young men who formed close emotional ties with the monarch and were frequently to be found in the company of the king. Like principal ministers, they benefited from lavish gifts, noble titles and other favours. Provided a favourite was satisfied with honours and material gain, his status ruffled no ministerial feathers, but if he developed political ambition he was bound to create tensions between himself and the principal minister. The 'royal favourite' was a European, not a uniquely French, phenomenon, and the history of the seventeenth century brought forth several notable cases where the aspirations of favourites resulted in political crisis. In England, for example, Charles I's promotion of his favourite the Duke of Buckingham provoked the hostility of other royal advisers and resulted in the assassination of Buckingham in 1628. Louis XIII, too, was to prove susceptible to the attractions of favourites, some of whom, as will be seen, attempted to extend their influence to the realm of politics. In so far as their actions threatened to undermine the trust between king and principal minister, they drew resolute, uncompromising responses from the latter.

France: Government and Administration

If we concentrate on Richelieu for the time being, what instruments
were available to him as he assisted Louis XIII to govern the kingdom?
At the centre, alongside the *conseil d'état*, were administrative councils,
which put into effect the decisions that the king had taken. The principal
bodies were the *conseil des finances*, which, after its restructure in 1615,
handled the assessment and raising of taxation and all the other financial affairs of the kingdom, the *conseil privé* (known later in the century as
the *conseil des parties*), which dealt mainly with the administration of
justice, and the *conseil des dépêches*, which oversaw the transmission of
royal laws and other instructions to provincial bodies and assemblies. In
legal terms these councils had no independent existence but were an
extension of the *conseil d'état*. Moreover, because they had evolved histor-
ically in response to the demands of government, their functions were
not clearly defined, but coincided to a considerable extent; similarly it
was common for personnel to serve on more than one council. The
instruments of central government and administration in France had
not been created according to abstract principles that conformed to
some systematic philosophy of government; they had developed organ-
ically over the centuries and overlapped in their functions and personnel.
The people who staffed the councils were not 'civil servants' rendering
dispassionate service in a present-day sense: they were political appointees
attached to a powerful minister or some other adviser to the king.
French central government worked through the personal service of
'client' to 'master'. In the terminology of the day, great ministers placed
their *'créatures'* ('clients') in the central councils and other bodies, and,
when a minister was dismissed, his *créatures* went with him.

When royal legislation was issued, its application in the provinces, like
that of the authority that the king exercised in more general terms, was
filtered through an array of regional officers, institutions and bodies
which, like those at the centre, had evolved over time. Among them were
governors who administered the *gouvernements*, of which there were
twelve at the beginning of the century.[4] As representatives of the king,
governors were exceedingly powerful figures. They were responsible
for every branch of administration apart from law and, like ministers in
Paris, placed their *créatures* in key positions. Governors normally were
drawn from the royal family or great aristocracy, and certain families came
to monopolise particular *gouvernements*: the Bourbon family did so in
Languedoc, that of Albret in Guyenne, Condé in Picardy, and Guise in

Burgundy and Champagne. Although agents of the crown, governors exercised a *de facto* power in the provinces which rivalled, and on occasion surpassed, that of the king. From the point of view of the crown, one of the dangers inherent in the role of the governors was that they would become semi-autonomous 'rulers' in their *gouvernements*, resembling medieval magnates in their sense of independence. Aristocratic revolts were always dangerous to the crown, but if they involved governors who raised an entire province against the king, they could threaten the stability of the kingdom.

Some provinces, notably those in frontier regions, had their own assemblies, or Estates, composed of the three sections into which society traditionally was divided: Clergy, Nobility and Third Estate (commoners). The major *pays d'états* were Brittany, Normandy, Burgundy, Dauphiné, Provence and Languedoc, but some minor provinces at the foot of the Pyrenees also had Estates. Provincial Estates met when called by the king (usually annually, although the Estates of Burgundy met every three years), and spent much time discussing purely local affairs. However, they also received legislation from the crown. After examining the legislation to ensure that it conformed to local practice, they officially registered it, at which point it came into effect. If a royal law was deemed incompatible with local custom, a provincial Estates could 'remonstrate': that is, return it to the king with a request that it be amended. Although provincial Estates regarded themselves as channels through which royal authority was exercised, they also took seriously their role as guardians of local liberties. If the crown introduced laws which the provincial estates deemed to run counter to those liberties (for example, in matters of taxation), they could put up considerable resistance through the practice of remonstrance.

In certain parts of France, *parlements* – the principal, or 'sovereign', law courts of the kingdom – also registered legislation. There were nine *parlements* at the beginning of the seventeenth century;[5] others were created at Pau (1620) and Metz (1633). It should be emphasised that the chief responsibility of the *parlements* was the exercise of royal justice, and to this extent they were instruments of royal control. This is why the crown, if possible, introduced *parlements* into territories which were absorbed into the kingdom, as in the cases of Pau and Metz. However, like the provincial estates, they received royal legislation which had to be registered and they also wielded the weapon of remonstrance and confronted Richelieu when he attempted policies which, in their opinion, were contrary to traditional 'liberties' and 'rights'. In sum, although

Louis XIII and Richelieu possessed effective means whereby policy could be decided and laws created, the implementation of policy and law depended heavily on the attitude of assemblies and institutions in the provinces.

One sphere in which decision-making by the central government was vulnerable in its execution was that of finance. For purposes of taxation the country fell into two main categories: the aforementioned *pays d'états* and the *pays d'élections*. With regard to the former, there was no uniformity in their fiscal systems. The provinces in question had become part of the kingdom at different times and retained diverse fiscal practices. Broadly speaking, the *pays d'états* were taxed differently from the rest of the country, usually under the guise of a *don gratuit*. This, as the wording indicates, was supposedly a 'free gift' which the provincial estates voted for the crown. Crown agents attended meetings of the provincial estates and negotiated the amount to be raised as a *don gratuit*, after which the estates collected the money themselves – again there was no uniformity in the methods by which they did so – and passed it to the crown. The provincial Estates were not the only bodies to operate this way: the General Assembly of the Clergy likewise voted *dons gratuits* to the king. The rest of the country, the *pays d'élections*, was divided into *généralités*, which in turn were composed of smaller areas, *élections*: in the early 1620s there were about 150 *élections* in total. In these parts of France the crown collected taxes and other impositions through its own apparatus. Each year the central government decided how much direct taxation was to be raised; it divided this global sum among the *généralités*, where financial officers subdivided it among the *élections*; there, other officers divided their portion among the parishes, and it was at that level that taxes were collected.

In practice this division between *pays d'états* and *pays d'élections* was not clear-cut, for by the beginning of the seventeenth century the crown was engaged on a process of creating *élections* in *pays d'états*. It imposed *élections* on Guyenne in 1603 (they were suspended in 1611 but reintroduced between 1621 and 1627) and on Dauphiné, Burgundy and Provence in 1629. It explained these actions by claiming that the crown's procedures on taxation were less oppressive than those of the Estates, and that the new *élections* were expressions of royal magnanimity towards the king's subjects. In reality they were a means of subverting the financial independence of the provinces and of raising levels of taxes without having to go through the Estates. Thus, whereas in 1629 the crown imposed taxes on Dauphiné totalling 439,000 livres, that figure rose to over 593,000 livres in 1631.[6]

The system was open to numerous confusions, of which three may be identified here. First, the distribution of taxes among *généralités*, *élections* and parishes was complicated by the special pleading that came in every year: bad harvests here, floods there, destruction of property because of riots, the calamitous effects of epidemics which devastated a local population, and a host of other afflictions which were cited by parishes and *élections* appealing against their assessments. It was difficult to arrive at an agreed apportioning of direct taxation, and long delays were thereby built into the system. It was common for *élections* and *généralités* to be several years behind in their payments. Secondly, the assessment and collection of taxes was notoriously vulnerable to corrupt practices. At every level, financial *officiers* creamed off money through accepting bribes, favoured their friends or home parishes in the distribution of taxes, falsified receipts, claimed heavy expenses and employed a host of other subterfuges to defraud the government and line their own pockets. Dishonesty on the part of *officiers* was integral to the government's financial procedures and was a major cause of discontent among tax payers. Many of the riots and revolts of the 1620s, 1630s and 1640s were reactions to the activities of tax officers, and although the government was aware of the problem, it was powerless to do other than make an occasional example of *officiers* who went too far. Thirdly, the structure of taxes was itself extremely complex. The principal direct tax was the *taille*, but it existed in two forms: *taille réelle* (assessed on a person's property) and *taille personnelle* (assessed on an individual), neither of which was easy to estimate accurately, for taxpayers in both categories were adept at disguising or hiding the true worth of their property or income. A further complication arose in that certain sections of society were exempted from paying the *taille*: they included the clergy, nobility, inhabitants of certain privileged towns including Paris, military personnel and other groups. This is not to say that they paid no taxes at all: they were liable for indirect taxation, and the government found other means of tapping into their wealth; but their exemption did mean that the *taille* was paid chiefly by peasants and the inhabitants of unprivileged towns.

Similar problems of inequity occurred with respect to indirect taxes. One such tax was the *gabelle*, a charge on salt. In some parts of France, especially the north, every household was required to purchase a fixed minimum of salt each year; in these areas the *gabelle* was, in effect, a direct charge. In other regions tax was put on salt, but there was no compulsion to buy prescribed amounts; and some areas paid no *gabelle* at all. Similar inconsistencies affected other indirect taxes, notably *aides* (duties on wine, paper, cloth and other commodities) and *traites* (customs duties on goods coming into the country or moving within the kingdom). The regime of indirect taxes was distinctive in another sense: the government 'farmed out' or leased indirect taxes to groups of financiers (*'fermiers'*). It negotiated contracts with *fermiers*, who paid the agreed amount directly to the government but collected the dues themselves, retaining excess revenues as profit. Private enterprise thus was an integral part of the French taxation system, and added to the diversity already manifested in the *pays d'états* and *pays d'élections*.

If one were to present a detailed description of taxation in France, it would confirm that structural disparities and corrupt practices existed at every level; the procedures for creating, assessing and collecting taxes had developed through no consistent or coherent philosophy, and presented serious problems to any minister whose policies necessitated a rapid increase in expenditure. A speedy expansion of regular revenue was impossible, and the minister had to devise other means of meeting the resultant deficit: borrowing on the national and international money markets, the invention of new taxes or other charges, forced loans, the multiplication of offices to be put up for sale (a subject discussed below) or the issuing of government bonds (*rentes*). The sale of offices and of bonds was referred to technically as *extraordinaires*, but by the seventeenth century it had become a regular means whereby the crown raised money; and, rather like indirect taxes, *extraordinaires* were leased out to financiers (*traitants*), who paid the government and then handled the administration of these sales. Finance was to be a perpetual problem facing Richelieu and Mazarin. We shall see in later chapters how they responded and with what consequences.

One other conditioning factor in the government and administration of France should be noted. The majority of the personnel who staffed law courts or the fiscal institutions of the state, and held other public positions, were *officiers* who had bought their posts. The practice whereby the government sold offices (*vénalité d'offices*) went back at least to the fifteenth century, and was a means of raising money quickly, especially in time of war. So extensive did the practice become that in 1522 there was created a special government department to administer the sale of offices: the *recette des parties casuelles*. By then, *vente d'offices* had become a standard, if strictly speaking irregular, part of royal fiscality, and it continued to occupy an ever-increasing proportion of governmental revenue. In order to meet its financial commitments, the crown could not resist creating offices, irrespective of whether they were needed for bureaucratic reasons. Whereas in 1515 there were some 4000–5000 *officiers* in France, that number had risen to 25,000 by 1610 and increased even more under Louis XIII and the young Louis XIV. Richelieu and Mazarin had recourse to the sale of offices, and by the early 1660s there were some 46,000 *officiers*; so many that in the mid-1660s Louis XIV's minister, Jean-Baptiste Colbert, took steps to reduce their number.[7] Offices were eagerly sought by purchasers, not only because of their financial returns (when he bought an office, the *officier* received an annual payment which was, in effect, the interest paid by the government on the capital sum paid for the office; he also received other payments in the course of his duties), but also because they conferred social status and opened up routes both to social ascension and to careers.

A major innovation occurred in 1604. Thereafter, by paying an extra annual sum to the government, known as the *paulette*, an *officier* in effect could turn his office into private property. He now could dispose of the office as he wished and bequeath it in his will along with other property. *Officiers* routinely paid *paulette*; it brought in more revenue to the government, but, by allowing *officiers* to become owners of their offices, greatly increased their property and capital wealth. By the time Richelieu became principal minister, *vénalité d'offices* was an integral part of government finance, accounting for almost 40 per cent of royal revenue. The *officiers* were a powerful interest group which the government alienated at its peril.

The kingdom of France was in many respects a collection of diverse provinces and regions with their own legal systems, languages (Occitan in Languedoc, Breton in Brittany, and Provençal in Provence, were spoken more than French), patterns of land-owning and representative assemblies. The crown had to acquire skills of management and manipulation in handling this plethora of provincial institutions and assemblies; it was not sufficient simply to issue legislation and expect it to be registered and obeyed. A process of constant negotiation, persuasion, cajoling, flattering, threatening and bribing had to be undertaken. Of course, in the last resort the crown could and did resort to force to impose its will, but this was always a dangerous and unpredictable course of action which it preferred to avoid. Instead it made increasing use of special commissioners ('*intendants*') who were sent to the provinces to oversee the imposition of the royal will. *Intendants* were not new; as far back as the thirteenth and fourteenth centuries the crown had despatched commissioners on specific missions to the provinces; it was the ascending scale on which they were employed under Louis XIII and Louis XIV which was different. They were not systematised until the second half of the century, but Richelieu and Mazarin both acquired the habit of sending *intendants*, who carried the full authority of the king, to provincial bodies or assemblies to ensure that the royal will was obeyed. Under Louis XIII the *intendants* were not a separate class of administrator: most of them were lawyers seconded from a central council of government, or even from a provincial financial body, to undertake a specific task. Once the task was finished, they returned to normal duties. Under Louis XIV, *intendants* did evolve into a new layer of administration, but for most of the period covered by this book they should be understood in the limited sense just outlined.

France in the 1610s was still recovering from the Wars of Religion, and indeed many of the socio-political tensions which the wars had generated remained only just under control. Experience was to show that all too easily the potential for further conflict could turn into reality. Furthermore, France's international standing was to be complicated by the outbreak of the Thirty Years War in 1618. This war began as a rebellion by Bohemian Protestant magnates against their Austrian Habsburg king, but it quickly evolved into an international conflict which had repercussions in France. To assist him in guiding his kingdom through the difficult years of his reign, Louis XIII had several would-be principal ministers. He eventually banked on Richelieu and in so doing selected a figure of towering importance to the history of France. It is appropriate, therefore, to turn to Richelieu and examine his origins and rise to political eminence.

Chapter 2: Richelieu: Bishop and Emerging Political Leader

The Family Inheritance

Although certain features of the family background of Armand-Jean du Plessis, Cardinal Richelieu, predisposed him to a position of some eminence in the ecclesiastical hierarchy of France, they did not signal the remarkable political career which he went on to pursue. The du Plessis family were minor nobility, most of whose land was in Poitou in the region around Loudun; among their estates was that of Richelieu, from which Armand-Jean later took his name. Armand-Jean's parents, François du Plessis and Suzanne de la Porte, grew up and led their married life amidst the conflict and vicissitudes of the Wars of Religion. Ironically, it was the violence of the period which transformed the prospects of François, and by extension those of his children. Being the younger son he had no expectation of inheriting land, but his elder brother Louis was killed in the wars in 1565, and in consequence François became heir to the family estates. He could now seek a wife, and in 1569 he married Suzanne who came from a well-to-do family of Parisian lawyers. As a commoner she was of lower social status than François, but brought a respectable dowry and in due course other financial gifts from her father, all of which added much-needed financial capital to François's resources.

In early modern France, the course of a nobleman's career depended heavily on his ability to attract powerful protectors or patrons. In this regard the du Plessis family was fortunate in that it held some of its lands from the great Montpensier dynasty, which belonged to the Bourbon–Vendôme branch of the Bourbons. During the Wars of Religion, François du Plessis

fought alongside the Montpensiers: Louis de Bourbon, Duc de
Montpensier, who was governor of Anjou, Touraine and Maine, and
after his death in 1582, his son François. It was probably the Montpensiers
who brought François du Plessis to the attention of Henri, Duc d'Anjou
(later King Henri III), into whose household he subsequently passed.
Anjou became king in 1574 and retained François in his circle of
confidants, appointing him Grand Prévôt de France in 1578. This was
a post with considerable responsibilities: the incumbent oversaw security
arrangements at the royal palaces, and the provision of food, wine and
other necessities, and was head of a special tribunal of justice to which
members of the royal household were privileged to bring cases. The post
conferred significant financial rewards: in addition to the salary of 8000
livres a year, the holder received gifts of money from the crown, and
other payments from businessmen seeking contracts to supply the royal
palaces or from litigants involved in the law court. Although François
diverted some of his new income into the purchase of more land in
Poitou, his expenditure at court used up many of his revenues; moreover,
he had to maintain his family in Paris where he was normally based, and
even when he was absent fighting in the Wars of Religion (as he was
intermittently in the 1580s), this too proved a heavy financial drain.
Furthermore, François, punctilious in his management of the king's
affairs, neglected the administration of his own property and finances.
When he died in 1590 his affairs were so confused that it took his children over thirty years to sort them out. The legend later grew that
Armand-Jean du Plessis was born into a poverty-stricken noble family.
This was not so: his father left a disordered inheritance rather than one
consumed by debt. Moreover, he had brought up his children in Paris,
and made their names known in royal circles.

François and Suzanne had three sons and three daughters. To the
eldest son, Henri, fell the chief responsibility for restoring order to his
father's estate. Henri had made considerable progress to this end by the
time he too died in 1619.[1] The two younger sons of François and
Suzanne – Alphonse-Louis and Armand-Jean – entered the priesthood.
When only thirteen (1595), Alphonse-Louis was nominated to the
bishopric of Luçon, contiguous to the principal family estates in Poitou,
in succession to an uncle who had held the benefice since 1584. However,
although he had a religious vocation, Alphonse-Louis had no desire for
ecclesiastical honours and in 1601 entered the Carthusian order to lead
the life of a monk. Henri IV allowed the nomination to pass to the
youngest du Plessis son, Armand-Jean. Alphonse-Louis remained in his

monastery until 1623 when his younger brother, by now a cardinal, persuaded him to become Archbishop of Aix; two years later Alphonse-Louis was translated to Lyon, and in 1629 he also became a cardinal.

The three daughters of François and Suzanne married, but in differing circumstances. Marriage was a means of cementing alliances between families and of preserving, even enhancing, social status. Brides had to be provided with suitable dowries, but the experiences of the three du Plessis daughters illustrate problems facing noble families in this regard.[2] The eldest, Françoise, married twice. Her first marriage lasted less than a year, cut short by the death of her husband (1597), but the second, in 1603, lasted until her own death in 1616. The second husband was René de Vignerot, sieur de Pont-Courlay, a nobleman from Poitou. Since her dowry was probably small, this was an alliance between two noble families from the same province and of similar social standing. The marriage, in other words, confirmed their social status. René and Françoise had two children, who, when Armand-Jean was at the height of his political power, were advanced financially and socially by their uncle: the son, François, was made Général des Galères (1635) and the daughter, Marie, was made Duchesse d'Aiguillon (1638).

The second daughter of François and Suzanne was Nicole. In 1618 she made an excellent match when she married Urbain de Maillé, Marquis de Brézé. An aristocrat of his standing normally would not have married somebody from the lesser nobility, but he was heavily in debt and Nicole (who was ten years older than he) was provided not only with a large dowry – 80,000 livres – but also with the promise that in due course even more of Brézé's debts would be paid. Her chief benefactor was her brother Armand-Jean, who already had amassed considerable financial resources. He provided three-quarters of her dowry (the remainder coming from her brother Henri), and gave the promise concerning Brézé's debts. The du Plessis family was buying its way up the social scale thanks to Armand-Jean. The third daughter, Isabelle, caused a scandal and was, in effect, erased from the family's collective memory. She defied convention by eloping with, and marrying, the son of a doctor from Poitiers. Her family cut off all contact and, as far as they were concerned, she ceased to exist.

For all its individual characteristics, the history of the du Plessis family in the late 1500s was representative of that of many provincial noble families. François advanced their interests by attaining a position at court, but left a confused inheritance which his eldest son had to unravel. The two younger sons entered the priesthood, and the daughters achieved mixed success in their marriages. By all the usual indicators, the family would have continued in this vein, managing its estates in Poitou and attending to the careers and marriages of its sons and daughters. That their prospects were transformed is explained by the achievements of one man: Armand-Jean.

Armand-Jean du Plessis: his Youth and Rise in the Church

Armand-Jean was born on 9 September 1585. After spending his earliest years in Poitou, he went to Paris to be educated at the prestigious Collège de Navarre. Given the incertitude surrounding his father's legacy, it was his mother's family who paid most of the costs of his education. This experience taught him a lesson which he never forgot: that a noble title meant little if it was unsupported by sound finances. In the course of his career he not only accumulated immense wealth, but paid careful attention to its management. He began his studies with a military career in view, but family concerns propelled him into the priesthood. In the 1570s the du Plessis family had used its aristocratic and courtly contacts to acquire the bishopric of Luçon. These manoeuvres had borne fruit in 1584 when the aforementioned uncle of Alphonse-Louis and Armand-Jean was made bishop. Luçon, on the Atlantic coast, was one of the poorest dioceses in France and contained a large Huguenot (Protestant) population. Whilst the financial returns of the diocese were modest[3], the du Plessis family prized it for the social prestige which it conferred and the influence in the social, political and ecclesiastical affairs of Poitou to which it led. The family was anxious to retain the bishopric and accordingly secured the succession for Alphonse-Louis. His decision to turn it down caused consternation in the family. Pressure was now put on his younger brother, Armand-Jean, to enter the priesthood and accept the bishopric of Luçon. He agreed and began to study theology. In 1606 Henri IV acknowledged him as bishop-apparent. Since, according to the normal provisions of the Church, Armand-Jean was under age, he had to go to Rome to seek special dispensation. In April 1607, while in Rome, he was consecrated bishop even though he was aged only twenty-one.[4] Having been precipitated directly into the episcopate, he took his study of theology seriously,[5] and all the signs are that his religious faith was genuine and a constant guide to his thought and conduct, both private and public. Herein lay the origins of one of the most controversial aspects of his later career: the interplay between his religious commitments and ecclesiastical obligations on the one hand, and his duties as a political leader on the other. It was not always easy to reconcile the two, but he made strenuous efforts to do so. In 1608 Armand-Jean travelled to Luçon, where he spent most of the next six years. By temperament the bishop proved to be a reformer. This was a time when the Counter-Reformation was making headway in France. It emphasised not only the combating of heresy, but the revival of spirituality and social action among the Catholic clergy and laity. Richelieu[6] established a seminary, conducted regular visitations to the parishes of the diocese, strove to improve the intellectual and spiritual quality of the clergy, and encouraged attendance at Mass by the laity. For inspiration he turned to two leading figures of the French Counter-Reformation, both of whom were to figure in his later career: Pierre de Bérulle and François le Clerc du Tremblay, known as Père Joseph. Bérulle introduced the Oratory[7] into France in 1611, and after organising his first group in Paris, established the second in the diocese of Luçon. Bérulle, who was made a cardinal in 1627, was one of the most energetic reformers in the French Catholic Church and was prominent in the *dévot* movement, which advocated the submission of the domestic and foreign policies of the crown to the cause of Catholicism. Bérulle's collaboration with Richelieu was to give way to criticism when the latter, as principal minister of Louis XIII, followed policies based on Reason of State. Père Joseph was a Capuchin monk who, before he took holy orders, had served in the army and performed diplomatic services on behalf of the crown. He too was a reformer, but he was also involved in moves to convert Huguenots to Catholicism through missions. He argued against the persecution of the Huguenots on the ground that compulsion either drove people into stiffer resistance or secured only false 'conversions'. Père Joseph organised several missions to Huguenots in Poitou, including the diocese of Luçon. In later years when, as a minister of the crown, Richelieu had to grapple with the Huguenot problem, he modelled his policy on Père Joseph's strategy. Richelieu also turned to the monk for advice in the sphere of international relations, and was to send him abroad as a diplomatic representative of France.

Steps to Political Office

Richelieu's first appearance on the national stage came in 1614 when he attended the Estates General, held in Paris, as a representative of the

Clergy. The Estates General – composed of three Estates: Clergy, Nobility and Third Estate (commoners) – had been conceded by the crown in response to pressure mainly from aristocrats, especially the Prince de Condé. Elections were held in the summer of 1614, and Richelieu was chosen by the Clergy of Poitou. The Estates General assembled on 27 October, but it was not until mid-November that it turned to serious business. The details of the debates and discussions that took place over the next few months need not detain us.[8] Richelieu conducted himself with a composure and skill that impressed not only other members of the Assembly but also the Queen Mother, Marie de' Medici, and her chief adviser Concino Concini. In February 1615, shortly before the Estates General dispersed, it was Richelieu who gave the closing speech on behalf of the Clergy, outlining their final resolutions and petitions.

He remained in Paris, increasing his contacts with the government in the hope of political advancement. The key figures whom he hoped to cultivate were the Queen Mother, Marie de' Medici, and her Italian favourite Concino Concini, for they more than anybody controlled the formation of policy. Concini's wife, Leonora Galigaï, had been a childhood friend of Marie, and with her husband had accompanied Marie to France in 1600 when Marie married Henri IV. Marie showered Concini with honours. He received the governorships of several fortified towns, the noble title of Marquis d'Ancre, and in 1613 the supreme military honour, the rank of Marshal of France. Marie also admitted him to the innermost royal council wherein policy was formed. The ostentatious and politically powerful Concini and his wife were detested by great aristocrats, especially the Prince de Condé, who regarded them as Italian upstarts who had risen scandalously above their station by exploiting the vulnerability of Henri IV's widow. The young Louis XIII too viewed them with distaste. On numerous occasions the conduct of Concini and Leonora towards the king was little short of insulting. Marie failed to correct them, for she too seems to have had scant regard for the abilities of her son. She made little attempt to disguise her opinion that, in every respect, he was much inferior to his father. The Concinis could display disrespectful attitudes while Marie was Regent, but both she and they were curiously oblivious to the implications of two events in October 1614: on 2 October the Regency ended, with the proclamation of the majority of Louis XIII, and on 20 October the king's coronation took place. Henceforth Louis was fully king and empowered to act independently, yet the conduct of his mother and Concini towards him did not improve. Richelieu, not privy to such tensions, stayed in contact with Marie and her favourite, regarding them as best placed to advance him politically.

One question that Marie and Concini had to resolve was that of finding a wife for Louis XIII. They sought one within the Spanish Habsburgs, and in 1615 travelled to Bordeaux where negotiations with the Spanish took place; en route they stayed at Poitiers, to which Richelieu travelled in order to pay his respects to them. The talks were a success and agreement with the Spanish was reached. In November 1615 a double marriage took place, between Louis XIII and Anne ('of Austria'), the elder daughter of Philip III of Spain, and between Louis's sister Elisabeth and the future Philip IV. The marriages delighted *dévots* like Bérulle, who saw them as the foundation of a long period of concord between these two great Catholic monarchies. France and Spain, the *dévots* anticipated, would combine their forces in the cause of Counter-Reformation, and jointly assail Protestant heresy. Conversely, but for precisely the same reason, Huguenots and Protestants elsewhere in Europe feared the implications of the marriages: the unions portended renewed religious oppression and would underpin a new phase of Spanish Habsburg aggression. Provoked by such prospects, Huguenots burst into rebellion in November 1615 and received support from the Prince de Condé. He too took exception to the marriages, less because they brought France and Spain together than because they were a triumph for the hated Concini, upon whom Marie lavished yet more honours (he was awarded the governorship of Normandy). Condé, with the support of aristocrats such as the dukes of Mayenne, Longueville and Bouillon, decided that the only way to break Concini's hold over Marie was by force. They joined, and gave leadership to, the rebellion of the Huguenots, and continued fighting until Marie bought them off with financial subsidies and grants of land, in the Peace of Loudun (3 May 1616).

From Luçon, Richelieu too had observed the progress of the discussions in Bordeaux, and their success corroborated his conviction that Concini was the all-powerful figure in government who must be courted. Notwithstanding the rebellion of Huguenots and disaffected aristocrats, Richelieu maintained his contacts with the Queen Mother and her Italian adviser; his solicitations were rewarded when he was appointed chaplain to Louis XIII's sixteen-year-old bride Anne of Austria. On 1 September 1616, Marie and Concini struck back at Condé by having him arrested. In November they made changes in the government, and appointed the Bishop of Luçon as Secretary of State. Richelieu accordingly was admitted to the innermost council advising the king, but did so as a '*créature*' of Marie and Concini.

The Assassination of Concini and its Consequences

Aristocratic resistance to Concini was lessened by the Peace of Loudun and arrest of Condé, but an alternative focus of danger, which Concini underestimated to his ultimate cost, was the king. Louis, still an adolescent, had formed a close friendship with his chief falconer, Charles d'Albert, Duc de Luynes. Louis was passionate about hunting and in Luynes, twenty-three years his senior, found a charming mentor who built up his self-confidence. Luynes also spoke to him about politics. Louis revealed that he wanted to dispense with Concini but did not know how, for Concini not only was the favourite of the Queen Mother, but had substantial military resources at his disposal. Luynes brought three associates into his confidence: Louis Tronson, a lawyer; the Baron de Modène, who was a cousin of Luynes; and Guichard de Déagent. This last figure was attached to Claude Barbin, *contrôleur général des finances*, who in turn was a follower of Concini. Déagent learned of Concini's movements from Barbin and passed on the information to Luynes, who finally convinced Louis XIII that Concini could be arrested before he had an opportunity to organise resistance. Déagent added a further observation: if Concini resisted an order of arrest executed in the name of the king, he should be killed. Louis did not speak in favour of this proposition, but neither did he countermand it. Luynes and the others took this as consent.

The plotters struck on 14 April 1617. Nicolas de l'Hôpital, Baron de Vitry, a captain in the royal body guard, was charged with the task of seizing Concini, which he did as Concini was entering the Louvre. Vitry took him by the arm and announced that he was under arrest. Concini began to speak and put his hand on his sword. Vitry and his companions interpreted this as resistance; they shot him five times and plunged their swords into his corpse. Vitry cried 'Vive le roi!', and the news of Concini's death spread quickly around the palace. The king was overjoyed and spent most of the rest of the day in a state of near-delirium. Courtiers crowded in to declare their loyalty to Louis and congratulate him on the death of Concini. Richelieu presented himself, but was dismissed brusquely as an ally of Concini. Louis refused to receive the Queen Mother, who left the Louvre accompanied by, among others, Richelieu. Luynes later had Concini's widow tried for witchcraft; she was found guilty and executed. The Parlement of Paris proclaimed that the killing of Concini was not an assassination, but an act of justice on the king's part. Concini's possessions were confiscated, many going to Luynes, who acquired the governorship of Normandy, the marquisate of Ancre and a large residence in Paris. Marie retired to Blois, where she was told to remain at the king's pleasure. For a few weeks Richelieu stayed with her, attempting to rescue his political career by informing on her to Luynes and sending messages of loyalty to the king. It was to little avail, for in June he too received royal instructions to return to his diocese. In April 1618 more orders arrived: he was exiled to the papal territory of Avignon, where he was to remain at the king's pleasure.[9]

How long he would have remained there cannot be known, but within a year he was inadvertently rescued by the actions of Marie. Frustrated by her incarceration in Blois, she secretly established contact with one of her former husband's most trusted lieutenants, the Duc d'Épernon. On the night of 21–2 February 1619, in a cloak-and-dagger operation which involved Marie clambering down a rope ladder, Épernon rescued her from the château at Blois and took her to Angoulême, where they raised an army. The king mustered his own forces, and it looked as if a civil war might begin. Luynes intervened and convinced Louis that he should avoid war by negotiating with Marie; moreover, contended Luynes, the one person who could persuade her to do likewise was Richelieu. Louis consented, and Richelieu was instructed to leave Avignon, go to Angoulême and persuade Marie to negotiate. Richelieu obeyed. On behalf of Marie he met royal representatives and agreed the Treaty of Angoulême on 30 April 1619. By its terms, Marie was permitted freedom of movement and she received the governorships of Anjou and Normandy. On 5 September, again advised by Richelieu, she was formally reconciled with her son.

Tensions nevertheless remained. Marie established her residence at Angers, but was still smarting over Louis XIII's refusal to allow her a role in government. She was further incensed when, in October 1619, her former enemy, the Prince de Condé, not only was released from prison but was received by the king. Over the winter of 1619–20 relations between mother and son became increasingly embittered. Louis decided on military action, and in 1620 he personally led an army to Angers. On 7 August he defeated her forces at Ponts-de-Cé on the outskirts of the city. Richelieu once again was called on to intervene. He secured a second peace between Louis and Marie on 10 August. Richelieu was given to understand that as a reward for his mediatory efforts he would be made a cardinal. After a delay, which caused Richelieu to fear that the king might change his mind, Louis accordingly sent a request to the pope, who made the appropriate announcement on 3 September 1622.

Now that he was a cardinal, Richelieu resigned as Bishop of Luçon. His promotion encouraged him to think again in terms of political advancement, which duly came in 1624. Before that is discussed, however, a digression into wider political developments in France and abroad is advisable, for they created the context into which he entered when he was readmitted to the king's inner council. Both within France and on the international stage, violent conflict had reached dangerous heights, forcing Richelieu and the king's other advisers to confront difficult decisions.

Béarn, Huguenot Rebellion and International Developments

After overcoming the forces of Marie at Angers, Louis XIII continued south to the province of Béarn, which he proceeded to incorporate fully into the kingdom of France. In so doing he provoked another rebellion by Huguenots. Béarn was a Bourbon possession which formed part of the medieval kingdom of Navarre, whose territory ranged across the Pyrenees. By the late sixteenth century, that part of the kingdom which was south of the Pyrenees had been absorbed by Spain; only the northern, 'French', side remained to the Bourbons. Henri IV ruled Béarn independently of France, but Louis XIII decided to unite it with France for dynastic reasons. France could be ruled only by a king, a queen regnant being inadmissible. Navarre, by contrast, permitted a queen to rule. It was possible, therefore, that future vagaries of births, marriages and deaths affecting the Bourbons might lead to different monarchs in France and Navarre. By bringing Béarn fully into France and subjecting it to French succession law, Louis would prevent any future confusion. There was also a religious motivation behind his action. Béarn was overwhelmingly Protestant in religious complexion and its governing council was monopolised by Huguenots. As a Catholic monarch of deep personal conviction, Louis felt called to restore his Protestant subjects to the Catholic Church; in 1617 he accordingly reintroduced Catholic worship into Béarn. When he arrived with his army in the autumn of 1620 he put his unification plan into effect. He proclaimed the union with France, abolished the governing council of Béarn and replaced it with a *parlement* staffed exclusively by Catholics.

These measures alarmed Huguenots elsewhere in France. Their status was defined by the Edict of Nantes (1598), which had guaranteed liberty of conscience, freedom of worship in specified places, the right to fortify about 150 'places of security', and special law courts to resolve disputes with Catholics. Religious division and sectarian tensions nevertheless continued, and although Béarn, because of its special constitutional status, did not come within the terms of the Edict of Nantes, the espousal by Louis XIII of a 'Catholic' policy there raised wider Huguenot fears. In November 1620 a Huguenot General Assembly met in La Rochelle without royal permission (normally a condition of such gatherings) and discussed the implications of recent events in Béarn. Supported by leading Huguenot aristocrats, notably the Duc de Rohan and his brother the Duc de Soubise, the Assembly called on Huguenots to resist the government by force. Most of Huguenot France from Poitou to Languedoc, and even Montpellier in Provence, responded; armies were created and wide areas of Huguenot France were put on a war footing. Louis counter-attacked in 1621, but to little effect. In 1622 he launched a second campaign which, amidst much bloodshed and numerous atrocities including the notorious massacre of the population of Nègrepelisse on 10 June, succeeded in quelling the rebellion. The last significant stand of the Huguenots was at Montpellier, defended by Rohan, which surrendered in October 1622. Louis decided to negotiate with Rohan, and by the Treaty of Montpellier (18 October 1622) renewed the Edict of Nantes, but reduced the Huguenot places of security by eighty. This was only a temporary cessation, for within a few years Huguenot rebellion broke out again; but when it did so, Richelieu was a member of the *conseil d'état*, and it was one of the first major challenges which he had to face.

The uprising of 1620–2 occurred at a time when, in international affairs, the crown was embroiled in the Valtelline crisis, which was to confront Richelieu also in due course. The Valtelline was a strip of territory linking Milan – a Spanish possession and military stronghold – and Austria; it also served the Spanish as a crucial stretch of the 'Spanish Road' by which they supplied their forces in the Spanish Netherlands by land from Milan. Most of the inhabitants of the Valtelline were Catholic, but their rulers were Protestant lords united in an organisation known as the Grey League (or 'Grisons'). In 1620 the Spanish occupied the Valtelline, expelled the Grisons and installed a Catholic government. Neighbouring states – Venice, Savoy, Mantua – were alarmed at this strengthening of Habsburg power. German Protestant states likewise were apprehensive, for the Thirty Years War had broken out in 1618 and the seizure of the Valtelline by the Spanish threatened closer cooperation between the Austrian and Spanish Habsburgs in the war. The Dutch Republic was especially fearful. In 1609, after more than forty years of war, the Republic had signed a twelve-year truce with Spain. The truce would expire in 1621, and the Dutch interpreted the Spanish seizure of the Valtelline as a prelude to a new war. In spite of the 'Spanish' marriages, the French government had no desire to see the Spanish tighten their grip on northern Italy, and urged them to restore the Grisons and avoid an international crisis. This the Spanish agreed to do, by the Treaty of Madrid (1621), but soon afterwards they once again occupied the Valtelline. In 1623, France, Venice and Savoy formed a league whose aim was to force the Spanish to abide by the Treaty of Madrid. No declaration of war was made, but over the next three years, forces of the league, including French troops, engaged in a series of military campaigns as they tried to force the Spanish out of the Valtelline.

Richelieu enters the Conseil d'État

Richelieu's ecclesiastical promotion to the rank of cardinal whetted not only his own political ambition, but also that of his protector, the Queen Mother. Excluded from political life herself, she worked to have Richelieu restored to Louis's *conseil d'état*; through Richelieu, she calculated, she could exert influence on policy. Circumstances looked propitious. Luynes had died in December 1621, and Louis had recalled some of his father's former ministers to office, including Nicolas Brûlart de Sillery, the Chancellor, and his son Pierre Brûlart, Marquis de Puisieux, who ran foreign affairs. Most of these figures were well advanced in years and in no position to bring in a long-term strategy at a time when rebellion by the Huguenots and crisis in the Valtelline called for resolute government. Other developments on the international scene gave cause for concern. In the Thirty Years War, the forces of the Holy Roman Emperor continued their advance in Bohemia and the Palatinate, and in 1621 Spain resumed its war against the Dutch Republic; on every side, the Habsburg cause was in the ascendant. To *dévots* in France this was cause for rejoicing as they looked forward to France joining the Habsburgs in a religiously inspired campaign against Protestantism. Others thought in *bon Français* terms and advocated the political principles espoused by Henri IV: the interests of France, not those of the Catholic Church, must decide policy at home and abroad. According to this view, neither Austrian nor Spanish Habsburg policy was governed by disinterested service to Catholicism; rather, the Habsburgs used the vocabulary of religious crusade to legitimate dynastic ambition. Habsburg successes in Bohemia, the Rhineland and Italy in the early 1620s brought to the surface of French political debate the tensions between *dévot* and *bon Français* strategies of government.

Against this background, a struggle for political power in France was fought.[10] In 1619, Louis had appointed a new *surintendant des finances*, Henri, Comte de Schomberg, but his office was coveted by the captain of the royal bodyguard, Charles, Marquis de la Vieuville, who as well as a being a military man of *bon Français* political persuasion, had connections among French financiers. The government's finances were in a parlous state, and Schomberg resorted to borrowing on a frightening scale. La Vieuville, and indeed the Brûlarts, warned the king that Schomberg was mishandling the king's financial affairs. In January 1623 Louis dismissed Schomberg and replaced him with La Vieuville. The latter, having overthrown Schomberg, now set his sights on the Brûlarts. His machinations led to the king removing the function of Keeper of the Seals (*garde des sceaux*) from Sillery in January 1624 and conferring it on La Vieuville's candidate, Étienne d'Aligre; when Sillery died later in the year, d'Aligre replaced him as Chancellor of France.[11] In February 1624, Sillery's son Puisieux was dismissed from his position in charge of foreign affairs, which were placed in the hands of a triumvirate, all supporters of La Vieuville.[12]

Louis XIII, whose memories of Concini had left him with an antipathy towards over-mighty ministers, was alert to the dangers implicit in La Vieuville's rise, and looked for somebody to counterbalance him. The Queen Mother was still pressing for Richelieu's admission to the king's inner council, but while Louis was aware that the cardinal was a man of outstanding political gifts, he was deeply suspicious of somebody who had been so closely associated with Concini and was a confidant of the Queen Mother. Ironically, it was La Vieuville who persuaded Louis to admit Richelieu to the council. La Vieuville too looked back to the experience of Concini, but as a warning to be heeded. Concini had been assassinated because he wielded too much power and alienated powerful aristocratic factions. La Vieuville recognised that it was essential to avoid any suggestion that he was aspiring to be a new Concini. If Richelieu were admitted to the council, this would serve to refute any suggestion that La Vieuville and his 'clients' were monopolising government; it would also help to reconcile Marie and her entourage to La Vieuville's role as principal minister. Louis consented and on 29 April 1624 Richelieu was once again invited into the king's inner council.

La Vieuville's hopes that Richelieu's presence would help to stabilise his ministry were mistaken, for within four months La Vieuville was under arrest and Richelieu had replaced him as principal minister. Financial crisis and rebellion continued at home and the Habsburgs continued to flourish abroad. La Vieuville's handling of these problems drew criticism from many quarters, including Richelieu himself. When La Vieuville tried to arrange an alliance with the Dutch Republic, it was Richelieu who slowed down negotiations by insisting that the Dutch be required to extend full religious rights to Catholics in the Republic. It was Richelieu, again, who complicated La Vieuville's negotiations with the English regarding a proposed marriage between Charles, Prince of Wales (the future Charles I), and Louis XIII's sister Henriette, by insisting that, if she did marry the Protestant Charles, Henriette must be allowed full rights of Catholic worship and her household should contain priests and other appropriate persons to minister to her spiritual as well as material needs. La Vieuville complained that Richelieu, by acting the enthusiastic cardinal, was pursuing the *dévot* line of Marie rather than the *bon Français* strategy which La Vieuville favoured.

It would be an exaggeration to claim that Richelieu alone engineered La Vieuville's downfall, for criticism of the principal minister was coming from many quarters by the summer of 1624. Nevertheless, there is no denying that after joining the royal council in 1624, Richelieu made life difficult for La Vieuville. It was Louis personally who decided that the principal minister lacked the ability to solve the problems facing the country, but this was a sentiment which Richelieu did nothing to discourage. Aware that the king was losing confidence in him, La Vieuville was prepared to resign. However, the king moved first and on 13 August had him arrested. Richelieu was made principal minister.

Richelieu in 1624

The trajectory of Richelieu's ascent from the Estates General of 1614 to the position of principal minister ten years later cannot be presented as a simple, perpendicular motion. There were many pauses, diversions and setbacks along the way, and there was more than a little luck involved in his triumph. His association with Concini could have been fatal to his prospects, but the disputes between the Queen Mother and Louis XIII provided him with other opportunities to be politically useful. The crucial factors were the abiding support of the Queen Mother, and Richelieu's nomination as cardinal. Marie de' Medici may have quarrelled with her son, but her regal status ensured that she could not be ignored as a political force; as one of her chief confidants, Richelieu too was never utterly alienated from the centre of power during these years. However, had he remained the bishop of a minor diocese, he could easily have been overlooked by La Vieuville and others in the political infighting of 1623 and 1624. As a cardinal he commanded a prestige and authority which could not easily be discounted. This supreme ecclesiastical honour enabled him to move in the most elevated political and social circles in a way that a bishopric could not have equalled.

He was also fortunate in that, just when Louis XIII was faced with formidable problems at home and abroad, the government was riven by faction. When Richelieu entered the royal council in 1624, he did not join a well-established, solid and cooperative team of ministers; it was one whose members were politically vulnerable and whose leader could no longer presume to have the support of the king. In the ten years since 1614 Richelieu had acquired masterly political skills, not only of survival but of advancement, and he deployed these skills to decisive effect in 1624. The political contingencies of that year enabled him to undermine La Vieuville while apparently doing no more than seek to uphold the interests of France. That he emerged at the summit of political power owed not a little to the infighting that preceded La Vieuville's dismissal in 1624. On the other hand, other figures had found themselves in a similar situation in recent years, and none had survived at the top for very long. Given the volatility of French high politics, could it be expected that Richelieu would be other than yet another transient minister, raised by political circumstance but unable to survive more than a few years at that rarified level?

Richelieu had no illusions about the fragility of his position. Although he had no serious doubts as to his intelligence and political ability, he lacked serious experience of government, his first period in the king's inner council having lasted only a few months in 1616 and 1617. His proximity to the Queen Mother undoubtedly had assisted his ascension, but although she and her son had undergone formal reconciliation they remained inveterately suspicious of each other; was it likely that Louis XIII would retain any longer than necessary the services of one of

Marie's closest advisers? Richelieu also knew that Louis had little liking for him on a personal level; the king found Richelieu austere in manner and inclined to instruct under the guise of offering advice. Richelieu's poor health counted against him. Even by the early 1620s he was subject to frequent bouts of illness, and it was by no means obvious that he could support for long the physical strains of government. That he did so until 1642 was a testimony to his mental toughness, for throughout the rest of his life he was dogged by one infirmity after another. Such considerations made Richelieu's immediate task self-evident: he must overcome the king's antipathy, or at least persuade Louis to set it aside; he must earn the king's trust by persuading him that he, Richelieu, was utterly and unequivocally devoted to his service; and he must convince Louis that Richelieu was the only man capable of developing a political strategy which would advance the interests of king and country. Here, then, was the objective. What principles and qualities did Richelieu bring to the task?

Chapter 3:   Richelieu as Minister

Richelieu and Principles of Government

Time was to show that Richelieu possessed mental and psychological attributes essential to his tenure of office, not least of which was a philosophical turn of mind. This had been cultivated in him by his studies at the Collège de Navarre and his intellectual formation in theology; his experiences as a bishop further developed in him a reflective approach to public affairs. In his diocese he had learned how to organise his pastoral and administrative programmes around well-thought-out principles deriving from two main and interlocking sources: the reforms emanating from the Council of Trent and the strategies of mission and conversion developed by Bérulle and Père Joseph. Richelieu brought the same mental attitude to government: domestic and foreign policies must correspond to logically consistent principles which, in turn, arose from bodies of theological and philosophical thought. This was not to deny that principles must be adapted to circumstance, or that much political business would be reactive to the actions of others; but Richelieu was consistent in his conviction that government must have strategic purposes which were explicable in philosophical and theological terms. The alternative was the kind of aimless government which, in his view, France had suffered since the death of Henri IV.

Accordingly, his ministry generated an extraordinary volume of literature to explain and disseminate the principles underpinning his policies, especially when those policies were controversial or provocative. His critics and enemies replied in kind, and for modern students of French political thought, the 1620s, 1630s and 1640s are decades extremely rich in polemical as well as dispassionate books and pamphlets dealing with great issues of politics during Richelieu's ministry. Richelieu made his own literary contribution to the debates. His immense correspondence, his *Memoirs* and his *Political Testament* (published posthumously in 1688) testify to a minister who never ceased speculating about government by drawing upon his theological and philosophical training. Richelieu developed into a master politician in a 'technical' sense: that is, somebody who proved adept at wielding and manipulating the powers that ministry conferred on him; but guiding his political actions, great and small, was a mind which subjected his actions to abstract principles that could be expounded in theological and philosophical terms.

Richelieu came to political prominence at a time of intense agitation in the practice of science. The 1620s and 1630s are central to that phenomenon which, for convenience of expression, is known as the Scientific Revolution. Some European natural philosophers (the word 'scientist' was not commonly used until mid-century) were advocating new methods of creating knowledge, based on experiment and observation, and were developing new theories concerning the structures and actions of matter. French natural philosophers were at the forefront of this movement. Famous names such as René Descartes and Pierre Gassendi were prominent in the Scientific Revolution, and groups of philosophers and scientists met informally but regularly in Paris from the 1620s and 1630s (the Dupuy brothers, Pierre and Jacques, hosted one such circle) to discuss the latest ideas in science and epistemology. The 'new science', among other things, generated the Mechanical Philosophy. This held that matter is composed of minute particles ('atoms'), and that variations which exist between the many forms of terrestrial matter, including all forms of life, are to be explained by differences in the number, size and shape of the atoms. It is not that forms of terrestrial matter are qualitatively different (they are all composed of the same types of atoms); variations in the nature of material objects are the product of differing numbers and relationships of the atoms.

The influence of the Mechanical Philosophy, of which Gassendi was a prominent exponent, extended far beyond the sciences into the social and political thought of the period. Richelieu who, as will appear later, patronised learning and the literary and visual arts, was himself well versed in the latest trends in science and was familiar with the content and implications of the Mechanical Philosophy. He attempted to adapt that philosophy to his practice of politics. He came to think of French society, and indeed the international community of which France was part, in 'mechanical' terms. Just as the scientist, by understanding the structures and properties of matter, could manipulate matter to particular effect, so the statesman who understood the structure and behaviour of the various societies and governments of which France and Europe were composed, could achieve great things by an analogous process of manipulation. The Mechanical Philosophy raised awkward questions of determinism (if human beings also are composed of atoms, are there any essential differences between human and other forms of existence; and can there be such a thing as free will?), but Richelieu did not allow them to confuse his attempts to apply the Philosophy to politics and diplomacy. Without being reductionist, it was possible for him as a politician to envisage the domestic and international arenas in which he operated as a vast laboratory in which, like the scientist, he strove to achieve understanding and exercise control.

None of the foregoing comments should be taken to imply that Richelieu came to office in 1624 with a fixed blueprint for action which he then resolutely followed over the next eighteen years; in 1624 he was still hesitant about the conduct of central government and recognised that he would have to develop policies as circumstance allowed. However, his memoirs, political testament and correspondence show that, as well as turning to philosophical, theological and scientific sources for guidance, he held certain purely political commitments which also inspired his actions. The most fundamental was his commitment to monarchy as a form of government. In itself this was unremarkable, for it can be said that, to all intents and purposes, everybody in France was a monarchist. The key question was: what kind of monarchy should France have? Richelieu never wavered in his conviction that, for France, not only was monarchy the one form of government capable of holding the country together; France possessed no institutions capable of sharing sovereignty with the king. There existed a plethora of law courts and other legal bodies, but in Richelieu's view they were instruments of royal authority, not participators in sovereignty. Richelieu, in other words, was committed to 'absolute' monarchy: that is, monarchy in which sovereignty was vested exclusively in the king. All law and all policy should be decided by the king. The king might take advice from ministers or from other quarters, but it was for him alone to take decisions. Richelieu was faithful to this concept of monarchy, partly because he believed that the fundamental laws of the state required it, but also because, for him, the dictates of religion did so. For Richelieu, it was God's will that France should be ruled by an absolute monarch. Legitimate forms of government, he believed, were less products

of historical evolution or accident than instruments created by God to
fulfil His purposes. God might punish unworthy monarchs by allowing
rebellious subjects to overthrow them (as happened in the Dutch Republic
when the Spanish monarchy was expelled); but provided that the kings
of France ruled according to divine law, God would preserve them in the
plenitude of their glory and powers. Richelieu saw his own task as being
to assist Louis XIII to fulfil this vocation; but first he had to persuade the
king that, in the cardinal, Louis had a principal minister utterly devoted
to him. This would be no easy matter given Richelieu's traditional
attachment to the Queen Mother; indeed, his emergence as principal
minister raised a most embarrassing question: could Richelieu's allegiance
be given equally to a master and a mistress, or would he have to choose?
Perhaps the price of Richelieu's remaining as Louis's principal minister
would be a break between the cardinal and Marie de' Medici.

In his social thought, Richelieu was a traditionalist who regarded
social hierarchy, just as much as monarchic government, as divinely
ordained. In its ideal form, he believed, French society was a unified
body composed of various groups, each of which had its rights and
responsibilities; by observing their mutual obligations, the groups which
constituted French society would coalesce into a united whole. The basic
social division was that between Clergy, Nobility and Third Estate, each
of which was itself subdivided: the Clergy had its hierarchy of archbishops,
bishops and so on; the Nobility had its hierarchy of titles; and the many
groups that comprised the Third Estate had their own hierarchical
structures. However, sinful human beings undermined the social order
which God desired; they engaged in disobedience, crime and rebellion,
and so challenged not only socio-political stability, but the social structures
which God ordained. One of the main goals of the monarch, abetted by
his principal minister, must be to preserve or restore traditional social
structures. The Catholic Church had a central role to play. The Church
must urge the faithful to live in peace and harmony, and to respect the
hierarchies of which society was composed, esteeming those who stood
higher and showing due regard to those who were below. The social, as
against the strictly religious, responsibility of the Church was to rein-
force stability by its teaching and example. Richelieu's social vision did
not preclude change or mobility. Indeed, as somebody who drew inspiration from the Mechanical Philosophy, he also thought of the millions of
individuals who comprised French society as the equivalent of 'atoms',
who constantly interacted with each other. He therefore understood
and expected that some individuals and families would rise in the social

hierarchy (indeed, he devoted much energy to supervising the ascension of his own family), while others would decline; but the dynamic elements in French society did not imply that the hierarchies and social divisions were themselves no more than impermanent epiphenomena: on the contrary, they were an expression of the divine will and as such were sacrosanct.

On such foundations Richelieu constructed his approach to government. In practical terms he had to reflect on topics such as how to preserve the prerogatives of the crown against the ambitions of aristocrats, *parlements*, provincial estates and other 'intermediate' legal bodies; how to enhance the prestige of the king at home and abroad; how to furnish the crown with the financial resources necessary for government; how to respond to movements of domestic protest, intrigue or rebellion which endangered social stability; what to do about the Huguenots, whose very existence was a challenge to the Catholic Church and its ability to bind society together; and in a Europe much of which was engulfed by war in the 1620s and 1630s, how to preserve the interests of the King of France, especially against aggressive Habsburg intentions. Moreover, as later chapters will show, the instruments of government and administration available to Richelieu, and the financial resources at his disposal, often were either unsuited to, or inadequate for, the task in hand. It was one thing to conceive grand strategies, but quite something else to put them into effect. France, at this stage of its history, was not a centralised state, and neither the king nor his principal minister was so naïve as to assume that the royal will would be executed unambiguously and without resistance.

As Richelieu developed his policies, he came to conceptualise them also through notions of *raison d'état* or 'reason of state'. This phrase will be discussed more fully later,[1] but in the present context it can be noted that 'reason of state' was a term widely used in the early seventeenth century; it was by no means unique to Richelieu. However, because the meanings attached to the term were disparate, in due course it will be necessary to define what Richelieu came to mean by it. 'Reason of state' was controversial because it was associated with the political thought of Machiavelli,[2] who was commonly thought to have contended that, because the over-riding responsibility of the ruler was to maintain his authority and the security of the state, he might do so at whatever cost: he might resort to any actions, even those which would be considered immoral or criminal if undertaken by his subjects. The prince was under no constraints, be they 'constitutional', religious, legal or moral; in other words, princely politics and conventional ethics were separate spheres, the latter having no application to the former. Such a brief characterisation of Machiavelli's thought distorts its subtlety, but it was in such crude terms that he was widely represented in the seventeenth century. Any statesman – and this applied to Richelieu – who allowed his policies to be justified in terms of 'reason of state', exposed himself to the charge of Machiavellianism. Richelieu took considerable pains to explain to Louis XIII's subjects the rationale behind his policies, and to deny that his understanding and implementation of *raison d'état* was a modern version of Machiavellianism, whatever his enemies alleged. Richelieu was to contend that, in his hands, the practice of *raison d'état* was compatible with Catholic doctrine and conventional ethical norms.

Richelieu and Louis XIII

Since, from 1624 onwards, Richelieu was acutely aware that his tenure of office was dependent on the king's will, the question arises of how he succeeded in earning the king's trust and avoiding the kind of fate that had befallen Concini and La Vieuville. To begin with a negative point, Richelieu never did succeed in establishing a warm personal relationship with Louis XIII; they were strictly formal in their conduct towards each other (their correspondence is peppered with ornate expressions of mutual esteem, but such effusions were customary in letters between a king and principal minister) and, so far as we know, rarely, if ever, slipped into an attitude of easy informality. This absence of mutual empathy was not necessarily a consequence of their difference in age; after all, Luynes, seven years older than Richelieu, had enjoyed a close rapport with the king. It was rather a matter of temperamental incompatibility. Richelieu, especially in the early years of his ministry, did turn upon the king the kind of charm with which he had courted the Queen Mother, but in this case it did not work. Louis found the cardinal a forbidding presence and the possessor of an overpowering personality. Richelieu regarded the king as unpredictable, having to be managed carefully and treated with circumspection. The fact that Louis did retain Richelieu for so many years should not cause us to underestimate the anxieties that Richelieu experienced, for he was never totally sure that his relationship with the king could survive all possible crises.

If personal amity did not hold the key to Louis's retaining Richelieu for so long, what did? The answer lies in their mutual political dependence. Louis came to recognise in his principal minister a figure of exceptional ability. For all his hesitation and procrastination in other respects, Louis did grasp the essential reality that Richelieu was that rarity among statesmen: somebody with a sense of the movement of the history of his times, combined with gifts of strategic management, foresight, tactical flexibility in the pursuit of his goals, and the capacities of a first-rate administrator. Moreover, after Louis rescued Richelieu from disgrace in 1630 on the so-called Day of Dupes (see chapter 4), Louis knew that his principal minister was utterly dependent on him and therefore could be trusted to serve the royal will and no other. Richelieu, for his part, was careful to consult the king on all major policies, to explain the reasoning behind his proposals, and to leave the final decision to Louis. Thereby, all policy unequivocally was royal policy; there was never any question of Richelieu acting in defiance of the king's wishes. This consultation formed an essential part of the king's political education, but it would be a mistake to dismiss it as indoctrination. Louis had an independent turn of mind, and the fact that he came to share his principal minister's priorities should not be interpreted as an indication that mentally or psychologically he was captivated, Svengali-like, by Richelieu. On the contrary, the minister never ceased consulting, persuading and cajoling the king, who invariably retained the right of decision. Louis XIII also applied himself to the detail of government and was able to comment on Richelieu's proposals intelligently and in an informed manner. Although never close at the personal level, Richelieu and Louis created an ideal political relationship, and it was this which bound them together for so many years.

This did not mean that Richelieu was in constant attendance on the king. He rarely attended the royal court unless required to do so for reasons of governmental duties, and his poor health often consigned him to the sickbed from where he remained in touch with Louis by letter. As early as the summer of 1625 he was writing to the king that,

> I have not the words to acknowledge the honour that your majesty does me in all respects, and even when the day comes that I have as much good health as I now have bad, my actions will not be sufficient to do so. What consoles me, Sire, is that...healthy or unwell...I will have no thought, movement or action which does not have your service as its aim.[3]

So frequent were Richelieu's bouts of illness, even at this stage of his career, that in 1626 Louis lessened the pressure on him by absolving him from having meetings with visitors, petitioners or other individuals who took up the cardinal's time. The document in which the king so informed Richelieu says, specifically, that its aim was to preserve the health of the minister so that he could concentrate on major affairs of state without being distracted by unnecessary interruptions. On the other hand, there were occasions when Louis insisted that Richelieu accompany him on military campaigns, even though the experience did place an enormous strain on the minister's health. Thus, when Louis personally directed the siege of La Rochelle in 1628, Richelieu was with him, even though the inclement weather and the military life took their toll.

Of course, the king, although he did not find court life congenial and kept his appearances there to a minimum, was surrounded constantly by attendants, members of the royal court, secretaries, visiting dignitaries and a host of petitioners and visitors; he also had his favourites: usually young noblemen whose company he enjoyed and upon whom he bestowed gifts and honours. This was something that Richelieu understood; he was also aware that he must therefore encourage the king in friendships with people who were acceptable to himself, Richelieu, and who posed no political danger. A favourite who was hostile to the principal minister could create difficulties and undermine that political relationship between king and principal minister which was essential to effective government. Accordingly, in 1625 Richelieu consented to Louis's friendship with one of his pages, François de Barradat, who seemed an innocuous young man. Barradat, however, developed ambitions beyond his station and had to be dismissed in 1626. Claude de Rouvroy de Saint Simon was a more discreet and longer-lasting royal favourite; although he had quarrels with Richelieu, they were kept within acceptable limits and Saint Simon remained a favourite until 1636.[4] Ironically, one of the greatest dangers to Richelieu from a royal favourite came towards the end of his life. In 1638 he brought into the royal court the eighteen-year-old Henri d'Effiat, Marquis de Cinq-Mars, son of a friend of the cardinal who had served in the king's inner council. Louis adopted Cinq-Mars as his favourite and conferred lucrative honours on him. However, Cinq-Mars developed political ambitions and urged Louis to allow him to attend the inner council. Richelieu strongly opposed the young favourite, who foolishly allowed himself to be drawn into a plot with the king's brother, Gaston d'Orléans, to have Richelieu assassinated. The cardinal learned of the conspiracy and had Cinq-Mars arrested and tried. He was executed on 12 September 1642, a few weeks before Richelieu himself died.

The Cinq-Mars affair was a late example of another danger with which Richelieu contended from his earliest years in office: the intrigues of aristocrats and princes of the blood. We should remember that Louis XIII was only the second Bourbon king of France and that he and his wife were childless until 1638; before the birth of the future Louis XIV, the king's heir was his younger brother Gaston, Duc d'Orléans. Gaston was a figure upon whom some disaffected aristocrats pinned their hopes: should the king die (and, like that of Richelieu, Louis XIII's health gave constant cause for concern), Gaston would succeed, sweep away Richelieu and his acolytes and heap rewards on his, Gaston's, acolytes. Other leading aristocratic houses, such as that of Condé, even had aspirations to the crown itself and saw Gaston as an obstacle. When Henri IV became the first Bourbon king on the extinction of the male line of the Valois dynasty in 1589, his claim was only marginally better than that of the Condés. They did not regard Henri IV or Louis XIII as qualitatively different from, or superior to, themselves; in their view the king was *primus inter pares*. If both Louis and Gaston died without male heirs (not an inconceivable prospect; after all, the last three Valois kings had done just that), then it was possible that the house of Condé would rule. To the Condé, Guise and other great aristocratic dynasties, the cabals which they formed and intrigues into which they entered were not acts of political betrayal; on the contrary, they were legitimate activities for persons of their social rank.

When Gaston reached his eighteenth birthday in 1626, Louis XIII and Richelieu wanted him to marry an heiress of the wealthy Montpensier family. If he produced sons, this would guarantee the succession of the main Bourbon line. It was for this reason that the opposite stance was taken by members of the Condé clan (who preferred both Louis and Gaston to be childless, whereby the chances of a Condé succession were kept alive), supported by others including the Duchess de Chevreuse and Gaston's governor, Jean-Baptiste d'Ornano, Comte de Montlaur. They entreated Gaston to refuse the marriage, while Ornano also urged Gaston to demand admission to the king's inner council. Richelieu persuaded Louis to dismantle the opposition by having Ornano and several of his associates arrested on 4 May 1626; and when the Chancellor, d'Aligre, showed some hesitation over the arrest, he was exiled to his estates and Richelieu brought two of his own supporters into the council: Michel de Marillac and Antoine Coiffier de Ruzé, Marquis d'Effiat (father of the Cinq-Mars executed in 1642). Gaston's marriage to Marie de Montpensier went ahead on 6 August 1626,[5] and later in the year several arrests took place: they included the Vendôme brothers (natural sons of Henri IV), the Comte de Soissons, and Henri de Talleyrand, Comte de Chalais (who was implicated in a plot to kill Richelieu, and was executed). The king's resolute action deterred aristocratic factions for the time being, but they were to reappear later in his reign. Louis gave Richelieu a bodyguard, but the cardinal could never relax his vigilance; the danger of assassination was ever present.

Yet it is important to stress that Richelieu was not anti-aristocratic or anti-noble as a matter of principle. He came from a noble family himself, and held conservative social views: he did not question the social status of the nobility, the privileges and wealth that they enjoyed, or their functions as military commanders and governors in the provinces. What he did resist was their capacity to create political and social disorder. He interpreted aristocratic intrigue and rebellion as a disastrous consequence of the disorder bequeathed by the Wars of Religion. Too many aristocrats and nobles assumed themselves to be above the normal constraints of law and morality; they had created spurious and misbegotten values and inhabited a perverse moral world. Symptomatic of this moral corruption was their propensity to engage in duels.[6] The duel had evolved from being a means of settling serious disputes formally and legally in cases where law courts were unable to reach a judgement (for instance, in cases involving charges of incest), to being a private and extra-judicial contest between young nobles, often fighting over trivial insults. Duels had become widespread by the early seventeenth century and led to the death of large numbers of young noblemen. The Catholic Church denounced duelling, and the state sought to curb it by issuing edicts against it: major edicts were forthcoming in 1602, 1609, 1614 and 1623; others came in 1643 and 1651. The crown proclaimed duelling to be a crime punishable by death. Nevertheless, noblemen who killed opponents in a duel usually escaped justice, and whereas commoners with grievances were expected to go to the law courts, nobles too often ignored the courts and settled their quarrels violently in duels. Duels rejected the principle, upheld by church and king alike, that society must resolve its disputes peaceably and within the law; duels showed that aristocrats and nobles considered themselves above the law and justified in employing violence to resolve even trivial disputes.

Richelieu approached duels as providing a test-case for the imposition of royal authority over the aristocracy and nobility; and in 1627 the requisite incident occurred. François, Comte de Montmorency-Bouteville, was, as his name indicates, a member of the great Montmorency clan; he was well known at court and had served Gaston d'Orléans. He was hot-headed, and by the age of twenty-four had fought over twenty duels. After his most recent, which involved the death of his opponent, he had fled to Brussels. In 1627, however, he not only returned to France but on 12 May fought another duel. He did so openly and as a direct affront to the anti-duelling edicts of the crown: he and two seconds fought the Marquis de Beuvron, with his seconds, in the Place Royale (now the Place des Vosges) in Paris. One of Bouteville's seconds was badly wounded, and one of Beuvron's was killed. Bouteville and his other second, the Comte Rosmadec des Chapelles, fled but were arrested before they got out of the country. They were tried by the Parlement of Paris, which condemned them to death. The king and Richelieu were subjected to immense pressure from Gaston, the Queen Mother, the Montmorency family and numerous other aristocrats, including Boute-ville's mother, to quash the judgement. The king and his minister stood firm. They both recognised that their insistence on the primacy of obedience to the crown was at stake, and refused to interfere in the court's judgement. Bouteville and Chapelles were executed.

The consequences of the affair were various. In the short run the incidence of duelling declined considerably as young noblemen heeded the warning; in the 1630s, however, duelling gradually spread again as the former laxity in the application of the anti-duelling laws resumed. By the late 1630s Richelieu was reminding the king of the necessity to enforce anti-duelling legislation, but amidst the array of other problems confronting the crown by this stage, this seemed a relatively minor matter to Louis XIII, who showed little inclination to act decisively. The Bouteville affair affected two other sets of relations. Members of the royal family and aristocrats who had pleaded in vain for Bouteville's life were left embittered at judges in the Parlement, who had not found some technicality on which to dismiss the charges; but more specifically, *les grands* blamed Richelieu for, allegedly, having controlled the mind of the king and having closed it to the entreaties of his mother, brother and other aristocratic petitioners. The Bouteville affair fuelled hatred of Richelieu among some aristocrats, and contributed to the attempts they made to unseat him.

Chapter 4: The First Years of Richelieu's Ministry, 1624–30

No statesman begins his public career with a *tabula rasa*; he inherits the problems that had faced his predecessors and the policies that they had pursued. He does not necessarily have to continue those policies, but even the process of modifying, or if necessary reversing, them can be difficult and time-consuming. The head of government has to be persuaded of the necessity for a new policy, the resource implications have to be assessed, and the mechanisms for change have to be set in motion. In the international sphere, Richelieu was faced with a context which, on the whole, was unfavourable to France, but with two major developments excepted: the creation of a defensive alliance with England and the Dutch Republic in 1624 and the successful outcome of negotiations, conducted by La Vieuville before his dismissal, for a marriage between Henriette and Charles I of England. The wedding took place on 1 May 1625.

In other respects the outlook was ominous, for the Habsburgs, in both their Austrian and Spanish branches, had achieved much success in recent years. In central Europe, where the Bohemian rising of 1618 and its aftermath had escalated into what later generations were to call the Thirty Years War, the armies of the Holy Roman Emperor, Ferdinand II, carried all before them. Christian IV of Denmark intervened in 1626, but to little avail: the Imperial forces drove the Danish army into retreat and even invaded Denmark itself. By the Treaty of Lübeck (1629), Christian withdrew from the war, leaving Ferdinand in control of the whole of Germany. Acting in a manner which appealed to *dévot* opinion in France, Ferdinand issued the Edict of Restitution, which provided for extensive tracts of Protestant territory to be restored to Catholicism. In the other main war, between Spain and the Dutch Republic, the Dutch proved capable of liberating provinces which the Spanish had occupied in the mid-1620s, and by 1629 had once again rendered their frontiers reasonably secure; but the threat from Spain remained and the war, which dovetailed with the Thirty Years War at numerous points, had many years to run. France, in spite of its alliance with the Dutch, had remained formally neutral in both of these conflicts, and Richelieu for the time being could do little about them apart from signing an accord in 1625 with a Protestant mercenary general, Mansfeld, by which Mansfeld received French subsidies to attack the Spanish in the Palatinate. The early to mid-1620s unquestionably were years of Habsburg triumph in Europe. France was exerting little influence in the international arena, being reduced to observing the two major wars from the sideline.

Northern Italy: the Valtelline and Mantua

One problem which Richelieu inherited concerned the Valtelline. Since the Treaty of Madrid (1622) the Spanish had enjoyed easy passage of their troops through the valley. In 1623 France entered into a league with Venice and Savoy, but neither had much confidence in their French partner. One of Richelieu's first tasks was to restore their faith in the French government, along with the faith of other interested parties. In 1625 and 1626 he sent envoys to Switzerland to convince the governing councils of the cantons and the Grisons-in-exile that the recovery of the Valtelline was possible. A small French force was despatched to the Valtelline where, over the next three years, it fought a sporadic campaign against the Spanish. To the Republic of Venice, Richelieu sent Étienne d'Aligre, son of the Chancellor, as ambassador, to reassure the Venetian Senate of French resolve. D'Aligre's task was made all the more difficult when news arrived that, in the war between the Dutch Republic and Spain, the city of Breda had surrendered to the Spanish (5 June 1625), while in France itself another Huguenot rebellion had begun. Meanwhile, Richelieu opened secret contact with Count-Duke Olivares, his counterpart in Spain, about a negotiated settlement. It was signed on 5 March 1626 and ratified on 2 May. By this Treaty of Monzón the Valtelline in effect was neutralised: the Grisons were restored as rulers, but Catholic worship was guaranteed and Catholic magistrates were allowed to practise. The forts in the valley would be destroyed, but because the wording of the treaty was vague on the question of Spanish right of passage through the valley, it was evident that the Spanish would resume the practice when it suited them. When the terms of the treaty became known, the Venetians were indignant at what they considered their betrayal by France. D'Aligre protested that Monzón was not inimical to Venetian interests, but there was no disguising the fact that Richelieu had kept the Venetians in the dark and then presented them with a *fait accompli*. The Treaty of Monzón was unsatisfactory from the French point of view: it did not exclude the Spanish from the Valtelline and it alienated the governments of Venice and other north Italian states. In Richelieu's defence it might be said that he inherited the Valtelline question and that the treaty was the best he could get in the circumstances; but it marked an inauspicious beginning in international affairs.

The Mantuan succession crisis was, however, of a different order. Mantua was of considerable strategic importance, for it comprised two territories: Mantua itself on the south-east border of Milan (Spain's main military base in northern Italy) and Montferrat, with the fortress of Casale, on the western frontier of Milan. On 25 December 1627, Vincent II Gonzaga, Duke of Mantua, died without a direct male heir. Two claimants emerged. Vincent's sister Eleanor was married to Emperor Ferdinand II; with his support and that of the Spanish Habsburgs, she insisted that the succession should pass to a junior branch of the Gonzaga line, and that accordingly the Duke of Guastalla (a tiny territory bordering on Mantua) should succeed. However, within Mantua itself, the Grand Chancellor, Alessandro Stiffi, and his colleagues concluded that a stronger claim lay with a French aristocrat: Charles de Gonzague, Duc de Nevers, the governor of Champagne. In January 1628, Nevers stole a march on his rival by travelling to Mantua and assuming government. Mantua had an unusual constitutional position, for although it was ruled by a duke, ultimate suzerainty over the territory lay with the Holy Roman Emperor. The Spanish Habsburgs were alarmed at the prospect of a French ruler in such a sensitive territory. Philip IV persuaded the Emperor to withhold recognition of Nevers. Philip brought Charles-Emmanuel of Savoy (who also felt betrayed by the Treaty of Monzón) over to his side by offering him Montferrat. In 1628 Spanish forces occupied most of the duchy of Mantua, leaving only the fortified towns of Mantua and Casale in the hands of Nevers. At the end of the year the Spanish besieged Casale.

Richelieu was in favour of military intervention in Mantua, although he did not intend a declaration of war, for France was in no position to undertake a full-scale conflict with Spain. Nevertheless, by now Richelieu had come to the conclusion that France must do all in its power to weaken the Habsburgs, especially the Spanish branch of the family. A Spanish preponderance in western Europe was fundamentally hostile to France's interests; France must resist the Spanish Habsburgs at every turn. Louis XIII agreed with this analysis, and in March 1629 he and Richelieu headed an army whose aim was to relieve the siege of Casale. The fighting was hard and in 1630 spread to territories of the Duke of Savoy, from whom the French took the fortress of Pinerolo. In 1630 the Spanish withdrew from Casale upon a promise from Louis XIII that he would refrain from further attacks on Spanish or Savoyard territory.

The Emperor still did not recognise Nevers as legitimate Duke of Mantua. Richelieu sought to force Ferdinand II's hand by exploiting his imperial difficulties. Although he controlled Germany militarily, the Emperor was faced with three major problems: first, he was concerned to secure for his son, Ferdinand, the succession to the Imperial crown by having the Electors choose him King of the Romans;[1] secondly, the Electors were demanding that he dismiss his leading general, Wallenstein, whose conduct was deeply offensive to Catholic and Protestant princes alike; thirdly, Gustavus Adolphus of Sweden was threatening to intervene in Germany on behalf of the Protestant cause, and indeed did so in July 1630. Ferdinand II called the Electors to Regensburg to discuss these matters. Richelieu sent Brûlart de Léon as ambassador and Père Joseph as an observer with the task of securing the Mantuan succession for the Duc de Nevers. At Regensburg, Père Joseph met representatives of the Electors, who agreed to support the claim of Nevers in return for subsidies from France. True to their word, they urged Ferdinand II to recognise Nevers. The Emperor gave way and indicated his readiness to recognise Nevers, hoping that this would help to secure the election of his son as King of the Romans.[2] Meanwhile, fighting between France, Spain and Savoy was continuing in Italy, with the pope trying to mediate a settlement. One of the chief papal representatives was Giulio Mazzarino, whose peregrinations between the contending sides first brought him into contact with Richelieu. After many setbacks and hesitations, France and Spain agreed on the Treaty of Cherasco (1631). The fighting ceased, the French agreed to restore to the Duke of Savoy the territory which they had taken, and all sides recognised Nevers as Duke of Mantua.

Richelieu could be more satisfied with Cherasco than with Monzón, but while the treaty signified a certain degree of progress in the struggle to weaken the Habsburgs, it was peripheral to the main conflicts then going on in western and central Europe. Sooner or later, France would have to involve itself openly in those wars if it were to challenge Habsburg predominance.

Domestic Issues: the Huguenots

The most serious domestic problem to confront Richelieu early in his ministry was another rebellion by Huguenots. Although peace had been signed with the Huguenots at Montpellier (1622), those in La Rochelle remained intensely suspicious of Richelieu's intentions. Their fears were as much economic as religious. Richelieu took a close interest in the economic revival of France, to which end he advocated the development of an extensive and aggressive maritime commerce and the creation of overseas trading companies capable of rivalling Dutch and English enterprises. In 1626 he was appointed *Grand Maître de la Navigation et du Commerce*, an office which also conferred on him administration of the colonies. As early as 1625 he presented to the king a *règlement pour la mer* in which he called for the expansion of the Mediterranean fleet to protect French shipping and to secure access to northern Italy by sea.[3] He lent his support to the creation of trading companies: in 1626 the *Compagnie du Morbihan* (or *Compagnie des Cent Associés*, as it came to be known) was founded to trade in the West Indies and Canada, and also the *Compagnie de Saint-Pierre* whose aim was to trade with Canada. Richelieu placed most of his hopes for North America in the *Compagnie de la Nouvelle France* (1628): it would not only conduct trade in North America, but also establish colonies, transport emigrants, oversee the construction of towns and ports and generally advance the interests of France in that part of the world. His attention also turned to the war fleet. Plans were laid for the expansion of fleets to serve in the North Sea and Atlantic as well as the Mediterranean. While such projects might have served the greater good of France, they caused disquiet in ports such as Saint Malo and La Rochelle, whose merchant communities and municipal authorities saw them as a danger to their traditional trading patterns and hence their prosperity. Viewed from political circles in Paris, Richelieu's proposals appeared to contain much merit; to ports in western France they represented danger.

Richelieu's intentions were also followed abroad. The Spanish, Dutch and English governments were apprehensive over the growth of French commercial and military maritime activity, for it signalled a more aggressive French presence than hitherto. It was the English who took the initiative by contriving a crisis whose aim was to deal a pre-emptive blow at Richelieu's maritime ambitions. In 1627 the Duc de Soubise, a Huguenot military leader, was in exile in England. He appealed to Charles I to send military help to the Huguenots of La Rochelle to secure their remaining liberties. In June 1627 Charles I, allegedly in the name of the defence of the Huguenots, sent to La Rochelle a fleet of eighty ships and 8000 soldiers under the command of the Duke of Buckingham. The plan was to occupy the city, initiate a wider rebellion and force Louis XIII and Richelieu to agree to terms which would include a promise to abandon the programme of maritime expansion. The fleet arrived in July and landed troops on the île de Ré, just off the coast from La Rochelle. Two forts on the island, held by French troops, were besieged.

Within La Rochelle itself there was consternation. Neither the Huguenots nor the municipality of La Rochelle had invited the English, but who would believe such protestations of innocence? The very presence of foreign troops implicated La Rochelle in the invasion. Popular agitation broke out in the city, where fear of a decline of the port – seen as a strong possibility if Richelieu's commercial plans bore fruit and other Atlantic ports flourished at La Rochelle's expense – combined with the religious fears of Huguenots to produce a mass movement of panic, which then called for the city to throw in its lot with the English. By September 1627 the city was in a state of rebellion triggered by the intervention of the English, which had heightened the religious and economic fears of the populace.

Louis XIII and Richelieu arrived at the head of an army of 20,000 and laid siege to the city. This proved to be a shrewd decision for reasons both of principle and of pragmatism. In their public pronouncements, Louis and Richelieu portrayed the rebellion as political, not religious, in nature; thereby they obviated any pretext for a general rising of Huguenots or for calls to Louis XIII from the governments of Protestant states to show restraint. It also enabled Louis and Richelieu to present the English as invaders, not protectors of the Huguenots. In practical terms, the siege threw the onus for continuing the rebellion onto the inhabitants of La Rochelle, and reinforced the alleged political, as against religious, nature of their resistance. It also minimised the chances of a massacre, something that almost inevitably would have occurred had Louis attacked and captured the city. In November 1627 Buckingham, having failed to take the forts on the Île de Ré, retreated to England leaving La Rochelle to its own devices. Richelieu received letters of felicitation from

Queen Anne and Bérulle, the latter attributing English failure to divine intervention.[4] Two further attempts were made by the English in 1628 to relieve the city, but they too ended in ignominious failure.

Louis and Richelieu personally directed the siege, taking up their residence in the encampment (the king went to Paris for a few weeks in the spring of 1628, but then returned to La Rochelle). The city was cut off from the sea by the construction of a dike across the bay in which the city was situated, and the siege aroused international as well as national interest, commanders of armies in Germany travelling there to inspect its progress. The inhabitants of La Rochelle suffered appallingly. Food supplies ran out, disease was rampant, and people were driven to the most desperate measures to survive. The population had been some 28,000 at the beginning of the siege, but by the autumn of 1628, deaths mainly through famine and disease had reduced it to about 6000. As winter approached it was evident that the population was in no condition to continue resistance. On 29 October 1628 La Rochelle surrendered to the king. On 1 November he formally entered the city. Louis would have been justified in imposing the most draconian punishment upon the rebels, but he and Richelieu opted for clemency. Some leaders were exiled, but otherwise a general amnesty was granted; there was neither massacre nor mass executions. The municipality was deprived of its privileges, but had expected no less. The Huguenots retained their rights of worship, although Catholicism was restored to the city.

As news of the fall of La Rochelle spread, messages of congratulations to Louis and Richelieu poured in from many parts of Europe. The international prestige of the king and his minister reached unprecedented heights; even more importantly, perhaps, their confidence in each other was confirmed. The siege had been a sustained test of nerve, for had La Rochelle been relieved by the English, and the king forced to retreat, the damage to Louis's standing would have been incalculable, Richelieu would have been dismissed, savage political infighting around the crown would have taken place and civil war would have been a distinct possibility. As it was, king and minister saw in each other not only somebody who had passed through a shared experience of extreme danger and hardship, but somebody who had demonstrated exceptional powers of tenacity and resolution. The siege of La Rochelle sealed their relationship as no other episode had or could. The generous terms which Louis extended to the city, especially his confirmation of Huguenot rights of worship, were consistent with the crown's proposition that this had been a political rather than a religious rebellion. This being so, there was no

need to impose religious penalties. To many *dévots* this was a false differ-
entiation, and Louis and Richelieu had squandered a golden opportunity
to eliminate Protestantism in La Rochelle. In private, Richelieu might
have conceded that he had indeed made a fine distinction, but it allowed
him to abide by the principle that he had learned as Bishop of Luçon:
persuasion rather than persecution was the way to deal with the Huguenots. To have imposed abolition on Huguenot worship in La Rochelle
might have satisfied short-term Catholic triumphalist instincts, but it
would have stored up trouble for the future. An act of generosity was
more likely to undermine the Huguenots than one of severity.

This same conciliatory mentality was displayed the following year,
only this time it was preceded by an ominous example of the harsh
alternative. While the siege of La Rochelle was progressing, Soubise's
brother, the Duc de Rohan, raised the Huguenots of Languedoc. He
gathered an army and took control of Nîmes, Montauban, Castres and
other towns. Against him the crown sent the Prince de Condé and Duc
de Montmorency. In 1628 the two sides fought campaigns in which each
committed appalling atrocities, massacres, mass hangings and the
destruction of crops and property. The royalist forces were reinforced
by Louis XIII himself in 1629 when he returned from the campaign in
Italy. He besieged Privas in May, but whereas he had shown restraint
and clemency in his treatment of La Rochelle, he made an example of
Privas. When it fell, after a siege of two weeks in which over 600 defenders
were killed, the town was pillaged by royal troops, sixty prisoners were
hanged, over a hundred were sent to the galleys (in addition to several
hundred more who had earlier fled the town and been taken prisoner),
and the property of all the inhabitants of the town was seized.[5] As news of
the treatment of Privas spread, other Huguenot towns quickly capitulated. They included Alès, which surrendered to the king on 17 June
before a shot had been fired. Louis, following the advice of Richelieu,
used this opportunity to bring the entire Huguenot rising in Languedoc
to an end. By the 'Edict of Grace' of Alès, he guaranteed full rights of
worship to all Huguenot towns which submitted to his authority; on the
other hand their fortifications had to be dismantled as a guarantee that
they would not rebel in future. A general amnesty was extended to
Huguenots who had fought against the crown. The military penalty apart,
the Huguenots of France retained, in addition to their rights of worship,
the other privileges which the Edict of Nantes had accorded them.

The Grace of Alès followed logically on the settlement at La Rochelle.
It affirmed the principle that the king offered peace, clemency and

freedom of worship to his Huguenot subjects, whereas Soubise, Rohan and other Huguenot military leaders had brought nothing but disaster. The attitude of Louis and Richelieu contrasted with that of the Emperor Ferdinand II, whose Edict of Restitution, also issued in 1629, sought to deprive many of the Protestants of Germany of their rights of worship. *Dévot* groups in France were scandalised at the Grace of Alès, for once again, in their view, Cardinal Richelieu had turned down an opportunity to serve the Catholic Church by following the example set by the Emperor. Richelieu's defence was that the chief domestic priority in 1629 was peace (especially since other parts of the country were experiencing social instability arising out of economic distress); and peace would be achieved through clemency, not oppression. The cardinal's argument proved to be remarkably prescient: thereafter the Huguenots as a group remained loyal to the crown; 1629 marks the end of a long phase of Huguenot rebellion which went back to the earliest days of the Wars of Religion; and in Germany, the Edict of Restitution had the opposite effect to what Ferdinand II intended, for it drove German Protestants into the hands of the Swedes, who, with French help, proceeded to drive back the Imperial troops and force the Emperor onto the defensive. The Grace of Alès and the Edict of Restitution represented contrasting approaches to the question of Protestantism. Richelieu and Louis XIII desired the conversion of Huguenots as much as any Catholic, but opted for the way of preaching and mission. Ferdinand II chose compulsion backed by political and military force.

Challenges to Richelieu: the Day of Dupes

By the end of the 1620s, the broad contours of Richelieu's approach to France's foreign and domestic problems were emerging: diplomatic and military resistance to Spain in Italy, the frustration of Austrian Habsburg purposes in Germany, and compromise with the Huguenots at home. His critics included aristocrats, *dévots*, his colleague Marillac in the king's council, and even his former protector, the Queen Mother. Marie de' Medici accused Richelieu of having betrayed his position as a cardinal by pursuing anti-Habsburg policies (as Regent she had tried to uphold good relations with both Vienna and Madrid), and by treating the Huguenots with what she considered a scandalous laxity. Marie also resented Richelieu's closeness to Louis XIII, and the influence which he exercised over the king. Richelieu's enemies advocated an alternative strategy: close relations with the Spanish and Austrian Habsburgs, and the forcible eradication of Protestantism from France.

They justified their stance by reference to principle, but also to the financial and social cost of Richelieu's policies. The financial aspect was pressed by Marillac, who, in addition to being *garde des sceaux*, was in charge of the administration of government finances under Richelieu's direction. After the fall of La Vieuville, Richelieu had instituted a *chambre de justice* to investigate malpractice by financiers who loaned money to the crown. The tribunal probed as far back as 1607 (when a similar *chambre* had operated), but concentrated on recent years. Although the *chambre* of 1624–5, as a result of its investigations, imposed fines totalling 10,800,000 livres and initiated legal proceedings against thirteen financiers (five of whom were executed), the exercise was designed to complete La Vieuville's disgrace rather than pave the way to fundamental fiscal reform. It did not investigate structural problems in governmental finance, nor was it authorised to make recommendations on taxation and tax farming.[6] Expenditure continued to rise – it was 36 million livres in 1624 and over 44 million in 1626 – and in 1626 the anticipated revenue for 1627 had already been spent.[7] The cost of military intervention in the Valtelline was a major factor in this increase in expenditure, and the fiscal disruption caused by the Huguenot rebellions also added to the government's burden. Richelieu was sensitive to the need to control expenditure, and in 1626 and 1627 began planning to do so (his office of *Grand Maître de la Navigation et du Commerce* was intended, among other things, to give him control of maritime and colonial finance); but the course of events over the next few years frustrated his efforts, and in the 1630s he found himself having to resort to the kinds of fiscal devices of which he had been so critical when they were practised by La Vieuville.

The financial strains imposed by his policies in the 1620s also contributed to the social unrest of the later years of the decade. The 1610s and early 1620s had been years of relatively good harvests and food supplies in France, but the later 1620s saw a downturn which was part of a general European pattern. Inclement weather caused widespread harvest failures in 1627, 1628 and 1629, and the hunger which followed made people vulnerable to the onset of disease. There had been sporadic and localised revolts, mainly against government fiscality, every year since 1623, but from 1627 to 1629, many provinces and provincial towns experienced food riots on a large scale: Bordeaux and other towns in the south-west, Amiens, Auxerre, Troyes and Paris to the north, Lyon, Dijon and their respective hinterlands, Aix, Marseille and many other towns and regions;

and these risings, it should be remembered, coincided with the Huguenot rebellions in La Rochelle and Languedoc. In the late 1620s much of
France was in turmoil; critics of Richelieu at court and within the *dévot*
community placed the blame squarely at his door.

In the autumn of 1630, Richelieu's enemies sensed that they were on
the verge of overthrowing him. The talks at Regensburg between the
Emperor and the Electors were progressing, but the word was that the
French plenipotentiaries were making little headway over the Mantuan
succession question. The campaign in Italy looked to be bogged down as
the Spanish besieged Casale. In September, Louis XIII was in Lyon
when he fell dangerously ill; he was given the final rites and his death
was expected. Gaston d'Orléans prepared to become king and Marillac
anticipated being principal minister. The king confounded all expectations by recovering and returning to Paris, where Richelieu joined him.
When he got there, the king required Gaston and Condé to swear to
keep faith with Richelieu. On 11 November he met his mother at her
Parisian residence, the Luxembourg Palace, where a stormy scene took
place. Marie denounced Richelieu to her son and demanded that he
dismiss the cardinal. Richelieu managed to gain entry to the meeting
and was subjected to a tirade by the Queen Mother, who accused him of
having abandoned every principle for which she stood. Louis, shaken by
his mother's explosion, ordered Richelieu to leave and retired himself to
his rural retreat at Versailles. Word spread that Richelieu was finished.
In scenes reminiscent of the aftermath of the murder of Concini, crowds
of courtiers and political advisers, including Marillac, rushed to the
Luxembourg Palace to congratulate Marie on having destroyed Richelieu.
The cardinal himself was in despair, and appeared at a loss as to what to
do. His friend Cardinal de la Valette persuaded him to go to Versailles
and seek an interview with the king. He did so and spent four hours in
private discussion with Louis. Louis assured the minister of his complete
confidence. The next day word reached the Luxembourg Palace that
Richelieu was confirmed as principal minister. Marillac and other critics
of Richelieu were arrested; the crowds around Marie dispersed rapidly;
Louis refused to see his mother. One of Marie's courtiers, remarking on
this remarkable turn of events, observed that 11 November had been the
journée des dupes, and it is as the Day of Dupes that it has passed into
history.

At the end of 1630 Richelieu was in, not an unassailable position, for
Louis could dismiss him at any time, but a position immeasurably
stronger than ever before. The Day of Dupes signalled uncompromisingly

that Louis XIII was persuaded of the virtues both of Richelieu as an individual and of the political strategies for which he stood. The king, in short, would pursue the *bon Français* policies advocated by his father and continued by Richelieu, rather than the *dévot* policies demanded by his mother. The siege and capture of La Rochelle had brought king and minister closer together; the Day of Dupes sealed their union and confirmed the strategic route along which Richelieu was taking government.

The Consolidation of Richelieu's Power

After the dramatic events of 11 and 12 November 1630, Richelieu seized the opportunity to purge the ranks of those implicated in plots and manoeuvres against him. Marillac was imprisoned and his brother Louis, commander of the French forces in Italy, was tried and later executed (1632). Gaston d'Orléans fled the country and went to Lorraine. In 1632 he attempted an invasion to 'rescue' Louis XIII from Richelieu, but the attempt failed and one of his generals, Montmorency, was seized, tried and executed. The Queen Mother was held in detention at Compiègne; in 1631 she escaped and fled to Brussels. She never saw France or her son again, eventually dying in Cologne in 1642. The household of the Queen, Anne of Austria, was emptied of advisers and attendants suspected of being hostile to Richelieu; they were replaced with figures loyal to the cardinal. François de Bassompierre, confidant of Marie and Gaston d'Orléans, was imprisoned in the Bastille and remained there for twelve years. The Duc d'Elbeuf lost his governorship of Picardy, and other aristocrats were variously punished.

The year 1630 did not mark the end of plots against Richelieu, for as long as Gaston d'Orléans was alive he remained a potential danger; but for the immediate future Richelieu's ascendancy was assured. He underpinned his position by advancing his own *créatures* or other loyal persons in governmental service. Changes at the centre included the promotion of Abel Servien to Secretary of State for War, and of Pierre Séguier to *garde des sceaux* in 1633 and Chancellor of France in 1635. As secretaries of state, Richelieu selected *fidèles* such as Léon Bouthillier, Comte de Chavigny, in foreign affairs and François Sublet de Noyers in war. To the department of finance he appointed Claude de Bullion and Claude Bouthillier.[8] In the provinces, governors loyal to Richelieu were nominated: Chevreuse succeeded Elbeuf in Picardy, Cardinal de la Valette replaced Marie de' Medici in Anjou, Richelieu himself assumed the governorship of Brittany and he appointed his brother-in-law, La Meilleraye, as his lieutenant. A second stratagem for bolstering his power lay in the marriages which he negotiated for members of his family on both its du Plessis and La Porte sides. Reference was made earlier to the marriage of Richelieu's sister Nicole to Urbain de Maillé, Marquis de Brézé, and Richelieu's role in financing that match;[9] the daughter of Nicole and Brézé, Claire-Clémence, achieved a spectacular marriage: her husband was Louis II de Bourbon, Prince de Condé. Richelieu's cousin Marie married the Duc de la Valette in 1634 and her sister married the Duc de Puylaurens. Richelieu's uncle, Amador de la Porte, was made Commander of the Order of Malta and Grand Prieur de France. His son and the minister's cousin, Charles de la Porte, became Duc de la Meilleraye and, in 1639, Maréchal de France. By such measures Richelieu created a web of alliances through whose own networks he could distribute patronage and extend his influence at court, in the government and in the provinces.[10]

One further observation is appropriate. The Day of Dupes was probably less the cause of this process than the occasion to accelerate it. Any statesman of this period knew that patronage and nepotism were essential weapons in the struggle to maintain office. The Day of Dupes created a climate in which Richelieu could proceed quickly to the promotion of his *créatures* in central government and to advantageous marriages for his relations; but he would have attempted to do so even without the Day of Dupes, although doubtless he would have moved more slowly and with greater circumspection.

Chapter 5: Richelieu and French Foreign Policy, 1630–42

Defence of the Frontiers

If the Day of Dupes enabled Richelieu to consolidate his power in government, it also freed him to develop a *bon Français* policy in the international sphere, relatively, although not completely, free from the ideological constraints to which the now-discredited pro-Spanish lobby had attempted to subject him. For the time being his motives in foreign policy were primarily defensive. The war in Germany was swinging in favour of the Habsburgs in the late 1620s, and although the Spanish were experiencing setbacks against the Dutch Republic (in 1628 the Dutch captured the Spanish treasure fleet and in 1629 took s'Hertogenbosch), their control of Flanders presented a permanent danger to the northern frontier of France. In formal terms France adopted a policy of neutrality towards these conflicts, although it had signed treaties with the Dutch and Danes to subsidise these states in their struggles against the Habsburgs. When it came to regions which Richelieu deemed crucial to the security of France, however, he did commit troops even though no declarations of war were made. One such region was Savoy and northern Italy; hence his intervention in the Valtelline and Mantua as described earlier. Another such area was Lorraine.

This independent duchy dominated the militarily sensitive zone between France's north-eastern frontier and the Rhineland. The dukes of Lorraine normally trod a wary path, seeking to antagonise neither the French nor the Habsburgs. However, in 1624 there succeeded to the duchy Charles IV, who was pro-Habsburg in his foreign policy and, as a devout Catholic, an advocate of the extension of Counter-Reformation Catholicism by every possible means; this too implied collaboration with the Habsburgs. Afraid that Charles IV would invite the Spanish or the Emperor to place Lorraine under their protection and establish military bases in the duchy, Richelieu sought to pre-empt such a move by urging him to allow French troops into fortified places in Lorraine; the French would guarantee Lorraine's independence. Charles entered into negotiations with Richelieu, but had no intention of consenting to the French proposal. The talks failed as Charles intended but, unwilling to leave Lorraine open to possible Habsburg intervention, Richelieu ordered the occupation of the duchy. In December 1631 French forces marched into Lorraine and in 1632 Charles IV reluctantly signed the Treaty of Liverdun, by which he ceded several crossing points over the river Meuse to France.

Matters did not end here. While the abortive negotiations were taking place in 1631, the disgraced and exiled Gaston d'Orléans travelled to Nancy, capital of Lorraine, and accepted the hospitality of the duke. Louis XIII was still childless, and the more years went by without Anne of Austria giving birth, the more Gaston's confidence grew that he would succeed his brother. However, he was a widower with a daughter, and because a female could not rule France it was necessary, for personal dynastic ambitions, for him to marry again and produce a son who could follow him as king. He covertly discussed with Charles IV a marriage with Charles's sister Marguerite. Charles agreed and the marriage took place in January 1632, but in secret. From Charles IV's standpoint the marriage eased the burden of the concessions he made in the Treaty of Liverdun, for if Louis XIII did die childless and Gaston succeeded, the queen of France would be a princess of the house of Lorraine.

The marriage could not be concealed indefinitely, and in the summer of 1632 Louis and Richelieu heard that it had taken place. They reacted with fury at an action which was certainly provocative and perhaps treasonable. A Prince of the Blood married only with the consent of the king, for, as in this case, the question of his wife was of political importance. Gaston's marriage was a blatant insult to Louis, but could also be construed as an act of rebellion. Louis and Richelieu appealed to Rome to have the marriage annulled on the ground that Gaston had been forced into it against his will. This was a form of wording used if a member of the royal family married without the king's permission, and, in French law was sufficient ground for an annulment. The Spanish and Austrian

Habsburgs, who saw the marriage as possibly serving their own purposes, put pressure on the pope to refuse the French request, and Rome entered into long negotiations with Louis XIII on the matter. Frustrated by this failure, and fearful that Charles IV would abrogate the Treaty of Liverdun at the first opportunity, Louis XIII invaded Lorraine again in 1633. Gaston fled to the Spanish Netherlands[1] and Charles IV was forced to abdicate. Although France did not formally annex Lorraine, it occupied and fortified the duchy, which now became a first line of defence on the north-eastern frontier.

The actions of Richelieu in northern Italy and Lorraine provide clues as to the evolution of his thinking on foreign affairs. His primary motivation at this juncture was defensive. By controlling routes or 'gates' through which France's enemies in the past had invaded, or might do so in future, the security of the kingdom would be enhanced. Richelieu was no nineteenth-century geopolitician ahead of his times, pursuing some grandiose scheme of extending the kingdom to France's 'natural frontiers'. Such concepts did not figure in seventeenth-century thought. In the early 1630s his ambitions were limited and determined by military strategy: he aimed to secure the frontiers and frustrate the Habsburgs. He still believed that France lacked the military preparedness to mount a direct military challenge to the Habsburgs. It could aspire only to weaken them by indirect means, meanwhile securing the frontiers.

Undermining the Habsburgs

Since the mid-1620s the French government had sent subsidies, for example, to the Dutch Republic and Denmark to support them in their wars against the Spanish and Austrian Habsburgs respectively. In 1630 and 1631, however, circumstances were emerging which indicated that a renewed diplomatic effort by France might bear fruit. In spite of the successes of the Emperor in Germany, there were signs that his triumph was fragile.[2] The Dutch controlled the major sea routes in the North Sea, Atlantic and Baltic, and Catholic princes of the Empire almost as much as Protestants were alarmed at the military successes of the Emperor. Catholic Imperial territories, led by Bavaria, suspected Ferdinand II of aiming to diminish the autonomy of all the princes; hence, at Regensburg, the Electors secured the dismissal of Wallenstein and refused to elect Prince Ferdinand as King of the Romans.

In 1630 and 1631 there were weaknesses in the imperial position which Richelieu could exploit. He made approaches to the English and Dutch governments, proposing that they renew their mutual commitments, but in 1631 he went further by signing an alliance (as against a looser accord) with Gustavus II Adolphus of Sweden. This kingdom too had adopted a policy of neutrality towards Germany during the Thirty Years War, but this policy was dictated chiefly by the fact that Sweden was engaged in a long war against Poland. However, thanks largely to Richelieu's diplomatic efforts, that war ceased in 1629 with the Truce (not peace) of Altmark. Richelieu already saw in Gustavus a desirable ally, for the Swedish armies had shown themselves to be an excellent fighting force; moreover, the Swedish government had observed the advance of the Habsburgs with concern. When Imperial forces reached the Baltic coast in 1629 and forced Denmark to make peace, and when Ferdinand II issued the Edict of Restitution, Gustavus Adolphus concluded that Swedish security was threatened. He agreed to the truce with Poland as mediated by France, invaded Germany in 1630, and signed the Treaty of Barwälde with France in 1631. The king of Sweden promised to maintain an army of 30,000 foot soldiers and 6000 cavalry. France would pay him 1 million livres a year. The alliance was for five years, to be renewed if necessary.[3] This treaty bound the two kingdoms in formal alliance and was an unambiguous expression of *raison d'état* on both sides. Richelieu and Gustavus were open to reproach from their respective Catholic and Protestant critics, but minister and king pointed to the higher purpose of their alliance: resistance to the mighty Habsburgs, the protection of the rights of the princes of the Empire, and the restoration of Protestantism in Germany (a point stressed by Gustavus but not by Richelieu).

This last aim was an embarrassment for Richelieu, who attempted to quell Catholic apprehensions at home and abroad by having it written into the alliance that Gustavus Adolphus would respect the religious rights of Catholics and would not use conquest as a pretext for extending Protestantism. Richelieu also helped to stem criticism by signing a second treaty in 1631, with Maximilian, Duke of Bavaria. The two sides promised to respect each other's neutrality in the German war. Bavaria was a staunchly Catholic principality, but its ruler was alarmed nevertheless at the growth of Habsburg ambition. He looked forward to cooperation with France as a counterbalance to the Emperor. Richelieu regarded the Bavarian treaty as a triumph, for it gave him a major associate within the Empire and showed that a foremost German Catholic prince viewed

Richelieu with favour. Like Sweden, France could claim to be acting in defence of the liberties of member states of the Empire.

The entry of Sweden into the Thirty Years War initiated a remarkable reversal of fortunes. Gustavus proved to be one of the finest generals of the age, but he also commanded an exceptional army. It was recruited on a systematic basis, the country being divided into regions, each of which had to provide a given number of recruits. Swedish soldiers were well trained and well equipped, and had acquired invaluable experience fighting the Poles. Although German Protestant princes were reluctant to ally with Gustavus (by doing so they turned themselves into rebels against the Emperor), they felt driven to do so by the disaster which befell Magdeburg in May 1631: an army fighting on behalf of the Emperor captured the city, and in the pillaging that followed, thousands of the inhabitants perished. 'Magdeburg' became a rallying cry of German Protestants, including the Electors of Brandenburg and Saxony, who now entered into league with Gustavus Adolphus. Gustavus inflicted a decisive defeat on the Imperial forces at Breitenfeld (1631), and as he advanced towards the Rhineland, Ferdinand II's hold over northern Germany collapsed. Gustavus proceeded to take Frankfurt, Mainz and Heidelberg.

Swedish successes continued into 1632, forcing Ferdinand II to recall Wallenstein as commander-in-chief. Meanwhile Gustavus invaded Bavaria and, deaf to appeals from Richelieu and Maximilian, laid waste to much of its territory before moving north to Saxony. Wallenstein gathered an army and headed for Nüremberg, which was being threatened by a Swedish force auxiliary to the main army of Gustavus. Aware of Wallenstein's presence, the Swedes avoided Nüremberg and turned north to join Gustavus. Wallenstein pursued them and on 16 November, at Lützen near Leipzig, met Gustavus in battle. Wallenstein was defeated but Gustavus was killed in the fighting. The death of the King of Sweden was a major blow to the anti-Habsburg cause. He was the one commander with the political and military authority to hold together the disparate collection of German princes, territorial rulers and city states which were aligned against Ferdinand II. The campaigns continued into 1633 and 1634, but although destructive of the German countryside, they brought neither side within sight of ultimate victory. When, in 1634, Wallenstein was murdered and the Swedish army was defeated at Nördlingen, it was evident that military stalemate had set in. Elector John George of Saxony, on behalf of the Protestant princes, proposed peace negotiations to Ferdinand II. Reluctantly accepting that he could not restore his victorious position of 1629, the Emperor agreed: peace was signed at Prague on 30 May 1635. Neither Sweden nor France contributed to the settlement.

France Declares War

Richelieu had followed the course of the war in Germany since 1631 with mixed sentiments. It was gratifying to observe the discomfiture of the Habsburgs as Gustavus Adolphus advanced, but Gustavus was no French puppet and Richelieu found him difficult to control. Gustavus's death forced Richelieu into a more active diplomatic role than he had anticipated. It was crucial to keep Sweden in the war, and when the Swedish Chancellor Oxenstierna, who now assumed direction of Swedish policy,[4] sought to persuade German princes to join Sweden in a military league, which would continue fighting the Emperor, he received Richelieu's support. When the resultant League of Heilbronn was formed (1633), Richelieu renewed the Franco-Swedish alliance, so confirming their united stance in Germany. The defeat of the Swedes at Nördlingen in 1634 subverted the prestige of the Franco-Swedish alliance, but Richelieu sought to offset this by a treaty of confederation with German territories in the Rhineland, Franconia and Swabia. He also signed another agreement with Sweden whereby the Swedes allowed the French to occupy strongholds in Alsace, which the Swedes had taken.

While this diplomatic offensive by Richelieu was taking place, the Spanish, still at war with the Dutch Republic, were strengthening their position in the Rhineland: late in 1634 and early in 1635 they took Philippsburg, Spire and Landau. In February 1635 Richelieu renewed France's alliance with the Dutch Republic, and by the spring of the year there was talk in French government circles of open war. The above-mentioned peace talks between the Emperor and the Elector of Saxony at Prague looked as if they would succeed, in which case the Emperor could be expected to release forces to support the Spanish. Their combined resources would be too much for the Dutch, whose collapse would be disastrous for France. The alliance between France and the Dutch Republic therefore implied that France would soon be at war against the Habsburgs. Richelieu signed treaties with several north Italian princes and in March 1635, French troops reoccupied the Valtelline. Richelieu also entered into an agreement with Bernard, Duke of Saxe-Weimar, a German mercenary commander formerly in the service of the Swedes. At the end of March there occurred the episode which took France into war. A French garrison was based in the electorate of Trier, whose ruler, the Archbishop-Elector, had requested French protection. A Spanish force occupied the electorate, drove out the French troops and imprisoned the Archbishop-Elector. In the face of this provocation Richelieu had no option but to respond: on 19 May 1635 France declared war on Spain.

Was the war inevitable? Ever since the Day of Dupes, which eradicated serious internal opposition, Richelieu had developed his anti-Habsburg policy with relatively little hindrance, and to this extent it may be said that the possibility of war increased. Yet he still preferred to fight through proxies, notably Sweden. One reason, as will be discussed shortly, was the condition of the French army, which was not ready to confront such experienced forces as those of the Spanish. It was one thing to engage in limited operations in the confined spaces of the Valtelline, but an entirely different matter to challenge the Spanish along the open frontier between France and the Spanish Netherlands. The death of Gustavus Adolphus and the moves towards the Peace of Prague propelled Richelieu towards war. Gustavus possessed the authority to hold the German Protestant princes together, but after his death only France could do so. This role of leadership was made all the more unavoidable in that Catholic princes, such as the Elector-Archbishop of Trier and Elector of Bavaria, sought French protection. There is also evidence that the Spanish government was seeking a war with France. Olivares was convinced that sooner or later Spain would have to fight France, therefore it was prudent to do so at an advantageous moment. In 1635 that moment seemed to have arrived. Spain could anticipate military help from Vienna after peace was signed in Prague, the French army was much inferior to that of Spain, and since Richelieu was fortifying Lorraine and Alsace it was necessary to move quickly. According to this analysis the Spanish attack on Trier was calculated to force France into a war which Olivares felt to be opportune and which Spain could win quickly. If all went well, Richelieu would be dismissed and a less anti-Spanish minister would be appointed.[5] In view of these circumstances it is difficult to see how Richelieu could have avoided war in 1635. It was forced on him sooner than he wanted, and the speed with which he signed alliances or other treaties in 1634 and 1635 indicates how much he felt under pressure. He sought to limit the conflict by declaring war on Spain alone, not the Emperor, even though Ferdinand II sent assistance to the Spanish.

It was Ferdinand II who declared war on France in March 1636, not
the other way round.

The Army and Navy

The early stages of the war went badly for France. The army which
invaded Flanders in 1635 won one victory, then collapsed into indiscip-
line and disorder. It retreated to the coast and had to be rescued by
Dutch ships. The French effort in the Valtelline stagnated, and
Bernard of Saxe-Weimar was kept loyal only by granting him land in
Alsace. Part of the problem was military. Whatever Richelieu's instincts
for reform in other spheres, they did not extend to the army. The major
change was in the size of the army. In the 1620s it normally comprised
around 20,000–30,000 troops, but in the early 1630s Richelieu began
expanding it. By the end of 1634 it stood at about 109,000 men. In 1635
it increased to 150,000 and in 1636 to over 200,000. Fluctuations
occurred (it reached its maximum of 211,000 in 1639), but in the period
from 1635 to 1642 the average size of the army was about 150,000.[6] At
its core were elite troops attached to the royal household and the 'great'
regiments named after the provinces where they traditionally fought:
the Normandy, Picardy, Navarre, Champagne and Piedmont regiments.
New units were created during the war, usually named after their
commanders.

The rapid expansion of the army was not, however, accompanied by
initiatives on such crucial matters as central or provincial military
administration, methods of recruitment, the payment of troops, the
provision of food and equipment for men and fodder for horses, the
guaranteeing of supply lines and all the other support mechanisms
necessary to a successful army. In these and other spheres, traditional,
and often very inefficient, practices were continued. In its manoeuvres
and tactics the French army attempted to learn from the Swedes, for
example by reducing the proportion of pikemen and increasing that of
musketeers;[7] but it was not noted for its own military innovations. The
quality of the troops was often poor (perhaps inevitably so in an army
expanded so quickly), desertion rates were high and mutinies could
occur all too frequently. If it is true that Richelieu, from an early stage of
his ministry, had anticipated war against Spain, it must be said that his
military preparations on land were far from adequate. The armies which
he put in the field were inferior in quality to those of Spain.

On the other hand, he had developed the navy as announced in 1626 and 1627.[8] The main governorships which he amassed, such as those of Brittany, were on France's coastline or included leading ports, especially Le Havre. He invested heavily in the extension of port facilities and fortifications: thus a tower was built at Toulon, ramparts at Brouage, and at Le Havre a floating dock and new locks were built. He also encouraged the shipbuilding industry, and to meet the demand for labour, carpenters, metalworkers and other shipyard workers were imported from the Dutch Republic and elsewhere. By the mid-1630s the fleet had been expanded to the point where three main Atlantic squadrons totalling thirty-five ships of the line and about the same number of lighter vessels were operating out of Normandy, Brittany and Guyenne. In the Mediterranean, a fleet of twenty-one galleys plus smaller craft had been created. An expanding fleet needed, of course, sailors and good commanders. In the army, officers almost exclusively were noblemen (although it was possible for commoners to rise in the ranks), but in the navy it was not possible to require captains and officers to be noble. In this latter service, insisted Richelieu, operational proficiency must be the criterion for appointment and promotion. For self-evident reasons, commanders with seafaring skills were to be found chiefly among the maritime communities of the ports; and although noblemen did join the navy and rise to positions of command (for example, Knights of Malta who had a background in naval warfare were recruited), most captains and officers in the French navy under Richelieu were commoners. Since its expansion began from a low base, the navy in the 1630s was still inferior in size to those of the Spanish and Dutch, but it did establish a significant presence in the Atlantic, North Sea and Mediterranean, and won notable victories such as that at Pont-de-Courlay near Genoa in 1638.

The Course of the War

It would serve little purpose to narrate the course of the war in detail,[9] but the principal phases can be identified. After the ignominious rescue of the French army by Dutch ships in 1635 the war swung in Spain's favour. Olivares regarded the front against the Dutch as the more important, and it was there that he concentrated most of his forces. For the time being he was content to fight a holding operation against the French.[10] However, when the French campaign of 1635 ended in ignominy, the Spanish crossed the frontier and in August 1636 captured Corbie near Amiens. The fall of Corbie caused panic throughout Picardy and down to Paris, for the route to the capital now lay open. Thousands of refugees flocked into Paris from the north, while from Paris itself others fled south to the Loire. Richelieu ordered an estimate of food supplies in anticipation of a siege. Louis XIII and Richelieu personally appeared in the streets of Paris to raise people's morale. An army of 40,000 was gathered, including some 12,000 volunteers from Paris, and marched north under the command of the king. In fact the Spanish had no intention of besieging Paris, for that would have been an immense undertaking requiring a concentration of resources which would have left them exposed elsewhere; and in any case, they still regarded the Dutch as the main enemy. Instead they launched attacks against Amiens and Abbeville, but when they heard that Louis was marching against them they withdrew towards the Spanish Netherlands. Corbie was recovered by the French in November 1636, an event celebrated in Paris both in the streets and in a service of thanksgiving held in the cathedral of Notre Dame.

The Spanish also invaded from the east in 1636. From their base in Franche Comté they penetrated Burgundy and came up against the small fortification of Saint-Jean-de-Losne near Dijon. There they met unexpected resistance as the garrison and townspeople held out for several days until reinforcements arrived, forcing the Spanish to retreat. This episode was one of the 'might-have-beens' of the war, for had the Spanish succeeded in invading Burgundy and central France in conjunction with the invasion of Picardy, they could have put the French government under intense pressure to make peace. As it was, the retreat of the Spanish from both zones eased Richelieu's position. Even so, the outlook for France gave cause for even more pessimism later in the year when Ferdinand II declared war and so threatened Louis XIII and Richelieu with the combined Habsburg forces. Richelieu himself was subject to another plot against his life in 1636, this time by confidants of Gaston d'Orléans and the Comte de Soissons. The plot was foiled, but was a reminder of the danger which the cardinal permanently faced.

In 1637 neither side established a clear advantage in the war, although by the end of the year Olivares was feeling optimistic. Within France, movements of violent protest against the financial and social costs of war reached alarming proportions. In the summer of 1636 the so-called Croquants of Angoulême and its neighbourhood had rebelled. The movement spread to Saintonge and Périgord, and in 1637 most of the south-west joined in. The rising of the Croquants compromised the French war effort by forcing the government to divert front-line troops against the rebels. So depressing was the outlook for the French government that Richelieu made approaches to Olivares suggesting a truce. The Count-Duke refused, for he detected encouraging signs. In Italy, the Spanish retook the Valtelline from the French, and when the French-born Charles, Duke of Mantua, died in September, both of the claimants to succeed him were pro-Spanish. Again, although Ferdinand II died in 1637, his son and heir, Ferdinand III, continued cooperating with Spain. Towards the end of 1637, Louis XIII invoked divine help. On 11 December he consecrated his kingdom to the Virgin Mary, seeking her intercession with God on behalf of France. The king's religious convictions were genuine and there is no reason to doubt the sincerity of his vow. On the other hand, it did surround the French war effort with an aura of divine benediction which was helpful in suppressing criticism at home; and to the public at large the efficacy of the vow was made manifest within a few weeks when it was announced that the Queen, after more than twenty years of marriage, was pregnant. She gave birth to a son, the future Louis XIV, on 5 September 1638.

By this time, the balance of the war was shifting in favour of France, even though domestic disturbances and rebellions continued to hinder Richelieu's prosecution of the war. In December 1638, Bernard of Saxe-Weimar took the fortress of Breisach on the Rhine (thereby compensating for a defeat which the French suffered against the Spanish at Fuenterrabía in September). Meanwhile the Spanish were experiencing setbacks in their war against the Dutch Republic. The Dutch retook Breda in 1637, and in 1639 inflicted a heavy naval defeat on the Spanish. Olivares had mustered a fleet of over seventy ships to transport soldiers to the Netherlands and establish Spanish maritime supremacy in the English Channel and North Sea. On 21 October 1639, Dutch warships encountered the armada just off the English coast and defeated it at the Battle of the Downs. Two further disasters hit the Spanish government. First, in 1640 the French besieged and took Arras, after which they proceeded effectively to annex this part of Artois. Secondly, the French advanced into Roussillon. This province on the southern border of France was a Spanish possession, with its chief city at Perpignan. French incursions took place from 1639 onwards, but in 1642 a concerted invasion was attempted. On 9 September, Perpignan fell to the French, who then extended their authority across the whole province.

The conquest of Roussillon took place at a time when Spain was in the midst of a domestic crisis. In 1640, Catalonia rose in revolt against Philip IV, and in Portugal, ruled by the King of Spain since 1578, there also began a war of independence. In 1641, leaders of the Catalan insurgents met French agents to seek military aid. Richelieu agreed, on condition that Catalonia formally accepted the protection of France. The Catalans consented and recognised Louis XIII as 'Count of Barcelona'. Likewise did Richelieu treat with the new King of Portugal, John IV: on 1 February 1641 an alliance between the two countries was signed. Philip IV of Spain and Olivares were now confronted by four major, but interconnected, conflicts: against France, the Dutch Republic, Catalonia and Portugal. They had no option but to spread their military resources, thereby weakening their capacity to fight any one of these wars effectively.

By the end of 1642, Richelieu could feel satisfied that France, having come through the difficult early years of the war against Spain, was making progress in certain key areas, notably Flanders and the Franco-Spanish border region in the south. The north-east and east, where the war between France and Spain merged with that between the Emperor, Sweden and various German princes, still presented difficulties; but on balance France was more secure than in 1635 and had proved itself capable of holding its own against Spain, even though that success depended in no small measure on Spain's internal difficulties. These last eventualities proved too much for Olivares. In January 1643 he resigned as principal minister of Spain, blaming much of his ill fortune on what he regarded as the machinations and intransigence of Cardinal Richelieu.

Richelieu's Legacy in Foreign Affairs

By then Richelieu himself had died. Since the summer of 1642 his health had been declining rapidly, and he expired on 4 December 1642, leaving France still at war and with no end to the conflict in sight. What verdicts may be passed on his handling of foreign affairs? His defenders during his lifetime portrayed him as a man of principle, a *bon Français* whose foreign policy was devoted to nothing other than the good of France. He certainly explained his policy through *raison d'état* but, contended his supporters, this was no morally blind concept and was far from the Machiavellianism with which his enemies charged him. His policy conformed unerringly to the precepts of Catholic doctrine and was entirely appropriate to a cardinal of the Church. His detractors accused him of the opposite: of pursuing a Machiavellian foreign policy bereft of moral principles and dictated exclusively by the demands of power, thus shaming the Catholic Church of which he was a priest and cardinal and deserving nothing other than the severest condemnation.[11]

Present-day commentators similarly include admirers and critics. To some, Richelieu's foreign policy was driven by a vision which transcended even the search for territory or the defence of France. He was seeking nothing less than a new international order for Europe. According to this interpretation, Richelieu viewed the Thirty Years War and its accompanying war between Spain and the Dutch Republic as products of the failure of Habsburg hegemony to form the foundation of European stability. What was at stake in France's war-by-proxy in the 1620s and 1630s, and its open war against Spain and the Emperor from 1635 and 1636 onwards, was the search for a new international order preserved this time by several powers, including France. The Europe which Richelieu envisaged was one in which no single dynasty or country would exercise hegemony; it was one in which several power bases would counterbalance each other and afford protection to smaller states. Here reference might be made to the influence on Richelieu of the Mechanical Philosophy of the 1630s and 1640s.[12] His compatriot René Descartes, for example, posited a universe composed of 'whirlpools' of celestial matter which carried moons around planets and planets around the sun. By analogy, Richelieu thought of a Europe in which smaller, 'satellite' states would 'orbit' larger, benevolent protectors, none of which would seek hegemony, but which instead would preserve in Europe a peace and equilibrium corresponding to the harmony of the heavens. Thus, according to this interpretation, when he afforded French protection to west German princes such as the Archbishop-Elector of Trier, he was pointing the way to a new European order. In short, whilst the defence of the interests of France remained its primary obligation, Richelieu's foreign policy displayed transcendental features which combined Cartesian cosmography and a religiously inspired vision of a 'new creation'.

A cynical alternative to this approbatory interpretation is that France's war against Spain guaranteed Richelieu's survival as principal minister to Louis XIII. The more he could convince Louis that Spain was an irreconcilable enemy who must be fought at no matter what cost, the more the king was dependent on him. Moreover, as has already been indicated, but will be stressed again later, Richelieu amassed enormous wealth in the service of the king and he lavished honours and money on his relations and *créatures*. By implication, had Olivares agreed to a truce in 1637 or had Richelieu sought and achieved peace in 1642, he would no longer have been indispensable to Louis XIII and would have been more vulnerable politically than at any time since the Day of Dupes.[13]

There is no compulsion to adopt either of these interpretations to the exclusion of the other, for Richelieu would not be the first, or the last, statesman to combine high-mindedness with self-interest. In objective terms it can be said that when he died in 1642, France's frontiers were more secure than for many decades. In the north, much of Artois was under French control; in the north-east, Lorraine, Alsace and several crossing points on the Upper Rhine likewise were held; key points in northern Italy were in French hands; in the south, Roussillon was occupied and Catalonia had placed itself under the protection of Louis XIII. The east was still vulnerable (and it is no accident that Louis XIV later made the seizure of Franche Comté a primary objective), but taken as a whole, the country was less open to invasion than in the past. Richelieu undoubtedly struck heavy blows against the Habsburgs, but even these were not decisive. The war against Spain had another seventeen years to run, for Spain proved resilient and did not collapse under the weight of foreign war and internal revolt. It is true that when peace eventually was signed with France in 1659, Spain's hegemony in western Europe came to an end, but Spain remained a major force in western Europe to the end of the century. In the longer term – that is, looking forward to the late seventeenth and eighteenth centuries – Richelieu's dream of a Europe in which no country would exercise hegemony perhaps was realised in the concept of a 'balance of power', but it would be too simple to attribute this notion to Richelieu alone. By the turn of the century statesmen everywhere in Europe were thinking in such terms. Richelieu may be seen as a harbinger of the concept, but its widespread adoption later in the century owed much to the international situation of that period. What is beyond question is that the wars of the 1620s and 1630s placed enormous strains on governmental finance and on the socio-political stability of France. The subjects of Louis XIII paid a heavy price for Richelieu's foreign policy, and this is a subject to which we now turn.

Chapter 6: Richelieu and the Internal Government of France, 1630–42

Problems of Finance

Richelieu's handling of the internal affairs of France was conditioned by the rising financial demands of warfare more than by any other single factor. He is often presented as the architect of a particular brand of monarchic absolutism: that is, one that took an uncompromising stand over the exclusiveness of royal sovereignty, but which also sought, controversially, to push to the limit the powers which, in Richelieu's opinion, ought to accompany sovereignty. This verdict has much to commend it, but it should be tempered by conceding that his approach to government was also shaped by pragmatism and financial realities; his innovations were as much a response to necessity as a product of ideology. The financial burden of war – the subsidising of allies before 1635 plus the cost of the French armies and fleets thereafter – forced Richelieu to increase the government's income by every possible means. He did not routinely concern himself with the day-to-day administration of finance, which he left to his subordinates, the *surintendants des finances*;[1] moreover, Louis XIII took a personal interest in finance and occasionally intervened to authorise expenditure. Richelieu, in consultation with the king, devised financial strategies, concentrated on their implementation, and relied on the *surintendants* to work out the details of accounting.

The principal strategy, of course, was to increase the volume of revenue and other forms of income. France was at war with Spain, a country whose king could draw on the resources of Spanish America, the Spanish Netherlands, Portugal, southern Italy and Sicily, in addition to those of Spain itself. Richelieu had to rely upon French domestic resources, supplemented with loans from international financiers. The French taxpayer therefore was subjected to rapid rises in taxation (especially in the first year of war), as the figures in Table 1 illustrate.[2]

Richelieu also pursued two secondary strategies. First, he tried to limit the burden on the frontier provinces where much of the fighting during time of war inevitably would take place. Not only did warfare entail the destruction of property and life, but the troops, who were constantly on the move, drained the economic resources of frontier regions. Richelieu dared not risk provoking fiscal rebellions in such militarily sensitive areas; hence for both humanitarian and practical reasons he attempted to minimise – in relative if not absolute terms – their financial contributions to the war. The corollary was that 'secure' provinces far from the war zones would have to carry an extra burden. Secondly, Richelieu cut back on the policy of his predecessor, Marillac, who had tried to introduce *élections* into *pays d'états*. This was a highly unpopular policy which provoked much resentment and resistance. Richelieu was prepared to abolish new *élections* if he could secure votes of money in return. In 1630 he persuaded Louis XIII to cancel the *élections* in Burgundy and Provence on condition that the Estates of those provinces voted compensatory *dons gratuits*. In 1631 a similar arrangement was reached in Languedoc. As regards Brittany, of which he was Governor and where he exercised considerable influence over the provincial estates, he secured royal promises to guarantee the liberties of the province and its Estates in return for *dons gratuits*. Willing to cooperate on this basis, the Estates of

Table 6.1 Money raised in taxation, 1630–42

Date	Total income of government (in livres)	Date	Total income of government (in livres)
1630	42,806,000	1637	85,179,000
1631	40,875,000	1638	96,791,000
1632	57,505,000	1639	89,141,000
1633	72,006,000	1640	90,659,000
1634	120,271,000	1641	115,967,000
1635	208,310,000	1642	86,607,000
1636	108,717,000		

Brittany voted a *don gratuit* of just over 1 million livres in 1632, 1.5 million in 1634, 2.5 million in 1636 and 3 million in 1640.[3]

Intendants

At one level, therefore, Richelieu cooperated with provincial Estates whenever he could: his priority was to raise money, not to turn *pays d'états* into *pays d'élections*. To this extent one might contend that he showed few signs of being 'absolutist'. However, he did make extensive use of *intendants*, and it is this practice which has often been cited as evidence of his 'absolutism'. Who, then, were the *intendants* and what were their functions? Although the origins of the *intendants* can be traced to the Middle Ages, for purposes of the present discussion we emphasise certain key developments that had taken place in the sixteenth century.[4] First, from the 1550s onwards the crown appointed advisers (*intendants*) to assist provincial governors with financial administration; these advisers usually were lawyers drawn from one of the great Parisian law courts, or administrators from a government central council. Secondly, during the Wars of Religion, the crown from time to time sent commissioners, again selected from one of the law courts or a royal council, on temporary missions into the provinces to supervise the various pacification edicts that were issued. Thirdly, Henri IV continued despatching *intendants* (the word was now in use) both to oversee the implementation of the Edict of Nantes and to assist financial *officiers* in the execution of their duties. By 1624, when Richelieu became principal minister, *intendants* were reasonably familiar figures and their duties were mainly advisory or supervisory. The *intendants* were not very numerous: between 1560 and 1630, only about 120 were appointed, and in 1624 there were only seven working in the provinces.[5]

During his first few years as principal minister, Richelieu made no significant difference to this pattern, but after the Day of Dupes (1630) he greatly increased the numbers of the *intendants*: between 1630 and 1648, somewhere between 120 and 150 were appointed (Mazarin continuing Richelieu's habits down to this latter year).[6] He was driven to do so, not by his philosophy of government (in his *Political Testament* he expressed hostility towards the use of extraordinary commissioners like *intendants*), but by circumstance. The rapid increase in France's foreign policy commitments in the 1630s, coupled with an equally dramatic rise in the incidence of domestic unrest and rebellion (to be discussed later in this chapter), forced Richelieu and his colleagues to send out more and more *intendants* until, by the early 1640s, they were to be found in all the provinces.

Among their duties, finance remained paramount. By the early 1630s, the government was receiving only about 25 per cent of the *taille* which it demanded; the rest was being creamed off by local financial *officiers*. In 1634 Richelieu created a commission to investigate the procedures whereby the *taille* was apportioned, collected and returned to Paris. In the light of its findings he instituted changes: the payments that financial *officiers* received were reduced by converting them into bonds drawn on the city of Paris; the number of people exempted from the *taille* was lowered; and the number and powers of *intendants* were increased. On this last point, *intendants* were issued with written instructions in 1634. When they went to the *généralités*, they were to interview senior financial officers to identify the major abuses in the collection of the *taille*, but it was for the *intendants* to take the necessary corrective measures. In the *élections*, the *intendants* were to check the lists of those who paid *taille*, to be sure that the correct assessments were made, especially of wealthy people; the *intendants* were to make themselves available to hear petitions from taxpayers who claimed to be victims of maladministration by financial officers; the *intendants* were to ensure that wealthy people were not evading the *taille* by such devices as claiming false titles of nobility, hiding ownership of property on which they ought to pay tax, or inventing non-existing debts which allegedly left them poor and unable to pay more than a small rate of *taille*.[7] Over the following years, *intendants* increasingly assumed the functions of financial *officiers* throughout France. They were authorised to over-rule financial *officiers* and, in effect, to become a new financial bureaucracy. This, in Richelieu's view, was the most effective means of countering corruption and keeping delays to a minimum. He even allowed the *intendants* to resort to force. They were permitted to raise companies of soldiers to protect tax collectors and seize the goods of taxpayers who refused to meet their obligations. This increasing use of *intendants*, backed up by military strength, generated widespread resentment, not only among the tax-paying public but also among *officiers*, members of provincial estates and other bodies who saw their functions being usurped by royal agents.

In addition to finance, *intendants* increasingly exercised judicial duties, especially regarding the punishment of the leaders of rebellions. They conducted investigations into the conduct of nobles, magistrates and others suspected of being implicated in sedition; they prepared court cases against them; and on occasion even conducted trials themselves to ensure that local court officials did not show undue leniency towards the accused. In these and other ways, the *intendants* more than counterbalanced the placatory effects of Richelieu's concessions on *élections*, and were a source of resentment among provincial *officiers* and of suspicions as to the government's long-term intentions. As long as France remained at war with Spain, and the kingdom remained vulnerable to riot and rebellion, there was no prospect of Richelieu or any other minister diminishing the use of *intendants*; however, the point of principle bears repeating: Richelieu regarded these commissioners as temporary expedients to circumvent, or even replace, the normal apparatus of financial and legal administration; he was not foreseeing them permanently usurping the functions of legal and financial *officiers*; they constituted an extraordinary response to extraordinary circumstances.

Tensions with the Parlement of Paris and Provincial Nobility

In addition to the provincial Estates, Richelieu had to contend with the *parlements*, which, like the Estates, registered royal legislation and possessed the power to remonstrate. The senior *parlement* was the Parlement of Paris, not only because it was based in the capital, but because its writ extended across much of northern France down to the Loire: roughly one-third of the kingdom. Relations between crown and Parlement of Paris normally rested on mutual respect. The Parlement regarded itself as the supreme court of justice in France, and although the crown never formally acknowledged it as such, it did enjoy special status. The Parlement believed that under certain circumstances it was the custodian of the kingdom. Its lawyers and judges contended that during the worst periods of the Wars of Religion, when monarchic authority had all but disintegrated, the Parlement had held the kingdom together, preserving it until royal authority was restored. In more recent times, it was the Parlement of Paris which conferred recognition on the Regency of Marie de' Medici immediately following the assassination of Henri IV, thereby preventing any politically corrosive disputes over the question of who should be Regent. These mutually supportive links between crown and Parlement should be borne in mind, for although Richelieu was to be involved in disputes with the Parlement, they were kept under control. Richelieu never questioned the Parlement as a judicial institution and had no desire to trespass on its purely legal territory; it was its political aspirations which he resisted, although experience not infrequently showed that little distinction, if any, between the legal and the political could be drawn.

Richelieu, perennially hard-pressed to raise finance, encountered numerous frustrations when the legislation announcing new taxes or charges was delayed by the Parlement as it exercised its right to scrutinise laws before registering them; it also 'remonstrated' with a frequency that caused more hold-ups. The crown took steps to speed up registration. The great codification of law, the Code Michau, which Marillac completed in 1629, contained a clause ordering all the *parlements*, including that of Paris, to exercise the right of remonstrance within two months of receipt of legislation; otherwise new laws would be registered automatically. At Richelieu's instigation, Louis XIII issued an edict in 1631 ordering the Parlement of Paris not to discuss legislation that was political in character, but to register it immediately. This instruction was provoked by the Parlement's refusal to register the crown's denunciation of Gaston d'Orléans as a rebel: to Richelieu here was a straightforward political matter in which the Parlement was meddling without justification.

Richelieu also sought to bend the Parlement to his will by resorting to the *lit de justice*. This was a procedure whereby the king went in person to the Parlement and registered laws himself. This ceremony rested on the proposition that the Parlement was the king's court and exercised its functions, including the registration of laws, on behalf of the crown. In a *lit de justice* the king became the embodiment of the Parlement and in that capacity registered legislation. Before the sixteenth century the *lit de justice* had occurred with considerable frequency, one of its principal purposes being to demonstrate harmony between king and Parlement: the fact of the king's presence in the Parlement manifested their special relationship. During and after the Wars of Religion, however, the *lit de justice* changed in significance; it was enacted increasingly when relations between crown and Parlement were strained. By the seventeenth century it had come to be seen as a ceremony wherein the king imposed his will on a recalcitrant assembly. Louis XIII held a *lit de justice* in 1633. A number of *officiers* had been dismissed because of peculation. Richelieu intended selling their offices immediately instead of waiting five years as the regulations required. The Parlement resisted, but by the *lit de justice* Richelieu's decision was imposed. Another *lit de justice* was held in 1635. The crown had created new offices to be sold, including twenty-four in the Parlement of Paris. The *parlementaires* objected, but by the *lit de justice* the decision once again was enforced. On this occasion, however, the resistance was so deep-rooted that the judges and magistrates went on strike from January to March 1636, and only returned when Richelieu compromised by reducing the twenty-four to seventeen (another strike occurred in 1638 over the dismissal by the crown of five lawyers in the Parlement; the crown backed down and reinstated the magistrates). The final *lit de justice* of Richelieu's ministry was in 1641: it comprised a general instruction from the king to the Parlement to refrain from interfering in political affairs.

Ironically, Richelieu's respect for the Parlement as a court of law contributed to his difficulties. Aware of the thoroughness of its procedures and its refusal to be a puppet dancing to the tune of the principal minister, he was forced to have resort to extraordinary tribunals; they, in turn, raised objection from *parlementaires* that he was tending towards 'absolutist' practices by circumventing the normal processes of the law. In 1624, for example, he wished to have several prominent financiers tried on the grounds that they had misappropriated public funds. He knew that if the accused appeared before a court of the Parlement, the trial would last many years and might not arrive at the verdict he desired. He therefore created a special tribunal, which tried and punished the financiers quickly. For similar reasons, in 1631 he set up another tribunal to try people accused of counterfeiting coinage. The Parlement protested, but was over-ridden by the crown. Magistrates of the Parlement viewed these and similar measures as highly provocative; at the same time, *intendants* were sitting on smaller courts in the provinces with increasing frequency, to ensure that the courts exercised justice in accordance with the royal will. This mounting sense of grievance felt by the Parisian and provincial legal communities exposed Richelieu to the charge of corrupting the regular apparatus of the law. Protests continued into Mazarin's ministry, and were a major factor in the Fronde of 1648.

Another group whom Richelieu alienated, needlessly as it turned out, was provincial nobles. In his zeal to increase the returns on the *taille*, he targeted 'false nobles' who, he suspected, existed in large numbers; they secured fraudulent immunity from the *taille* and denied the exchequer badly needed revenue. The general instructions given to *intendants* in 1634 ordered them to root out false nobles; however, Richelieu also instituted *recherches de la noblesse*: special commissioners were sent to a region to examine the titles of the nobility and subject impostors to the *taille*. Nobles greatly resented having to prove their credentials, especially those whose titles went back many generations. Richelieu sent one such commission to Normandy in 1634. Over the winter of 1634–35 it examined the titles of almost a thousand families, and judged that about 11 per cent were claiming their status spuriously. On close examination, it transpired that they were all poor. When the commissioners investigated the financial circumstances of the false nobles, a picture of poverty and misery emerged. The false nobles were inscribed on the *taille* rolls, but almost all were assessed at under 10 livres a year, while a few were so impecunious that they were assessed at zero. Richelieu's expectation that wealthy commoners were denying the state large amounts of *taille* by pretending to nobility proved to be mistaken. Later *recherches* confirmed the Normandy findings. False nobility existed, but it was of negligible financial significance to the state.[8]

Financial Deficits and Social Protest

Given the multiple sources of revenue, both regular and irregular, which Richelieu exploited, how successful was he in balancing income with expenditure? The answer must be, scarcely at all. Reliable statistics are difficult to establish, but one historian estimates that the government ran annual deficits throughout the seventeenth century (it only approached a balance in 1668), and that, in the period 1625–33, the deficit ranged between 21,532,400 and 38,214,500 livres a year. Table 2 shows the annual deficits between 1634 and 1642.[9]

It is evident from these figures that during Richelieu's ministry the French state accumulated colossal debts and that he bequeathed to his successor, Mazarin, policies which, in financial terms, were ruinous to the state. Indeed, it will be seen later that in 1648 Mazarin had to declare a bankruptcy. France could not sustain such deficits indefinitely. Richelieu spent, borrowed and engaged in financial manipulation on an immense scale, but argued that the aim – the ending of Spanish hegemony in

Table 6.2   Financial deficits, 1634–42

Date	Government financial deficit (livres)	Date	Government financial deficit (livres)
1634	95,350,000	1639	57,176,000
1635	50,347,000	1640	48,761,000
1636	84,785,000	1641	64,457,000
1637	56,799,000	1642	48,156,000
1638	64,906,000		

western Europe – justified the cost. Richelieu was willing to sacrifice financial probity and stability to his greater geo-political ambition. He was also willing to sacrifice social stability. Under any circumstances, the rapid acceleration which occurred in rates of taxation would have created social tensions, but in the depressed socio-economic conditions of the 1630s it proved explosive. France had a long history of urban and peasant communities resorting to violent protest as a means of expressing grievances. During the Wars of Religion, such protest was absorbed into the wider conflicts of the period, but it declined in the early years of the seventeenth century as the regime of Henri IV pacified the country. From the late 1620s, however, harsh climatic conditions produced a series of long, hard winters and short, cool, wet summers. Subsistence crises, often accompanied by epidemics of disease, occurred in many parts of France, and impoverished large areas when the burden of royal fiscality was increasing. This combination of harsh socio-economic conditions and increasing fiscal demands from the government created a volatile situation in which violence could be easily ignited. The episode which most often sparked an uprising was the arrival of financial officers bearing news of the latest tax. From the mid-1620s to the mid-1630s not a year went by without riot, revolt or rebellion against royal fiscality; in the 1620s this coincided with the Huguenot rebellions of that decade and thereby augmented the crown's problems. Between 1630 and 1636, there were serious uprisings in Aix, Paris, Lyon, Marseille, Bordeaux and Rennes, and lesser incidents in several small towns of Provence; in 1635 there were rural uprisings across the southwest. Given the history of revolt in France, Richelieu was not excessively disturbed by these outbursts, provided they remained local and uncoordinated. However, two rebellions occurred on a scale which worried the government and forced it to divert troops from the war: those of the Croquants in 1636 and the Nu-pieds in 1639.

The rising of the Croquants ('clod-hoppers')[10] began when groups of peasants formed ad hoc assemblies in the area around Angoulême. They sent petitions to the king, declaring their loyalty but requesting reductions in taxation and other fiscal demands. The movement spread to Périgord in 1637, where peasant assemblies began to arm and form military units. There emerged at the head of the Croquant forces a nobleman, La Mothe le Forest. Under his leadership, Croquant bands took control of villages in the region, and even seized the town of Bergerac. Although the nobility and priesthood of the Angoumois and Périgord did not support the rising in any significant numbers, neither did they take steps to suppress it. The scale and geographical spread of the Croquant movement forced the government to intervene. The Duc de la Valette was withdrawn from the war front with about 3400 cavalry and foot soldiers. This was not a large force, and it did not seriously compromise the war effort; but the fact that it had to be used at all, because of the inaction of local noblemen upon whom the crown could normally rely, indicated how far the alienation of local elites from Richelieu had gone. La Valette defeated the main Croquant force at La Sauvetat du Dropt, on 1 June 1637. He lost about 200 men, but about 1500 Croquants were killed. La Valette entered the village and burnt twenty-five houses with their inhabitants inside. Richelieu had no desire to provoke further trouble by excessively harsh treatment of the defeated rebels: forty were tried but only four executed; a general pardon was issued to the rank and file. The rising continued sporadically in Périgord and Quercy until 1641, and for much of the period between 1638 and 1645 little tax, if any, was received from this region. The rebellion supposedly had been crushed, but the region remained too dangerous for tax collectors to enter.

The rising of the Nu-pieds of Normandy was, if anything, a cause of even greater concern to the government because of its wider sociological appeal.[11] Normandy was the wealthiest of the provinces, with a varied economy based on maritime commerce, local industries and agriculture; accordingly it was heavily taxed. However, in common with other parts of France, it suffered a downturn in all these sectors in the late 1620s and early 1630s, and anti-fiscal riots occurred in Caen and its neighbourhood in 1631. Nevertheless, the government continued to impose new financial burdens. There were two *élections* in Normandy – Rouen and Caen – but in 1636 a third was created, based on Alençon. New offices were created and sold therein, and in that year the amount of *taille* demanded from Normandy was increased. In December 1636 another forced loan was imposed on the province; in 1638 a new law court was established at Caen, with offices again being created and sold. All sections of society were affected by these and other measures, and it is significant that it was the rumour of a tax, not an actual tax, which occasioned the rising of 1639.

It began in the Cotentin peninsula. This was one of the chief salt-producing regions of France; the labourers were known as Nu-pieds because they preferred to work bare-foot to avoid their shoes being corroded by the salt. The Cotentin had the privilege of paying no *gabelle*, but in 1639 the rumour spread that the government was about to cancel the privilege. In fact Richelieu had no such plan, but when a law officer arrived in Avranches in July, the story spread that he had come with an edict imposing *gabelle*. The officer was set upon by a crowd and beaten to death, and from this incident emerged an insurrection which eventually engulfed most of the province. In its early stages it was concentrated around two axes: one between Avranches and Coutances, and the other between Mortain and Domfront; these were areas in which the *recherche de la noblesse* of 1634–5 had been active, and the peasant demonstrators were joined by nobles, still resentful over the commission. The uprising spread to Caen and Rouen, where gangs of youths attacked and pillaged the homes of financial *officiers*. A populist leader emerged – he took the name Jean Va-Nu-Pied – and his followers took control of many towns and rural areas of Normandy. As in the south-west a few years before, the social elites either remained neutral or, in some cases, joined the movement. By the end of the year the *intendant*, Bouthillier, was writing in desperation to Richelieu requesting help.

In November soldiers were sent to the province; they occupied Caen and Avranches and scattered the Nu-pied army. Richelieu decided on a much more draconian treatment of the rebels than in the south-west. Under his orders the royal troops systematically pillaged the country-side, causing widespread destruction and loss of life. The Chancellor of France, Pierre Séguier, assisted by a team of special lawyers, was sent to Normandy to try the rebel leaders. About fifty were executed, seventeen were sent to the galleys, and about forty were banished from Normandy. Séguier made a special example of Caen and Rouen. Richelieu had been incensed at the failure of the municipal and legal authorities to resist the rioters. Séguier dismissed several members of the Parlement of Rouen; town councillors were made to pay arrears of town taxes which had accumulated and also to pay for the billeting of royal troops through the winter of 1639–40; the legal and fiscal privileges of the two towns were annulled, and several office holders were exiled. The severity of the repression was an unambiguous statement by the crown: it would no longer tolerate anti-fiscal risings on this scale, and it would hold to account those town councillors, lawyers, financial *officiers*, nobles and others who failed to rally to the crown. Fidelity to the crown must take precedence over local loyalties; social elites who failed to respond in future would feel the full weight of the state's coercive powers.

The revolts of the 1630s were sparked chiefly by royal fiscal policy, but even the most serious did not divert Richelieu from his foreign policy aims, and to that extent it might be said that their impact on the government was of little consequence. On the other hand, they flashed danger signals of insurrection on an even greater scale should warfare and its associated financial and social costs continue unabated. Even so, Richelieu – and in due course Mazarin – could rely on movements of insurrection being fractured and weakened by division. The different social strata might hold together against the crown for short periods, but both the Croquant and Nu-pied risings had shown tendencies towards fissiparation. It was significant, for example, that in Normandy, Nu-pieds had attacked the property and persons of financial *officiers*, and local tax assessors in all rebellions were vulnerable to the assaults of aggrieved taxpayers. The main subject of this book is Richelieu and Mazarin; popular risings are significant only in so far as they elicited responses from the principal ministers. Were this instead a study of popular risings, many pages would have to be devoted to divisions and conflicts between insurrectionists: nobles against peasants, wealthy against poor townspeople, one village against another and so on. The risings of the late 1620s and 1630s defy simple typologies; the most successful were those which were geographically limited and of short duration. The longer a rising lasted and the more it spread geographically, the greater was the chance that eventually it would disintegrate under the weight of internal division.

Richelieu and Patronage

This discussion so far has concentrated on the strictly political aspects of Richelieu's career, but it is important to recognise that he approached politics through other categories of thought and action. He placed strong emphasis on the patronage of letters and scholarship, both because of personal interest (we should recall that he was a writer of theology) and because of the demands of statecraft. He lived in an age which appreciated the power of the printed word to create and influence 'public opinion', and he himself subscribed to the adage that 'gouverner, c'est faire croire' (a phrase which implied that, in order to govern, he had to make his guiding principles believable).[12] He understood that the high culture of his day was a potential political force, an instrument with which he could convey political messages to the literate public. He therefore fought his battles through the printing presses as well as through government and administration. This meant patronising writers and other scholars who could assist him. Among those whom he employed were Mathieu Morgues (the Abbé de Saint Germain), Jean Baudoin, Scipion Dupleix and Jean Sirmond. These and other authors composed laudatory pamphlets and other publications applauding Richelieu's policies, saluting his gifts of statesmanship and waxing lyrical on his supposedly inimitable services to France.[13] Sometimes writers composed panegyrics of the cardinal on their own initiative, hoping thereby to earn his patronage. One such figure was Jean Louis Guez de Balzac. In *Le Prince* (1631), Balzac defended the cardinal against charges of tyranny and argued that Reason of State was a legitimate foundation of policy. Reason of State legitimated what Balzac termed 'prudence': that is, Richelieu, indeed any minister or ruler, was justified in taking pre-emptive action against individuals or groups suspected of treasonable or rebellious intent. It was better to punish or imprison potentially disloyal subjects before they acted, than to wait for them to rebel and then apply the rigour of the law. Justice, by definition, comes into force after a crime; 'prudence', argued Balzac, would prevent crime or rebellion in the first place and should be employed by Richelieu unsparingly.

In addition to individual writers, Richelieu used two leading periodicals as instruments of propaganda: the *Mercure François* and the *Gazette*. The first of these had been founded in 1603 as an annual review of significant public and political events. In 1624 Richelieu's friend and adviser Père Joseph became editor. He changed the character of the journal by turning it into an organ supporting the government's interpretation of national and international political affairs. Père Joseph occasionally published extracts from pamphlets written by authors hostile to the cardinal, but followed them with rebuttals demonstrating the errors and mis-representations which they allegedly contained. The *Gazette* was founded by Théophraste Renaudot, who had come to the attention of Père Joseph as a gifted publicist.[14] Renaudot originated in the same part of France as Richelieu and was about the same age as the cardinal (Renaudot was born in 1586). He travelled in Italy, the Netherlands and Germany, and when he returned to France he set up a free medical clinic in Paris, organised public debates on subjects of current interest, and in 1625 opened his Bureau d'Adresse et Rencontre: this was a mixture of pawnbroker, estate agent, medical agency and publiciser of business news. Renaudot founded the *Gazette* in 1631, partly through his own initiative, but also because he was encouraged by Richelieu and Père Joseph. It contained news and comment, but invariably followed the government's interpretative line.

As well as directing his own printed propaganda, Richelieu sought to deter hostile commentators by imposing strict censorship. There had long existed procedures for controlling the presses: printers needed licences to operate, and the Chancellor of France took responsibility for ensuring that books, pamphlets and other material remained within the law. At Richelieu's initiative, in 1623 censorship was tightened and the Sorbonne was confirmed as the body which would provide most censors. In theory, all books and pamphlets had to be submitted for approval by the censors before they could be printed. In practice, much clandestine printing of anti-Richelieu material took place and, of course, it was well nigh impossible to stop pamphlets being printed abroad and smuggled into France. Throughout his ministerial career, Richelieu fought the propaganda campaign, regarding it as crucial to the preservation of his policies and his own security as principal minister to Louis XIII. In 1640 Richelieu founded the *imprimerie royale* (royal printing press), which was installed in the Louvre. By this time his career was approaching its end, but the royal printing press equipped the crown with a further instrument through which to propagate its message and drive home to the literate public the rationale behind policy.

Richelieu's literary patronage extended to the world of *belles lettres*, and in this regard his most enduring creation was the Académie Française, founded in 1635. Its origins are to be found in informal meetings of writers in Paris at the residence of Valentin Conrart, to discuss matters of style and language. Such subjects were of more than narrow literary concern: they reflected a conviction that language exercises a formative influence on the nature, even the institutions, of a society. A society in which vocabulary is ambiguous in its meaning, grammar irregular in its construction, and differing forms of literary expression are cumbersome in their structure, is likely to be one in which disorder extends to the legal, institutional and other bonds of social cohesion. Richelieu learned of this group from the Abbé de Boisrobert and Jean Chapelain – two of the cardinal's friends and advisers on literary affairs – who suggested that here was the core of a formal literary academy whose services could be of value to the state. A state-sponsored literary society could bring to the French language an order, clarity and regulation which could have favourable social and political implications. Here one might perceive a variation on the Mechanical Philosophy, referred to in an earlier chapter: the proposition was – and Richelieu agreed – that the more people used language systematically, unambiguously and coherently, the more would their personal and communal behaviour become orderly and harmonious. The use of language influenced human conduct; and if leading writers of prose and poetry developed the French language through agreed rules and conventions, they could contribute to the stabilisation of society. The foundation of the Académie Française marks a conceptual leap by Richelieu from the notion of patronage as exercised by powerful individuals to that of patronage by the state. The Académie Française, of which Conrart was the first secretary, was to set a pattern of state patronage of scholarship, painting, architecture, music and the sciences that was to become a distinctive feature of French cultural life.

Richelieu also left an imposing architectural heritage, for, in accordance with the values of the age, he accepted that a great political figure must live in an appropriately grand manner and leave fine buildings to posterity. He undertook three main projects: his residence in Paris (the 'Palais Cardinal', now occupied by the Palais Royal), the church of the Sorbonne, and a new town on the borders of Touraine and Poitou named after himself, Richelieu. His chief designer on all these schemes was Jacques Lemercier, the foremost architect in France. Lemercier developed a style which blended French restraint – plain exterior walls, simple windows, high-pitched roofs – with Roman grandeur. Lemercier had studied and worked in Rome for seven years (1607–14), and introduced into France the large entrances and imposing façades that he had seen in Italy.[15] Lemercier's first building for Richelieu was a modest country house at Rueil, not far from Saint Germain where Louis XIII frequently stayed, but it was the Palais Cardinal, close to the Louvre, which presented him with a major enterprise. In 1624 Richelieu bought the Hôtel d'Argennes, had it demolished and in 1627 set Lemercier to work on an ambitious building scheme. Enough progress had been made by 1629 for Richelieu to take up residence, but the palace was not completed until 1639. When finished it was rectangular in shape, ranged around a courtyard at the entrance and a much larger open space behind, wherein were placed gardens, fountains and trees. The palace was filled with furniture, tapestries, paintings, statues, porcelain, silver and all the other adornments and accoutrements of a palatial residence; it contained a gallery devoted to famous men and women (the paintings were executed by Simon Vouet and Philippe de Champaigne) and a theatre. While work was progressing on the palace, Lemercier was commissioned to design the church of the Sorbonne at Richelieu's cost. Following the Roman style, he designed an imposing entrance using superimposed classical columns, and topped the edifice with a large dome.

Richelieu's most ambitious project of all was the building of a new town on the site of his ancestral home. In 1625 he charged Lemercier with the task of transforming the existing and somewhat run-down *château* into a fine, modern building. Meanwhile, Richelieu purchased more land adjacent to the *château*; his aim was to turn the estate of Richelieu into a duchy by expanding it in size and increasing its revenues. He succeeded: in August 1631 Louis XIII conferred the title on the estate and Richelieu thereby became Cardinal-Duc. He had an even more ambitious idea: to turn the estate into a town. The surrounding region was overwhelmingly agricultural in character, and a new town not only would enhance Richelieu's prestige, but would diversify the local economy and add to the wealth of the area. When completed in 1635, the town of Richelieu was rectangular in shape and had a main axis through the middle. Other streets were laid out in intersecting parallel lines so that the whole town was divided into geometrically regular sections. At either end of the main axis was a square, one of which served as the market and commercial centre. The town can still be seen, although the *château* was destroyed in 1805. It must be said that, as an exercise in urban development, the town of Richelieu was not a success. It lay off the main commercial routes in that part of France and never overcame its air of artificiality. The modern visitor who travels to Richelieu has to make a special journey to go there, and he or she can still understand how its tight, rigid design precluded further growth; it was a town whose limitations overcame its latent capacity for organic development.

The pages of this chapter have been dominated by themes of hardship, struggle and confrontation, and there is no doubting that the decades when Richelieu was principal minister were exceedingly demanding for France. Richelieu's decisions, concurred in by the king, first that France must eschew any notion of strict neutrality in the Thirty Years War and support the anti-Habsburg coalitions, and then, in 1635, that France itself must go to war, inevitably placed inordinate strains on a sociopolitical fabric still recovering from the Wars of Religion. Add to this the social and economic impact of bad harvests and epidemics in the late 1620s and early 1630s, and it is clear that the subjects of the King of France were undergoing exceptionally testing conditions, as the incidence of protest and rebellion indicated. Serious as rebellion often was in the 1620s and 1630s, the crown kept it within manageable bounds and did not permit it to exert a markedly detrimental influence on the conduct of war. Nevertheless, it was evident that the crown was, as it were, accumulating a mounting body of moral 'debt' towards its subjects: at some time in the future, the sacrifices of the king's subjects would have to be rewarded, especially in the sphere of finance. For the time being, there was no respite. Richelieu, through the king, made never-ending demands upon the people of France, engaging them in an anti-Habsburg struggle that was to extend well beyond the lifetime of the cardinal himself.

Chapter 7:   Richelieu: an Assessment

A brief study of any major statesman can do no more than deal with themes which 'define' his life and career. In the case of Richelieu such an exercise is all the more challenging in that, from his own lifetime to the present day, he has been the subject of debate and controversy which has prevented any lasting consensus emerging on the precise nature of his historical significance. Did he have fixed, long-term goals, and if so, what were they and how far did he realise them; how did he preserve his position and power in government; what was the nature of his relationship to the king, the Queen Mother and other notabilities with whom he had dealings; was he an 'absolutist', and if so, what is meant by that term; of what significance for his conduct of policy were his religious faith and his position in the ecclesiastical hierarchy; how did he square his adherence to the Catholic Church with precepts of *raison d'état*, tainted as they supposedly were by Machiavellianism; was he a radical reformer in domestic politics or a trimmer who adjusted his purposes to political realities; in foreign policy, was he driven only by detestation of the hegemony enjoyed by the Habsburgs, or did he have bigger purposes in prospect? These and other questions continue to be asked about Richelieu, and several have been touched on in preceding chapters.

Recent research has tended to emphasise the practical difficulties under which he laboured, and the extent to which they, as much as (if not more than) ideology, shaped his policies and actions. Thus, the newest and most comprehensive study of his handling of the army[1] concludes that Richelieu continued time-honoured, hand-to-mouth techniques of recruitment, payment, provision of ordnance, maintenance of communications and so on; he never overcame the corruption and inefficiency which weakened the army as a fighting force, and he shied away from the kind of fundamental reforms that commitment to 'absolutism' might have indicated. If royal 'absolutism' required a standing army, recruited, commanded and organised appropriately, was it not incumbent on Richelieu to adopt the requisite measures? That he did not do so implies either that he was less committed to 'absolutism' than has often been claimed, or that the pressures under which he worked were so intense that he had neither the time nor the inclination to take on yet another daunting task which would bring him into conflict with powerful vested interests. In the event, it was only later, under Louis XIV, that the army was subjected to systematic reform.

This absence of fundamental reform of the army can be extended to other institutions. It is true that he created the Académie Française and initiated a trend whereby other facets of French cultural life were incorporated increasingly into institutional structures; yet this propensity did not extend to the existing great legal and political institutions of the age. He preferred to work with, circumvent or manage the provincial Estates, *parlements*, municipalities and other bodies, rather than change their structures according to some grand scheme. He dealt with them on an individual rather than on a collective basis; his talents were to be found in the success with which he manipulated existing practices rather than in institutional innovation.

Nevertheless, the thesis that Richelieu was a pragmatist driven by circumstance does not preclude the proposition that, at the same time, he pursued strategic aims. They, however, rested on a paradox: he was utterly convinced that France must launch a sustained challenge to Spain, even though the cost in terms of socio-political stability and state indebtedness would be considerable; he was equally resolved that the work of Henri IV in overcoming the social divisions bequeathed by the Wars of Religion must be continued. It proved impossible to pursue both of these goals at once, and increasingly the latter gave way to the former, thereby provoking the resistance which was such a feature of the 1620s and 1630s. During the turbulent years of his ministry he was able to form few lasting alliances beyond the king and his own *créatures*. Given the shifting emphases of his policies, he had resort to temporary liaisons with members of the royal family, aristocrats, central and provincial assemblies, *parlements* and other bodies and factions which played a role in the political life of the kingdom; but with just as much frequency he found himself at odds with them. In the execution of his duties he made dangerous enemies and, at one time or another, was alienated from almost every great 'political' institution and faction in the land. When news of his death was disseminated, those who mourned his passing were heavily outnumbered by those who rejoiced.

The key to Richelieu's decisive position in government was the abiding confidence of the king. This was more than a personal relationship for, as was stated in an earlier chapter, Richelieu regarded monarchy as the only institution capable of restoring stability to France and of upholding France's position in the international arena. For Richelieu, faithful service to the king and the enhancement of royal authority reconciled the paradox of the conflicting imperatives of social stability and war against Spain. Herein lies a key to understanding Richelieu's 'absolutism'. It focused on the king rather than on an abstract entity entitled 'the state'. 'Reason of State', for Richelieu, was a concept subordinated to, and placed in the service of, royal authority. The ability of the king's will to be executed was, for Richelieu, the criterion by which his actions should be assessed; if the king's will could be implemented only by extraordinary means, so be it; but the king's will and its enforcement was the guiding principle to which Richelieu adhered. The question of where the limits of royal authority were to be drawn, or the point at which authority became authoritarianism, imposed few restraints on Richelieu the chief minister, whose primary obligation was to serve the king. He was little disposed to become embroiled in legalistic or constitutional wrangling, even though his theologically trained mind was familiar with fine arguments and distinctions. He was aware of the 'constitutional' fears and resistance which his actions provoked, hence his employment of pamphleteers who campaigned on his behalf; but he did not concede that he had pushed royal authority to limits beyond which it would become despotism.

Richelieu was characteristic of the age in that he also saw no impropriety in enriching himself in the service of the king. Earlier references were made to the marriages he arranged for his relations on both the Richelieu and La Porte sides of his family, and to the careers in which he advanced his nephews or cousins. All statesmen of the period behaved in this way, and Richelieu was unexceptional in so doing. What was remarkable was the scale of the wealth and property that he accumulated, even though the most up-to-date analysis of Richelieu's fortune has conceded that the task of fully estimating and detailing it may well be impossible.[2] His annual income from the crown and from his benefices, land, investments and other sources rose from 613,000 livres in 1631 to 1,099,000 in 1640; in the last two years of his life it dipped somewhat, but was still over

900,000 livres per annum. When he died, the value of his estate, estimated conservatively, was some 20 million livres, of which about 25 per cent comprised land and a surprisingly high 20 per cent was in cash. This latter figure reveals aspects of Richelieu's *modus operandi*: a large fund of cash from which he could make gifts and loans was essential to his system of creating political dependants. Money enabled him to maintain his *créatures*, exercise political and ecclesiastical influence, buy informants who would sell information on his enemies at home and abroad, preserve his interest in his home province, and cultivate members of the social elites in Paris and the provinces who were useful to him politically. Ready cash was essential to Richelieu's practice of statecraft, hence the proportion of his fortune which it constituted.

When one recalls the financial problems left by his father, the fortune that Richelieu bequeathed was a truly prodigious achievement. He lived in the grand manner as befitted the principal minister of the King of France, and his palace in Paris was one of the most sumptuous residences in the capital, apart from the Louvre itself. When he died he donated the palace to Louis XIII; otherwise his principal legatee was his grand-nephew Armand-Jean de Vignerot de Pont-Courlay, who inherited the Duchy of Richelieu and carried the family name into the next generation. Generous bequests also went to other members of the cardinal's family, including the Duchesse d'Aiguillon and Armand de Maillé de Brézé.

By present-day standards Richelieu was relatively young when he died, aged fifty-seven, but in seventeenth-century terms his death was not premature. Not only was life expectancy much lower than in modern times, but Richelieu suffered health problems throughout most of his lifetime and, even when allowances are made for his notorious hypochondria, was constantly aware of his mortality. Even when not laid low by particular ailments, he was vulnerable to migraines, insomnia and depressions. How far his indifferent health affected his personality and conduct towards others is difficult to define with precision, but it undoubtedly did so.[3] He preferred to assume an attitude of imperious self-control, but it is known that, when in private meetings with Marie de' Medici or even with Louis XIII, he would sometimes break down in tears; whether these losses of self-control were genuine or calculated is nevertheless a moot point. Equally dramatic departures from normality were sometimes reported by those who served him politically, or by ambassadors who encountered him in the course of their duties. Even under normal circumstances they found him a formidably domineering person, but he was liable occasionally to burst into a rage which could reduce all but the toughest personalities to submission. Once again, however, it is impossible to know how far, or how frequently, such frenzies were a pretence. Other comments on his character can be made with more confidence. His ambition, his capacity for hard work and his fortitude are beyond question; equally assured was his capacity to earn the genuine friendship of others. Père Joseph and, indeed, Mazarin in later years, held him not only in esteem but in affection.

One final observation can be made, and it reinforces points made in earlier chapters: Richelieu took his vows as a priest seriously, and found an abiding assurance and strength in his religious faith. It was not a faith that led to surges of emotion or mystical experiences, but was rather based on reason, intellectual consent, and a commitment of the will. He drew distinctions between his conduct as priest and bishop on the one hand, and as statesman on the other. In the former mode he led a life of exemplary piety and service, and was never involved in sexual scandals; in the latter, he exercised all the skills of contemporary statecraft, to the extent that his critics accused him of condoning actions inconsistent with his priestly vocation. Modern historians are ill-placed to pass judgement on such complex matters, but they should, and do, observe them. Whatever may be said about Richelieu, nobody who had dealings with him was left in a state of indifference. He affected people profoundly, be it in a positive or negative sense, and when he died, foreign as well as French commentators acknowledged that a figure of towering political importance had gone; somebody of exceptional, perhaps unique, gifts of statesmanship.

Chapter 8: Mazarin: Origins and Early Career

It was natural that a figure of the eminence of Cardinal Richelieu should keep a large household in addition to the many *créatures*, writers, artists and scholars whom he variously maintained, protected and patronised. In 1640 he brought into his immediate entourage an Italian diplomat with whom he had had dealings and who had impressed him as a man of singular political gifts: Giulio Raimondo Mazzarino (sometimes Mazarini) who, when he was naturalised in 1639, took the name Jules Mazarin. After Richelieu's death in December 1642, Louis XIII took Mazarin into the *conseil d'état*. There Mazarin remained after the demise of the king in 1643, and he was retained by the Queen Mother and Regent, Anne of Austria, as principal minister. The emergence of this Italian at the pinnacle of political power in France is one of the more unlikely eventualities of the period, and requires explanation and examination. Before that, however, his origins and early career should be sketched.

The Early Years

Although he always regarded himself as a Roman, since it was in that city that his parents lived and brought him up, Mazarin was born, on 14 July 1602, at Piscina in the Abruzzi region. His mother, Ortensia Buffalini, had gone there to join her brother, a priest, to escape the summer heat of Rome. Ortensia was well educated, wrote poetry, and was related to the powerful Colonna family. Mazarin's father, Pietro Mazzarino, originated from a well-to-do family in Palermo and was chief manager of the household in Rome of Filippo Colonna, Grand Constable of the King of Naples. Pietro and Ortensia ensured that their son Giulio received an excellent education, sending him to the Jesuit Collegio Romano. He proved to be academically gifted and in 1619 accompanied his friend Giralmo Colonna (son of the Constable, and later Cardinal-Archbishop of Bologna) to Spain to study at the University of Alcalà. He spent three years there, although he seems to have devoted more time to visits to Madrid, and to drinking, gambling and romantic entanglements, than to canon and civil law. When he returned to Rome, he opted for a military career and joined the Colonna regiment in the service of the pope. Most of his service was in the Valtelline, where he was based from 1623 to 1626, although he did return to Rome in 1625 to recruit more troops for the regiment and to visit his father, who was being tried on a charge of homicide (Pietro was acquitted).

It was while serving in the army that he acquired his first experience of negotiation and diplomacy. The commander of the papal troops in northern Italy, Torquato Conti, in 1626 sent Mazarin to Alessándria, where a large Spanish force was based. He was to meet the general in charge of the Spanish army and discuss ways in which they might coordinate their campaign against the French. In January 1627, Conti sent him on a similar mission to Milan to explore with the Spanish governor the most effective means of cementing papal–Spanish tactics after the Treaty of Monzón. In his report of their meeting, Mazarin stated that he had attempted to provoke the governor into losing his temper in the hope that, in the heat of the moment, the Spaniard would be indiscreet and reveal classified information. Shortly afterwards Mazarin left the army, returned to Rome and took his doctorate in canon law. He cultivated the friendship of Antonio and Francesco Barberini, cardinals and nephews of Pope Urban VIII. Urban – Matteo Barberini – came from a great Florentine family and had performed diplomatic missions himself as a younger man. His pontificate, which began in 1623, coincided with the Thirty Years War, and he found himself devoting strenuous efforts to keeping peace between the main Catholic states in order that they might concentrate on combating heretics. At the same time he feared Spanish hegemony, not least in Italy itself, and favoured a strong France as a balancing force. His military and diplomatic interventions in the Valtelline question aimed to secure, not a victory of one side over the other, but a resolution that both could accept.

When the Mantuan Succession crisis broke out after the death of Duke Vincent II in December 1627, Urban feared that the resultant fighting between Spain, Savoy, Austria and France would get out of hand; such fears were enhanced when Mantua itself was sacked in July 1630 by an Imperial–Spanish force. Among those whom the pope appointed to seek a diplomatic solution to the crisis was Mazarin, and it was in this context that he first met Richelieu. Already, in 1628, Mazarin had been sent back to Milan as apostolic nuncio, and in 1629 he held meetings with the Spanish general Spínola. Later in the year he was a member of the team, led by Antonio Barberini, which went to Bologna to discuss the Mantuan problem. In January 1630 he travelled to Lyon, and it was there that he had his first meeting with Richelieu. A second encounter followed in June at Grenoble.

Throughout 1630 Mazarin was heavily involved in the diplomatic bustle that took place between France, Spain and Savoy, and he was equally prominent in the round of negotiations and contacts which resulted in the Peace of Cherasco (1631). His most theatrical episode, which earned him a certain celebrity in diplomatic circles, occurred on 26 October 1630. On 4 September he had persuaded the Spanish and French to sign a truce whereby the French would surrender Casale to the Spanish if help did not arrive by the end of October. A hastily mustered French relief force was duly assembled, and on 26 October prepared to attack the Spanish. At the last moment, Mazarin arrived on horseback and rode between the two armies, waving his hat and crying 'Peace, peace!' He had just received a written agreement wherein the Spanish and French promised to withdraw from Casale, and the Emperor was prepared to recognise the claim of the Duc de Nevers to Mantua. The two sides drew back and battle was avoided.

Mazarin's diplomatic feats and enterprise were observed by Richelieu with growing admiration, a feeling that was mutual: in his meetings with the French cardinal, Mazarin likewise recognised that here was a statesman of uncommon ability, who would place his personal stamp on the international politics of the day. When Mazarin returned to Rome, Richelieu wrote to the pope acclaiming the contribution of Mazarin to the achievement of peace. Richelieu also instructed the French ambassador in Rome to press for Mazarin to be sent to France as papal nuncio. Mazarin was precisely the kind of figure who could cultivate harmonious relations between Rome and the French government; however, since normally a nuncio was a priest, Mazarin's appointment would probably require him to be in holy orders. In anticipation of a posting which he coveted, Mazarin took the first steps towards the priesthood, although events overtook him and he never completed the process. He did eventually become a cardinal, but was never a fully ordained priest.

From the Service of the Pope to the Service of Richelieu

The favour which Richelieu showed Mazarin was a mixed blessing, for within the political and diplomatic community of Rome, Mazarin was acquiring a reputation for pro-French leanings. Spanish envoys, in particular, were aggrieved that, as they saw it, somebody as hostile to their king as he, should be employed in the diplomatic service of the pope. For the time being Urban VIII nevertheless persevered with Mazarin and in 1634 sent him to Avignon as papal vice-legate. He spent little time there, for soon afterwards he was instructed to go to Paris to resolve the question of Lorraine. He was charged with the task of trying to persuade Richelieu to acknowledge the validity of the marriage between Gaston d'Orléans and Marguerite de Lorraine, and to restore the Duc de Lorraine to his duchy. Mazarin remained in France until May 1636, and although he failed to secure French concessions over Lorraine, he studied the background to Richelieu's decision to declare war on Spain and reported to Rome on the early development of the war as it affected France. In 1636 he was instructed to return to Avignon, and from there he was recalled to Rome, which he reached at the end of the year.

Now that war with Spain had begun, Richelieu knew that the influential Spanish faction at Rome would be applying pressure to Urban VIII, urging him to pronounce in Spain's favour. If the French cause were to be upheld in Rome, it needed effective advocates. Richelieu's aim was to use Mazarin, and he was delighted when Mazarin, with Cardinal Antonio Barberini, was appointed by the pope as an officer liaising with the French representatives. When the future Louis XIV was born in 1638, both Richelieu and Mazarin hoped that the latter would be chosen by Urban VIII to bear the pope's congratulations to Louis XIII and Anne of Austria. Urban refused. This was partly out of deference to the Spanish, but also because, if Mazarin went as nuncio to a kingdom as prestigious as France, he would have to be made a cardinal as well as a priest. Mazarin had ambitions to the cardinalate, and was encouraged to that end by Richelieu. The power politics of the papal court were such that the influence an individual exerted was commensurate with his rank. If Richelieu were to secure the most effective services from Mazarin, it would be a considerable advantage to have him appointed cardinal. Another factor arose in Richelieu's mind. On 18 December 1638 his friend, confidant and guide in German international affairs, Père Joseph, died. Richelieu began to think of Mazarin as a possible replacement for Père Joseph, and wrote to the pope formally requesting that Mazarin be nominated to the cardinalate. At first, Urban turned down the French request, but he finally consented in 1641. By this time Mazarin had left papal service and settled in France. In 1639 Richelieu invited him to perform diplomatic missions on behalf of Louis XIII, and procured for Mazarin letters of naturalisation.[1] After weighing up the advantages and drawbacks of such a move, Mazarin decided to accept the offer. He judged that his chances of advancement were greater in the service of Richelieu than they would be in that of the pope. He arrived in Paris in December 1639, and never saw Rome again.

The French court received him generously and Richelieu treated him with the warmest consideration, even seeking his advice on the design of the theatre in the Palais Cardinal. Mazarin's first mission on behalf of Louis XIV was undertaken in 1640 and concerned Savoy. The former duke, Victor Amedeo, had died in 1637, leaving his widow Christine, sister of Louis XIII, as Regent. Her regency was disputed by her brothers-in-law, princes Thomas and Maurice: they accused her of belittling the regency by affording too much authority to her favourite, Comte Philippe d'Aglié. Relations became embittered and civil war broke out. Richelieu despatched Mazarin to mediate a settlement. After assessing the situation, Mazarin concluded that as long as d'Aglié was at large, no peace was possible. He arranged to have d'Aglié arrested, but also worked to divide Thomas and Maurice. In 1640, French troops seized Turin, hitherto controlled by Thomas. Mazarin persuaded him to sign a peace agreement (31 December 1630) and acknowledge Christine as Regent. Maurice, now isolated, held out longer – he did not give up until 1642 – but it was evident that, once Thomas acknowledged Christine, it was only a matter of time before his brother followed suit. Mazarin returned to France in triumph in 1641 and received the news that the pope had agreed to award him his cardinal's hat.

By the turn of the year, potentially significant developments were taking place in the international arena. First, in the Holy Roman Empire, moves were afoot to organise an international congress in Westphalia with the aim of ending the Thirty Years War and, if possible, associated conflicts in the Baltic.[2] Secondly, news spread that the pope's health was failing; the next papal election probably was not far distant (although, in the event, Urban VIII survived until July 1644). In expectation of an imminent conclave, the Catholic powers began to make assessments of the potential candidates. Richelieu hesitated as to whether Mazarin should be assigned to only one or to both of these issues, but finally drew upon his services for the last political crisis of Richelieu's life: the Cinq-Mars affair.[3] When the young Cinq-Mars, with his friend François de Thou, foolishly allowed himself to be drawn into political intrigue against Richelieu, he left himself vulnerable not only to the vengeance of the principal minister but to betrayal by Gaston d'Orléans and other conspirators. When Richelieu learnt of the plot against himself, he put pressure on Gaston to reveal the names of his accomplices. Gaston submitted, and among those whom he named was the Duc de Bouillon, a marshal of the army operating in northern Italy. According to Gaston, Bouillon had promised to allow the enemies of Richelieu to use his fortified base at Sedan as a centre of operations. Bouillon was arrested and brought back to France. Mazarin was sent to interview him and make an offer: if he would instruct the soldiers at Sedan to admit royal troops, Bouillon would escape with his life, otherwise he would be executed. Faced with these options he chose the former. Later, having received a pardon, he left France to serve the papal army; he returned during the Fronde.

Over the two years or so that Mazarin worked closely with Richelieu, the latter did not disguise his admiration for the former papal diplomat. As a mark of his esteem, but also as a means of ensuring that Mazarin stayed in France after his, Richelieu's, death, he secured for his protégé the wealthy abbey of Corbie, whose revenues were about 80,000 livres a year.[4] There were, of course, other figures such as Sublet de Noyers, Servien and Bouthillier, Comte de Chavigny, who entertained aspirations to succeed Richelieu as principal minister. To them, Mazarin was a parvenu who had appeared, as it were, from nowhere; they observed his rapid political ascension with indignation as they planned their own moves in anticipation of Richelieu's death. As the latter's physical condition went into rapid decline towards the end of 1642, he had several visits from the king; and although he did not presume to instruct Louis XIII as to who should be the new principal minister, he did advise the king to retain the services of Mazarin.

When Richelieu died, Louis heeded his counsel and brought Mazarin into the *conseil d'état*. He refrained from naming a principal minister, and instead formed a triumvirate of Mazarin, Sublet de Noyers and Chavigny. Sublet de Noyers was dismissed on 10 April 1643 for having supposedly entered into a secret compact with the queen, Anne of Austria, to run the Regency after Louis's death. This was a subject about which Louis was extremely sensitive. At this late juncture of his life, his relations with the queen were, at best, formal; and although Louis accepted that after his death she would be Regent, his memory of the indignities which he suffered during his childhood, and of the calamities which attended his mother's Regency, made him determined to save his young son from similar experiences. As he felt that his end was approaching, he took steps to limit Anne's independence as Regent. On 21 April, Louis called a delegation from the Parlement of Paris to meet him at the royal *château* at Saint-Germain-en-Laye. He informed the *parlementaires* that after his death Anne should be Regent but must work through a council, in which decisions would be taken by majority vote. On the same day, his son Louis (soon to be Louis XIV) was baptised in the chapel of the *château*: the godfather was Mazarin and the godmother the Princesse de Condé. The Dauphin was baptised 'Louis-Dieudonné'. About three weeks later on 14 May 1643, Louis XIII died.

Chapter 9:   Mazarin in Government and the Conduct of War, 1643–8

Mazarin in the Conseil d'État

The deaths of Richelieu and Louis XIII created a sense of new beginning in French royal and governmental circles, or at least of a reassessment of the direction in which the French government should take the kingdom. This sentiment of expectation was all the stronger in that, in the few months before his death, the king had issued amnesties to prominent prisoners and allowed exiles to return to France. Gaston d'Orléans was readmitted to the royal court, Bassompierre and Vitry were released from the Bastille, and Vendôme and the Duchesse de Chevreuse returned from abroad. Louis's purpose was not only an act of reconciliation between *les grands* and himself; he was preparing the way for the next Regency. If Anne of Austria were to govern with the minimum of obstruction, she would need the compliance of great aristocrats; thus, the council of regency with which Louis XIII intended surrounding his wife included Gaston d'Orléans and the Prince de Condé. Given the traditional assumption by aristocrats that they should hold offices of leadership in the royal household and in central and provincial government, a 'counter-revolution', reversing the system favoured by Richelieu, looked a distinct possibility. It remained to be seen whether the returning 'exiles' could be reincorporated into the political system bequeathed by the cardinal, or whether they would confront it and pose to the Regent the kinds of problems they had presented to Richelieu.

When Louis XIII died, his widow imitated what her mother-in-law had done in 1610: she took the new king to the Parlement of Paris (on 18 May, four days after Louis XIII's death) to hold a *lit de justice*. With the support of Gaston and Condé, she proposed to the Parlement that the limitations imposed by her husband should be quashed, and that she should govern with the plenitude of powers attaching to the Regency. The Parlement so pronounced, but only after several speakers in the debate had implicitly denounced Richelieu and voiced the expectation that Anne would not employ in the *conseil d'état* people associated with him. The Regency was duly established, but although Anne brought Gaston and Condé into the *conseil d'état*, she also retained Mazarin. That she did so affronted some *parlementaires* and was a sign that, at the very least, she had not repudiated the policies of her deceased husband and his former principal minister. Anne, like all informed people, recognised that the war against Spain, and France's role in the wider Thirty Years War, had reached a crucial juncture, for talk of a universal peace settlement was in the air. The *lit de justice* coincided with a brilliant victory of a French army, led by Condé's son the Duc d'Enghien (later the 'Grand Condé'), over the Spanish at Rocroi, but it was evident that if military progress were to be matched in the political sphere, French policy must be guided by somebody skilled in international relations and with a gift for diplomacy. It was for this reason, as well as for others, that Anne brought Mazarin into the *conseil d'état*. Technically he was to assume responsibility for ecclesiastical affairs, but soon afterwards Anne recognised him as principal minister. Quite apart from the skills he offered, this choice made sound political sense. He had resided in France only since the end of 1639 and had been a devoted *créature* of Richelieu. He was beholden to none of the other factions or pressure groups at court or around the government. He was politically independent and able to extend his loyalty exclusively to the king and Queen Mother. Chavigny, who had hoped to be principal minister, was still a member of the council, but did not remain for long. Before the end of the year Mazarin had secured his dismissal; he was replaced in the conduct of foreign affairs by Loménie de Brienne.

Mazarin was promoted also for more personal reasons. Anne's temperament imposed limitations on the conduct of her duties. Most serious, perhaps, was her distaste for sustained work. She was capable of short bursts of energy, but lacked the stamina to apply herself unremittingly to the daily grind of government and administration. This character trait meant that she was heavily dependent on Mazarin to keep the wheels of government turning. Moreover, by 1643 their relationship was more than political. Since he first visited the French court in 1634,

Mazarin had cultivated the friendship of Anne. He had to proceed warily, taking care not to alienate Louis XIII. Over the following years, close emotional ties developed between Mazarin and the queen; even his enemies conceded that physically he cut a splendid figure and that he was possessed of uncommon charm and grace. His experiences in the Rome of the Barberinis had endowed him with all the attributes of the accomplished courtier, and Anne was profoundly affected emotionally by this elegant and alluring Roman. Almost inevitably, rumours about the nature of their relationship spread (there was ribald gossip among Parisians that Mazarin, not Louis XIII, was the father of Louis XIV), but it is certain that during Louis XIV's minority, Mazarin's relations with the queen were correct. She was a woman of profound religious devotion and piety; quite apart from preserving her reputation as queen, her personal convictions ruled out any irregular liaison. Later, there were stories that Mazarin and Anne secretly married in 1643 or 1644, but this report too was unfounded. Nevertheless, to observers knowledgeable about Mazarin and Anne, it was no surprise that he emerged as principal minister.

Among *les grands* were to be found disaffected figures for whom the presence of Mazarin spelled the continuation of everything that Richelieu supposedly stood for: ministerial 'absolutism' and their exclusion from their 'rightful' political roles. A group of so-called '*importants*' plotted to overthrow Mazarin before he settled in as principal minister. Prominent within the cabal were Augustin Potier, Bishop of Beauvais and chaplain to the Queen Mother, César de Vendôme, natural son of Henri IV who had been deprived of his governorship of Brittany by Richelieu but returned to court after the cardinal's death, François de Vendôme, Duc de Beaufort, who emerged as the leader of the group, Marie de Rohan, Duchesse de Chevreuse, who returned to court in 1643 after many years of exile, and Anne-Geneviève de Bourbon, Duchesse de Longueville. The cabal was far from secretive in its preparations for a *coup* against Mazarin, but its plans were frustrated by resistance from unexpected quarters: Anne herself displayed resolve in standing by Mazarin, but significantly Gaston d'Orléans and Condé refused to condone the intentions of the cabal. In September 1643, Beaufort was arrested and imprisoned for five years; other conspirators once again were exiled and the Bishop of Beauvais was ordered to return to his diocese. A potential crisis was forestalled, but equally importantly Anne had affirmed her confidence in Mazarin. In that year she performed another symbolic act. She and Louis XIV left the Louvre and took up residence in the Palais

Royal, as Richelieu's former palace was now known. Mazarin purchased a property nearby and, in imitation of Richelieu, began to turn it into a sumptuous residence. During its construction he too moved into the Palais Royal. The distance from the Louvre to the Palais Royal was but a stone's throw, but the Queen Mother's move and the presence of her principal minister in the same palace as herself and her son was a powerful statement of intent: the new regime had every intention of continuing the policies of the old.

War and Peace to 1648

While the adjustments that accompanied the shift from one reign to another were taking place in France, the Thirty Years War was reaching what proved to be its final phase. Although international peace negotiations began in Westphalia at the end of 1643, the war continued until the peace treaties of 1648; the prolongation of warfare complicated the negotiations as the various delegations hardened or softened their stances in accordance with the fluctuating military position. From a French point of view, the first three years of Mazarin's ministry saw heartening successes against the Emperor and Spain, and from 1645 onwards French strategy in the war was coordinated increasingly with that of Sweden. In the short run, Enghien followed his victory over the Spanish at Rocroi with a push towards the Palatinate, the aim being to drive out the occupying forces of the pro-Habsburg Elector-Duke of Bavaria. At the battle of Fribourg, which lasted almost a week in August 1644, Enghien finally overcame the Bavarians; he then occupied important fortifications and towns along that stretch of the Rhine: Philippsburg, Mainz, Worms and Spire. Mazarin and others lavished praise on the young Enghien, whose earlier, as well as most recent, victories inspired envy among other French princely houses, notably that of Orléans.

Gaston was jealous of the glory which Enghien's achievements conferred on the house of Condé, and when the question arose of who should command the French army in Flanders in 1644, Gaston insisted on being chosen. Mazarin consented, and Gaston began a campaign whose strategy was to take towns *en route* to Dunkirk, this port being the final objective. The first major town to be besieged was Gravelines, which surrendered to Gaston in August 1644. Later in the year, and during the next year's campaigns, other towns were occupied: Courtrai by Gaston; Mardyck, Furnes and, in 1646, Dunkirk itself by Enghien. The capture of Dunkirk had important implications for the war at sea, as it deprived the Spanish of a major port linking the North Sea and English Channel. Meanwhile, Mazarin continued Richelieu's policy of supporting the rebellions against Philip IV in Catalonia and Portugal, pinning down large numbers of Spanish troops who otherwise would be free to fight in the Netherlands.

Turenne, one of the French generals fighting in Germany, warned Mazarin that, Enghien's successes against the Bavarians notwithstanding, the military position of the Emperor (now Ferdinand III) in central Europe had not been seriously damaged, and would only be so if France cooperated more effectively with its ally, Sweden. Responding to Turenne's argument, Mazarin adopted three measures in 1645. First, he negotiated the Peace of Brömsebro between Sweden and Denmark. These two states had gone to war in 1643, forcing Sweden to divert military resources from Germany. The peace allowed Sweden once again to concentrate on Germany, and Mazarin followed up with an alliance with Denmark, thereby guaranteeing Sweden that no further danger from that quarter would be forthcoming. Secondly, Mazarin signed an agreement with George Rákóczy, Prince of Transylvania. George received French subsidies, and in return promised to support a rebellion against Ferdinand III that was taking place in Hungary, and to lend military assistance to the Swedes in Germany. Thirdly, Mazarin arranged the marriage between Wladislaus IV of Poland and a French princess, Marie de Gonzague-Nevers (daughter of the Duke of Mantua), thereby reinforcing the threat to Ferdinand III from the north-east.

Against this background of war and intense diplomatic activity, peace negotiations were taking place in Westphalia. The initiative had come from a meeting of the Imperial Diet, which Ferdinand III called at Regensburg in 1640. Emperor and Diet agreed that an international peace congress should be assembled involving the territories of the Empire and non-German governments, notably those of Spain, France, Sweden and the Dutch Republic. The Diet sent an invitation to Queen Christina of Sweden inviting her to nominate the location of a congress; after consulting Richelieu she proposed that it meet in two cities in Westphalia: Münster, where delegations from the Emperor, and from Catholic princes of the Holy Roman Empire and other Catholic states would meet, and Osnabrück, where Imperial representatives and those of Protestant princes of the Empire and other Protestant states would meet. In practice Dutch representatives went to Münster (since Spain and the Republic were at war, it made sense for them to negotiate directly), and French representatives attended both locations, although Münster was their principal base. The pope mediated at Münster and the King of Denmark at Osnabrück. The first meetings, mainly of a preparatory and organisational nature, took place late in 1643, but in 1644 and 1645 the major delegations arrived and began serious negotiations which lasted until 1648. When they finished, the settlements to which they led were transcribed into formal agreements, which were then collated into two texts, and signed by the delegations simultaneously in Münster and Osnabrück on 24 October 1648. The texts together comprised the Peace of Westphalia.

The long duration of the talks was a consequence partly of the magnitude and complexity of the task in hand, but also of procedural features of the congress. Ministers of participating governments did not attend in person, but remained at home and received regular reports from their delegations. Having studied the reports, they then sent back further instructions. Delay therefore was built into the system. The main French delegation was headed by the Duc de Longueville, but he was a figurehead charged principally with coordinating the efforts of the French representatives and keeping a vigilant eye on the comings and goings of members of other delegations in Münster. The two plenipotentiaries responsible for the conduct of the negotiations on behalf of France were Claude de Mesmes, Comte d'Avaux, and Abel Servien (later Marquis de Sablé). Although the younger of the two, d'Avaux was the more experienced in diplomacy. He had been ambassador in Venice and other parts of Italy, and had served as a diplomat in Denmark, Sweden, Poland, various German territories and the Dutch Republic. He knew several of the leading rulers and statesmen of Europe and, from Mazarin's point of view, was the ideal person to understand the personalities and proclivities of other negotiators in Münster. Although he had administered Richelieu's *bon Français* policies faithfully, d'Avaux was known for Catholic commitments which took him close to the *dévot* movement. Protestant delegations in Westphalia watched him carefully, suspecting that his presence might signify that France was about to realign its foreign policy in accordance with religious principles rather than those of *raison d'état*. D'Avaux's relations with his colleague, Abel Servien, were poor. Servien had diplomatic experience, but much less than d'Avaux; he had also fallen foul of Richelieu and spent several years in self-imposed exile at Angers. Although technically equal in status with d'Avaux in Münster, Servien complained that his colleague treated him as an inferior. On the other hand, his personal political views were much less 'Catholic' than those of d'Avaux, and Mazarin regarded him as a check on any tendencies of d'Avaux to stray beyond his brief. Indeed, in Mazarin's opinion Servien was a more gifted diplomat than d'Avaux, and it was Servien who signed the Peace of Westphalia on behalf of the French government.

The general instructions which guided the French negotiators had been drawn up by Richelieu, but were retained by Mazarin.[1] They emphasised the need to find, not just solutions to the problems of the last twenty-five years, but a general settlement of Europe based on new principles of international relations. Those principles must arise from two sources: the Christian impulse towards peace and justice, and international arrangements for collective security. Herein may be detected elements of Richelieu's wider political philosophy,[2] and his desire for what he called 'le repos de la chrétienté' ('the peace of Christendom'). Yet as the negotiations in Westphalia proceeded against a background of persistent warfare, d'Avaux and Servien found that the desirability, let alone the possibility, of adhering to such principles came into question. In the event, a general settlement of Europe was not achieved in 1648: France and Spain remained at war for another decade, and when Mazarin signed the Peace of the Pyrenees in 1659, it was on the basis that France was poised for even further expansion, as the first few years of the personal reign of Louis XIV were to show.

As the talks in Westphalia continued, how did France's wars progress after the successes of 1643, 1644 and 1645? In Flanders in 1646 important conquests were made, as noted above. In other respects, however, Mazarin showed signs of losing his touch, or at the very least of questionable judgement. Perhaps over-reacting to the successes in Flanders, he conceived the idea of annexing all or part of the Spanish Netherlands. He discreetly put a proposal to the Spanish government that if it would cede the Spanish Netherlands to France, the French would withdraw from Catalonia and use their influence to have the King of Spain's authority restored. The Spanish leaked Mazarin's proposal to the Dutch, who reacted vehemently to this 'betrayal' by their French ally. Within the Republic there were already political figures who advocated a separate peace with Spain. Their voice was all the more persuasive once Mazarin's action became known. The Dutch Republic thereafter had no compunction about seeking unilateral peace with Spain, which was signed early in 1648 and confirmed later in the year by the Peace of Westphalia.[3] It is possible to present the Dutch–Spanish settlement merely as a prelude to others signed later in the year, but it did encourage the Spanish to be bolder in their dealings with the French at Münster, and correspondingly made the task of d'Avaux and Servien harder.

In 1646, Mazarin also committed French forces to an Italian campaign, which was perhaps peripheral to France's international priorities but added to the fiscal burdens causing socio-political tensions on the domestic front. Mazarin decided to attack Spanish fortified ports on the coast of Tuscany. If some or all of these fortifications could be captured, so he reasoned, Spanish power and prestige in the Ligurian Sea would be diminished and that of France increased. In May 1646 a fleet of forty-five ships bearing soldiers sailed against the Spanish, but was driven back. A second expedition was undertaken later in the year, this time to greater effect. The French took Piombino on the Italian mainland and the fort of Porto Azzuro on the adjacent island of Elba; they held on to these prizes for four years. It may be submitted that Mazarin achieved his purpose of weakening Spanish primacy in the Ligurian Sea and succeeded also in forcing Genoa (whose shipping passed through the Ligurian Sea) henceforth to be circumspect in its dealings with France. On the other hand, the question must arise as to whether the benefits of the seizure of Piombino and Porto Azzuro were worth the expenditure in men, money and military resources, or whether this enterprise was little more than an expensive side-show to the strategic struggles being settled north of the Alps.

In Germany, Mazarin persisted with his strategy of increasing pressure on the Austrian Habsburgs while at the same time seeking to detach Maximilian of Bavaria from Ferdinand III. Franco-Swedish forces invaded Bavaria in 1646 and laid waste to much of the duchy. The devastation they caused was such that when they threatened Munich itself, Maximilian called for peace. The Swedes, whose earlier experience of dealing with Maximilian had taught them not to trust him, were reluctant to comply, but under pressure from Mazarin they agreed to a cessation of hostilities involving not only themselves, France and Bavaria, but also the Landgrave of Hesse and the Archbishop-Elector of Cologne. In March 1647 these states signed a truce by which they agreed to suspend fighting until a general European peace was reached. To Mazarin's chagrin, but not to the surprise of the Swedish government, Maximilian did indeed break the truce, but his army was decisively beaten in May 1648 by Turenne. Other French military successes continued well into 1648. In May, Enghien, now the Prince de Condé since his father had died on 26 December 1646, captured Ypres, and in August he defeated an imperial force at Lens. By this time the negotiations in Münster were well advanced, and the final settlement was within sight. As stated above, the Peace of Westphalia was signed by all the delegations on 24 October 1648. The 'French' portion of the general settlement was signed by Servien in the name of Louis XIV, representatives of Emperor Ferdinand III, and others of the princes and states of the Holy Roman Empire. The French presence in the Rhineland was strengthened, French occupation of Metz, Toul, Verdun and the fortresses of Breisach and Philippsburg being acknowledged. Most important, however, was the yielding by the Emperor of his rights in Upper and Lower Alsace, including ten Imperial cities including Haguenau, Schelestadt and Münster (not to be confused with the city in Westphalia). Exactly what those rights were, and how far they extended throughout the territories and cities which comprised Alsace, was left in a state of ambiguity; this was intentional, for any attempt to resolve the detail of such tricky questions would have prolonged discussions indefinitely; another complicating factor was that some cities, notably Strasbourg and Mulhouse, were excluded from the peace and retained their autonomous status. Nevertheless, the broad outcome was that France now possessed, to a greater or lesser extent, most of the Rhineland between the Swiss Confederation to the south and the Palatinate to the north. The longer-term geo-political implications of the acquisition by France of rights in Alsace were self-evidently considerable – France was bound, henceforth, to play an influential role in west German affairs – but what were those implications for France itself? Should Alsace eventually be fully incorporated into France or treated as a special case? After all, Alsace was a predominantly German-speaking region with a large Protestant population. Was it in France's interest to absorb this territory into a kingdom wherein differences of language and, even more so, religion had been major destabilising forces for so long? Although France derived considerable strategic advantages from the annexation of Alsace, the implications for the internal tranquillity of France were less positive.

The negotiations at Münster failed to achieve two of Richelieu's aims. First, France did not secure Lorraine, a duchy which Richelieu had regarded as crucial to France's security in the north-east. No agreement was reached over this territory, and the Duke of Lorraine remained at war with France on the side of the Spanish. This leads to the second and more important failure: France did not sign peace with Spain. Having ended the war with the Dutch Republic (which Spain now recognised as an independent state), the Spanish were less inclined to yield to French pressure. Neither side had a clear military advantage, and while it was true that Spain faced formidable internal difficulties as revolts continued in Catalonia, Portugal and Italy (although here Spain was reasserting its authority in 1648), France experienced a similar crisis when the Fronde rebellions began. Since neither side would give way, France and Spain remained at war until 1659. When the terms of the Treaty of Westphalia became known to the French public, Mazarin was criticised from many quarters, including his former colleague Chavigny. He was accused of having prolonged war to no great advantage, of having engaged in pointless Italian adventures, and of having bungled the negotiations with Spain. By October 1648 the city of Paris was immersed in the Fronde and the denunciations of Mazarin's handling of the peace negotiations added to the plethora of grievances which ignited that rebellion. Mazarin defended himself through pamphlets and celebrations of the peace, but in the highly-charged domestic atmosphere of 1648 the terms which he authorised in the Treaty of Westphalia had the effect of augmenting rather than diminishing the movement of protest against him.

Prelude to the Frondes

Mazarin came to government in France with a solid background in diplomacy and international relations, but his grasp of internal French politics was much less sure. Nowhere was this more so than in the realm of government finance, a subject on which he claimed limited expertise. For the administration of financial affairs he relied heavily on Michel Particelli, sieur d'Hémery, *contrôleur général des finances*, who sat on the *conseil d'état* from 1644. Technically Particelli was subordinate to the *surintendant des finances*, Nicolas le Bailleul, but it was from Particelli that Mazarin took advice.

Particelli's principal obligation was, of course, to continue finding money to fight the war, to which end he resorted to borrowing on an alarming scale, guaranteeing the loans which he took from financiers by pledging the anticipated revenues of future years. In 1645 he secured loans on the revenues for 1646 and 1647, and in 1648 did so on the revenues for 1650 and 1651.[4] As short-term expedients, such measures helped to keep French armies in the field, but they were no basis for sound financial management and raised governmental debt to dangerously high levels. Particelli also persisted with the kinds of extraordinary devices of the Richelieu years: the sale of offices, the issuing of government bonds, the tardy redemption of bonds which had matured, and at a rate lower than their face value, as well as reductions in the rate of annual interest paid on bonds, and the announcement of new taxes. He introduced, for example, a somewhat ill-defined tax on wealth, and in 1644, a charge aimed specifically at Paris, the *toisé*. In a sense this was not a new imposition, for it referred to a sixteenth-century law forbidding the construction of houses and other property close to the city wall, on pain of a fine. The motive behind the law was military defence; if houses, shops or workplaces abutted the city wall, they would make the defence of the city all the more difficult and correspondingly would be of use to an attacking force. In recent decades the statute had fallen into abeyance and much property had been erected in the forbidden locations. The *toisé* imposed fines on the refractory property owners, thereby incurring the hostility not only of those directly affected, but of the city's inhabitants more generally, who were complaining that they were being singled out because they were an easy target. This sense of persecution was heightened further by the *pancarte*, a duty which Particelli placed on certain foodstuffs coming into the capital.

Meanwhile, across the kingdom, the *taille, gabelle, aides*, and all the other sources of revenue that the government could exploit, were being assessed and collected through the clumsy and often corrupt procedures bequeathed by former ministers. Those procedures had fomented socio-political unrest in the 1630s and early 1640s and continued to do so throughout the 1640s. In Provence, for example, anti-fiscal riots occurred in Arles in 1644, Draguignan and Marseille in 1645, and Grasse in 1646. Similar outbursts occurred in Gascony in the mid-1640s. Taxes still were being farmed out to financiers, who made large profits from the government's financial desperation and were detested by taxpayers, who regarded them as exploiters of the worst sort. Many of the uprisings of the 1640s were directed specifically against them, the property of financiers and their agents frequently being attacked and despoiled by rioters.

The government's financial girations, especially the apparently endless introduction of extraordinary charges and forced loans, provoked much 'constitutional' resistance from the *parlements* and other bodies which registered royal legislation. They resorted to the well-tried practice of remonstrance, but the crown, in the case of the Parlement of Paris, responded by *lits de justice* in 1645 and 1648 to impose the registration of financial edicts. The *parlements* and other great law courts in the kingdom, such as the *chambres des comptes* and the *cours des aides*, and the provincial

Estates, also manifested growing resistance to the government's use of *intendants* and its practice of overruling the judgements of law courts when it found them politically unwelcome (for instance, if judgements went against financiers to whom the government was indebted). To *parlementaires*, other judges and magistrates, municipal officers across the kingdom, and all the other people involved in the administration of the kingdom's legal and financial affairs, it appeared that the 'absolutism' of Richelieu had in no way abated under Mazarin, and that the expectations of a new beginning which had attended the accession of Louis XIV had been thoroughly misplaced.

The episode which triggered the Fronde of 1648 and plunged France into five years of rebellion and civil war was a dispute over the *paulette*, the annual payment made by *officiers* to secure their offices as private property. The rate at which *paulette* was paid was fixed for periods of nine years, after which negotiations would be held between the government and representatives of the *parlements* and other bodies to strike a new rate. Naturally, the government wanted the *paulette* to be as high as possible and *officiers* tried to keep it low. The ultimate threat which the government could wield was to refuse to renew the *paulette*. If *paulette* were not paid, offices would cease to be the *de facto* property of *officiers* and would revert to the crown if an *officier* retired or died; his family then would have to repurchase the office, a move involving a heavy outlay of capital. The most recent cycle of *paulette* had ended in December 1647. On 30 April 1648, the government offered to renew it on condition that *officiers* in the *grand conseil*, the *cours des aides* and the *chambres des comptes* sacrificed four years' income from their offices. The *parlements* were exempted from this provision. This attempt by the government to withhold four years' salary from many *officiers* crystallised opposition to Mazarin and Particelli. Magistrates and other *officiers* saw the edict of 30 April as illegal, malicious and characteristic of a ministry which had lost all sense of responsibility to the king's subjects. They also interpreted the exclusion of the *parlementaires* from the requirement to lose income as a crude and pathetic attempt to divide them from their colleagues in other law courts. The resistance of *officiers* to the edict surmounted particular institutional interests and turned into a united movement against Mazarin. He, in response, bitterly claimed that the obduracy of the *parlements* and other courts over the *paulette* was making his task of securing a last-minute peace with Spain, at the Münster negotiations, all but impossible. The Spanish, he contended, were gambling that the French government would be paralysed by domestic disputes, which would cripple the major law courts of France and halt the entire process of legislation. The Spanish expected to exploit the situation to their military advantage and so refrained from signing the peace. In 1648, relations between Mazarin's ministry, the *parlements* and other bodies involved in the quarrel over *paulette* broke down; each side castigated the other, accusing it of bad faith and deceit. The affair had become a *cause célèbre* whose significance transcended the technical details of *paulette*: it had turned into a question of how, and according to which principles, France should be governed.

Chapter 10:   The Frondes

From the Fronde in Paris to the 'Peace of Rueil'

On 13 May 1648, the Parlement of Paris, the *grand conseil*, the Parisian *Chambre des Comptes* and *Cour des Aides* jointly issued the *Arrêt d'Union* by which these four great law courts agreed to elect representatives who would meet in a hall of the Parlement – the Chambre Saint Louis – to discuss the reform of the state. The Regency, which was following closely the collapse of the power of Charles I in England, feared that the *Union* might imitate what the Parliament in London was doing to the king. When discussions between representatives of the magistrates and the Regency failed to reach accommodation, the crown resorted to threats, which simply hardened the attitude of the *Union*. Anne relented and on 15 June accepted the Act of Union. The meetings in the Chambre Saint Louis aimed to dismantle the 'ministerial absolutism' which Richelieu allegedly had constructed and which Mazarin had preserved.[1] The assembly drew up a text of twenty-seven articles demanding reform. They included the suppression of the *intendants* and all other extraordinary commissioners not authorised by the courts of justice, a ban on the creation and sale of new offices, an end to royal interventions in the normal conduct of justice, a return to 'traditional' procedures in the creation of new taxes (i.e. fiscal legislation must be registered in the 'normal' way before being implemented), and a similar return to traditional means of collecting revenue (which meant dismissing the agents of the tax farmers). In July the Parlement of Paris added its own demand: contracts between the government and tax farmers must be revoked and the *taille* reduced by one-quarter.

Faced by a resolute Chambre Saint Louis and Parlement of Paris, just at a time when the negotiations in Münster were concluding, Anne and Mazarin made concessions. On 9 July Particelli was dismissed, much to the joy of the magistrates. He was replaced by an old soldier of little financial acumen, but of unquestioned honesty: Charles de la Porte, Duc de la Meilleraye. Most of his work was undertaken by two assistants with the title of *directeurs des finances*: Étienne d'Aligre, sieur de la Rivière, and Antoine Barillon, sieur de Morangis. On 18 July, all the extraordinary commissioners, including the *intendants*, were suspended (excepting those attached to the army in the frontier provinces); on the same day the *taille* was reduced by 12 per cent. The Parlement accepted this as a future projection, but still insisted on 25 per cent for 1647, 1648 and 1649. When they heard this, financiers panicked and refused to loan more money to the crown. Mazarin had no option but to declare a *de facto* bankruptcy, and the government ceased making payments on its bonds or towards its other debts. On 31 July, Anne and Mazarin gave in on the question of the *paulette*: they renewed it on generous terms and abandoned the requirement that magistrates forfeit four years' income.

By the end of July 1648, the Regency had yielded on all the major demands of the Chambre Saint Louis and the Parlement of Paris. It was possible to present these concessions, not as a retreat by the Regency, but as a return by the crown to traditional procedures in the government and administration of the kingdom now that peace, even though it was partial, was about to be signed in Münster. It could be argued that the Regent was turning the clock back to supposedly happier times when the crown was thought to have worked in collaboration with its *officiers*, its great courts of law and other bodies. Moreover, had the demands emanating from the judicial elites and their associates in 1648 ended there, this analysis would have carried much force and some form of accommodation with the Regency could have been found. However, having tasted success, the Parlement pushed on with what it termed 'reform', but what looked to the crown like the kind of revolution that was threatening England: a usurpation of royal prerogatives by the king's subjects.

So far the great questions at stake had been between the Regency on one side and the magistrates on the other, but in the background was a third force, and whoever acquired its support would be in a strongly advantageous position: the populace of Paris. On the occasion of the festivities which accompanied Saint John's Day (23 June 1648), Anne and Louis XIV had attended the municipal celebrations. The nine-year-old

Louis XIV had ceremoniously ignited the great bonfire which the city had built and he and his mother then attended the *fête* which was held. The Queen Mother made a point of meeting municipal notabilities, and the crowds attending the carnival had cheered and applauded the young king. On their side, the magistrates depicted the demands which they made of the Regency as aiming to serve the public good, not merely the sectional interest of *officiers*. It was in order to substantiate this claim that the Parlement continued to press further changes upon the Regent. The Parlement had another motive: the Regency appeared to be in retreat and in a mood to make even more concessions. In August the Parlement demanded that, in future, the *pancarte* be assessed by person-nel drawn from its own ranks, not by the *conseil d'état*. Although at first the Regency refused, a compromise was reached eventually: the tariff would be assessed by Gaston d'Orléans on behalf of the Regent, and two magistrates, Broussel and Ferrand, on behalf of the Parlement. Pierre Broussel had emerged as one of the sternest critics of the Regency, especially of what he considered its arbitrary and irresponsible financial practices. Personally he was a figure of the highest probity, who lived modestly and had a reputation as a public servant worthy of the highest esteem. He began to extend his newly acquired responsibilities beyond the *pancarte* to an investigation of the *gabelle* and the methods whereby contracts were agreed with tax farmers. On his recommendation the Parlement decided to institute proceedings against certain financiers. To the Regency this was an alarming development; not only because it threatened to expose chicanery and dubious financial practices in and around the government, but also because it was a move of revolutionary potential, for it implied that the crown was answerable to the Parlement for its conduct of public affairs.

The *conseil d'état* (or *conseil d'en haut*) decided that the time had come to retaliate, a sentiment encouraged by news that the Prince de Condé had won a decisive victory over the Spanish at Lens; it would now be feasible to withdraw troops from the front and deploy them in Paris. The council took a decision. A *Te Deum* to celebrate Lens was to be held at the cath-edral of Notre Dame on 26 August 1648, and would be attended by royalty, nobility, representatives of the city, the trades guilds and other corpor-ations, but also by members of the Parlement. The plan was to arrest leading parlementary critics of the government as they left the cathedral; among those to be seized was Broussel. On the appointed day the *Te Deum* was celebrated in a packed cathedral, with crowds outside having watched the processions and parades that preceded the Mass. When the service was finished, the royal family and leading ministers departed in their coaches, but only a minority of the royal bodyguard accompanied them, the rest remaining outside Notre Dame. This break with custom (members of the bodyguard only left royalty unattended under exceptional circumstances) alerted the congregation in the cathedral that something was afoot. Some members of the Parlement of Paris, suspecting a royal *coup*, tried to slip out of the cathedral by side doors; some escaped, but others on the list of those to be arrested were seized. Meanwhile troops had gone to the residence of Broussel, who did not attend the *Te Deum*; he too was arrested and led to prison.

There then occurred an eventuality which neither the government nor the Parlement of Paris had fully anticipated: a popular uprising in Paris to demand the release of Broussel and his colleagues. This dispute between crown, Parlement, other law courts and the Chambre Saint Louis, was a contest between crown and judicial elites, but Broussel's arrest was the catalyst which widened its social participation. On 26 August, barricades began to be erected in many parts of Paris, the city militias throwing in their lot with the demonstrators. Royal guards attempted to control the centre of the city, but were driven back to the Palais Royal by crowds using slings (*frondes*) to pelt them with stones, hence the origin of the sobriquet. Crowds remained in the streets overnight to defend the barricades. Members of the Parlement met Anne and Mazarin and urged them to release Broussel; so did the prelate who had conducted the service in Notre Dame, Jean-François-Paul de Gondi de Retz, Coadjutor-Bishop of Paris. He had been out among the crowds trying to calm them, or so he claimed; his later role in the Frondes convinced Anne and Mazarin that, on the contrary, he had been encouraging them to resist the government. At first, Anne's advisers assumed that the rioting would quickly subside, but on 27 August it became worse as barricades spread to other parts of the city. After more crisis meetings, Anne and Mazarin relented: on 28 August, Broussel and the other magistrates were released amidst an outburst of public celebrations.

In the present context it is the fact of the popular rising which is important, not so much the reasons behind it; they had much to do with hostility to the regime's fiscal programme, especially the recent duties on the movement of goods in and out of Paris; fears that the Regency was about to send the army into the city to exact reprisals; and equally strong fears that amidst the crisis, gangs of vagabonds and robbers would take the opportunity to rob and loot. A sense of civic solidarity with the Parlement also played its part; the government's 'assault' upon that body was popularly understood to be an attack upon Parisians themselves.[2] Quickly, this intermixture of apprehension and resistance was distilled into two names: Broussel and Mazarin, the one supposedly embodying the liberties of Paris and the virtues of 'traditional' and honest government, the other being the epitome of everything that was wrong with the regime. Mazarin was denounced as untrustworthy, corrupt, despotic and self-serving. Pamphlets, later known as 'Mazarinades', began to be published and soon were a distinctive feature of the Frondes. Over the next few years, several thousand were printed, mostly hostile to the Regency in general and Mazarin in particular. He was reviled as a foreigner who was enriching himself at the state's expense, and an adventurer who exercised a sinister influence over Queen Anne. As pamphlets continued to pour from the printing presses, the regime found itself facing a 'propaganda deficit', which it never effectively resolved.[3]

In September and October further meetings took place between delegates from the Parlement and, acting for the Regency, Gaston d'Orléans and the Prince de Condé (who had returned to Paris). Mazarin remained in the background, since his presence in the discussions would have been inflammatory. Once again the Regency was forced to make concessions. On 22 October it issued statutes (verified by the Parlement two days later, the day of the signing of the Peace of Westphalia) not only confirming the original articles adopted by the Chambre Saint Louis, but also abolishing *lettres de cachet*.[4] Queen Anne burst into tears when she signed the statutes, regarding them as a humiliation for herself and a disaster for the monarchy. Mazarin too believed that they spelt the death-knell of 'authentic' French monarchy unless they were reversed as soon as possible.

For several weeks the Regency lived with the defeats the Parlement had inflicted, and observed with growing concern the debates that took place in that body. Some *parlementaires* argued that 'reform' had gone far enough, but others contended that even more radical demands should be made of the government. Early in the new year, Anne and Mazarin decided on action. During the night of 5 to 6 January 1649, when the Epiphany or Twelfth Night celebrations were taking place in the city, the royal family slipped out of Paris and went to Saint-Germain. As news of their departure was carried around the city, alarm set in, for rumours also spread that Mazarin was about to order a military assault by Condé, who was in the vicinity with his troops. The resolve of members of the Parlement, the city fathers and inhabitants of Paris was stiffened when several princes and aristocrats, who had their own quarrels with Mazarin, offered their military services. On 9 January 1649, the Parlement issued a declaration denouncing Mazarin and demanding his exile. Condé now placed the city under siege. Mazarin's intention was to starve Paris into submission and annul the concessions which the crown had made under duress. De Retz, who had thrown in his lot with the Frondeurs, was prominent in organising an anti-Mazarin coalition. On 18 January, a group of leading aristocrats took an oath to support the Parlement against Mazarin. The group included Charles de Lorraine, Duc d'Elbeuf; Armand de Bourbon, Prince de Conti; François de Vendôme, Duc de Beaufort; François-Maurice de la Tour d'Auvergne, Duc de Bouillon; and de Retz himself.

The departure of the royal family and the siege of Paris placed enormous pressure on the municipal authorities and the Parlement. The latter was punctilious in avoiding any action that could be construed as rebellion against the king (it had been careful to insist that it was resisting the 'despotic' acts of Mazarin and his predecessor Richelieu, not Louis XIV himself), but the longer the siege went on, the more difficult it would be to maintain this stance. The news from England that Charles I had been executed further complicated the position of the Parlement: although within its ranks there were radical reformers, they were heavily outnumbered by judges and magistrates who loathed regicide and had no intention of allowing the French crisis to get out of hand. Moreover, municipal leaders and most members of the Parlement were alarmed at the behaviour of some of les grands, who were talking of inviting the Spanish to intervene; and when de Retz gave a series of inflammatory sermons calling for the overthrow of Mazarin, he too seemed to be legitimating popular disorder in the city.

For its part, the Regency did not want the siege to continue too long. Spring was approaching, and with it a new season of campaigns against the Spanish. Mazarin could not allow Condé and his forces to be tied down. When the First President of the Parlement, Mathieu Molé, proposed talks with the Regency, he found support on all sides, even though de Retz urged the Parlement not to sign peace with the Regency. In March, discussions took place at Rueil between the Regency, whose representatives included Gaston d'Orléans, Mazarin and Séguier, and the Parlement. Agreement was reached in the so-called 'Peace of Rueil' and was accepted by the Parlement on 1 April 1649. The crown confirmed the concessions made to the Parlement in July and October 1648, but the Parlement repealed its anti-Mazarin declarations. An amnesty to

Frondeurs was granted. By a narrow interpretation of the peace, the Parlement had more cause to be satisfied than did the Regency, for it had preserved all the advantages won in 1648. On the other hand, the Regency could derive a certain satisfaction. Mazarin had survived, and it now seemed probable that a limit to the demands of the Parlement had been reached. The Parlement had drawn back from the kind of revolutionary position that Parliament in England had adopted. The Peace of Rueil implied that the 'Fronde of the Parlement' was a struggle over the limitations within which French monarchy and its ministers should operate, not over the question of whether there should be a monarchy at all.

On 18 August 1649 the royal family returned to Paris in a triumphant procession which drew tens of thousands of cheering Parisians onto the streets. The celebrations apparently confirmed the restoration of relations between Regency, city and Parlement and gave cause for optimism that socio-political order would be restored. Such optimism soon had to be tempered. The Fronde of Paris had spread to the provinces, notably Provence and Guyenne, and the city of Bordeaux was in a state of tumult as Frondeurs there threatened to seize control. In Paris, de Retz and other aristocrats denounced the settlement at Rueil as an act of cowardice by the Parlement, and continued to intrigue against Mazarin. There was still an undercurrent of popular grievances to be exploited, and when riots occurred on 11 December 1649 as a reaction to rumours that the government once again was going to default on its payments on bonds, they served as a warning that the city could easily slip back into anarchy. On the international front, the war against Spain was still being fought, and Mazarin was having difficulty in defending the frontiers. Moreover, by the end of the year the Regency was faced with another challenge to its authority, this time from elements within the great aristocracy. From this clash came the 'Fronde of the Princes'.

Mazarin and the Queen Mother were badly shaken by the crisis of 1648–9; they had been forced onto the defensive and obliged to make concessions under duress. The coincidence of the Fronde of the Parlement and the final negotiations at Münster weakened Mazarin in both the Parisian and Westphalian arenas: the outbreak of the Fronde persuaded the Spanish not to yield to French demands; conversely, the failure of Mazarin to secure general peace at Westphalia complicated his dealing with the Parlement. His career was saved by external factors: the execution of Charles I, which discouraged most members of the Parlement from embracing a more radical political programme; Condé's military intervention in support of the Regency; and the fact that Anne of Austria held faith with him in spite of the temptation to buy off the Parlement with his dismissal. Mazarin's relative inexperience of French domestic politics showed through in 1648 and 1649; he was lucky to survive beyond the Peace of Rueil.

The Fronde of the Princes

A key figure in 1649 was the Prince de Condé, twenty-eight years old and exceedingly conscious of his status. He contended that it was he who had rescued the Regency earlier in the year. Without his military intervention, so he maintained, the Parlement would have imposed even more stringent terms on Anne and Mazarin. Posing as the 'saviour' of the Regency he sought rewards, honours and money for himself and his friends. He also demanded a political role in government. Anne and Mazarin resented his arrogance and the audacity of his claims, but for the time being dared not alienate him. Mazarin agreed to some of his demands: the principal minister promised to consult Condé before making important political, diplomatic or ecclesiastical appointments; he also agreed to secure Condé's consent before arranging the marriages of any of his, Mazarin's, nieces or nephews (in 1649 Mazarin negotiated the marriage between his niece Laure Mancini and the Duc de Mercoeur).

Mazarin and Anne concluded that they must deflate Condé's ambitions, but without driving him into the enemy camp. This latter danger was all the more real in that Condé had been reconciled with his sister, the Duchesse de Longueville, a leading Frondeuse. One factor working in Mazarin's favour was the hostility that existed between Condé and de Retz, and between Condé and the Vendôme dynasty. By playing on these tensions, Mazarin hoped not only to prevent a united aristocratic front emerging, but also to remove Condé from the political scene. Anne and Mazarin decided on a risky course of action: to have Condé arrested, along with his brother Conti, and brother-in-law, the Duc de Longueville. The problem was to do so without provoking the popular reaction that had occurred when a similar stroke had been attempted against Broussel in the preceding year. To prevent another Parisian uprising in the event of the arrest of the princes, Mazarin had a confidential meeting with de Retz. Knowing that de Retz had ambitions to be a cardinal, Mazarin promised to use his influence to have him nominated, on condition that de Retz help to keep Paris calm. The *coup* was executed on 18 January 1650. Condé, Conti and Longueville were imprisoned at Vincennes, just east of Paris. The news was received in Paris with, at most, indifference, and even with some rejoicing; certainly there was no Parisian rising in their support. This was not only because de Retz urged peace in the city, but because Parisians remembered that only a year before, Condé had besieged them. Condé was no Broussel. Mazarin's fears that the arrest of the princes might trigger violence on the streets of Paris proved to be unfounded.

The arrests did, however, provoke an aristocratic revolt which soon spread to the provinces. Her husband and brothers in prison, the Duchesse de Longueville mustered supporters whose aim was to secure their release and overthrow Mazarin. One of her earliest and most important moves was to persuade Maréchal Turenne, brother of the Duc de Bouillon, to join her cause. Turenne was an experienced soldier who had fought with distinction in Germany. That somebody of his smilitary calibre joined the Fronde of the Princes alarmed Anne and Mazarin, but it also showed how deep was the sense of disaffection among aristocrats. In April 1650, the Duchesse de Longueville and Turenne committed what could be interpreted as an act of treachery: they signed an accord with a Spanish representative whereby the government of Spain promised financial and military help. The stated aim of the agreement was to establish peace between the two countries and to secure the liberty of the imprisoned princes; the document named Mazarin as the principal obstacle to be overcome. Other partisans of the princes organised armed resistance to the Regency, especially in the provinces where the princes were governors or had estates. Condé's wife, Claire-Clémence de Maillé-Brézé (ironically, a niece of Richelieu), helped to raise rebellion in Burgundy and Berry where her husband was governor; she also fomented resistance in Guyenne, where the city of Bordeaux had risen against the Regency once more. In the summer of 1650, the Princesse de Condé took up residence in that city. Conti's wife was similarly active in Champagne, where her husband was governor, and the Duchesse de Longueville provoked risings in Normandy. Other parts of the country, including Provence, also rose until, by the summer of 1650, extensive areas were in a state of civil war.

Anne and Mazarin had to withdraw forces from the war against Spain to attack the rebels. Much of Burgundy was recovered by royal forces by late summer; in July, the Queen Mother and principal minister accompanied royal troops in an assault on Bordeaux, whose surrender Mazarin regarded as imperative to the wider cause of royal authority in the south-west. Gaston d'Orléans was left in charge of government in their absence, but only after he signed a promise not to release the imprisoned princes. Bordeaux was besieged and much of its surrounding area devastated by the royal army; large numbers of peasants took refuge in the city, so swelling the population and straining its supplies of food. Neither the city authorities nor Mazarin desired a protracted siege, and peace was agreed on 30 September. Mazarin promised an amnesty to the city, agreed terms for the peaceful departure of the Princesse de Condé to Anjou, and consented to the dismissal of the unpopular governor of the city and province, the Duc d'Épernon. On 5 October 1650, Anne and Mazarin entered Bordeaux.[5]

Against this background of political uncertainty and violence in 1649 and 1650, normal procedures of government were almost impossible. The collection of taxes at times all but ceased. D'Aligre, one of the *directeurs des finances*, sent numerous warnings to Mazarin that socio-political dis-order and the misconduct of troops on all sides was threatening to bring further financial ruin, so little money was reaching the government coffers. In some areas such as Touraine, Maine and Anjou, d'Aligre stated, the disorder was such that people were unable to pay taxes; and the situation in and around Bordeaux meant that no taxation of any description was being collected there. Because of these dire circumstances, government loans could be secured from *traitants* only at exorbitant rates of interest.[6] To add to Mazarin's troubles, word arrived that, in the north, the Spanish had invaded from the Netherlands and were being supported by Turenne. Turenne's Frondeur army had occupied Rethel to the north-east of Rheims. If the Spanish succeeded in joining him there and made this the base of further operations, Paris itself would be in danger. Bordeaux having capitulated, Mazarin personally accompanied an army to retake Rethel. He introduced another factor into the equation: he took Louis XIV with him. Like the other Frondeurs, Turenne claimed to be resisting Mazarin, not the king. The presence of Louis XIV rendered this pretence worthless and increased the political pressure on Turenne. It also proved an inspiration to the royal troops. When the two armies met on 15 December 1650, the royal force carried the day, raising the hopes of the Regency that, at last, the struggle was turning in its favour. Burgundy had been subdued, Bordeaux had capitulated, the risings in Provence and Normandy were subsiding, and now the leading Frondeur general had been defeated. Anne and Mazarin could face 1651 with some optimism.

As on other occasions, it proved to be misplaced. During the court's absence from Paris since the autumn, de Retz – incensed that he had not received the cardinal's hat which Mazarin had promised – and other Frondeurs had been busy intriguing against the principal minister. The weak link proved to be Gaston d'Orléans. De Retz persuaded Gaston that Mazarin was the cause of the ills of the state, and that if he were overthrown, peace with Spain and the internal stability of France would be achieved. De Retz held out a further allure to Gaston: in the event of Mazarin's dismissal, Gaston himself would be principal minister or adviser to the Regent. De Retz also contacted Broussel and other *parlementaires*, and urged them too to press for the dismissal of Mazarin. Mazarin, argued de Retz, could not be trusted. As soon as circumstances allowed, he would abrogate the concessions made to the Parlement in 1648 and 1649. De Retz and his associates succeeded in their negotiations.

At the end of January 1651 a series of agreements was reached between aristocratic Frondeurs and members of the Parlement of Paris. Gaston, the Duchesse de Chevreuse, other aristocrats, Broussel and some *parlementaires* agreed that the imprisoned princes should be released, Mazarin should be dismissed, Gaston should be head of the *conseil d'en haut*, and de Retz should be promoted to the cardinalate. Marriages to strengthen this accord were agreed: Condé's son (the Duc d'Enghien) would marry a daughter of Gaston, and Conti would marry the daughter of the Duchesse de Chevreuse. Early in February 1651 Gaston formally broke with Mazarin; the Parlement of Paris demanded that the minister go into exile. Faced with this 'union of the Frondes' – aristocratic Frondeurs supported by the Parlement of Paris – Mazarin, whose position a few weeks before had looked so strong, capitulated. On 6 February he left Paris and travelled first to Le Havre, to where the princes had been transferred. Condé, Conti and Longueville, aware that he was in retreat, refused any accommodation with Mazarin. He had no option but to order their release, after which he left the country. He stayed for a while in Liège, but in April 1651 was offered sanctuary by the Archbishop of Cologne. He settled at Brühl, not far from Cologne. Back in Paris, Gaston received information that on the evening of 9 February the Regent planned to leave the city again, taking the king with her. Gaston raised the militia and forced Anne to remain in the Palais Royal, a virtual prisoner. The Parlement took further steps to confirm the overthrow of Mazarin. On 17 February it announced that no foreigner, even if naturalised, henceforth should sit on the king's council; later in the month it pronounced Condé, Conti and Longueville innocent of any charges against them.

Divisions between Frondeurs, and the Revolt of Condé

From his retreat near Cologne, Mazarin kept in touch with Anne by clandestine communications. He had placed his personal affairs in the hands of a trusted household assistant, Jean-Baptiste Colbert, and in their correspondence Colbert kept his master informed of events inside France. The principal development was the rapid disintegration of Frondeur unity, a tendency which Mazarin encouraged through the Queen Mother. The exiled minister, who still considered Condé to be the most dangerous of the princes, took steps to isolate him. He was assisted by Condé's high-handed manner, which increasingly alienated other aristocrats. Condé resumed his governorships of Guyenne and Berry, and restored his younger brother, Conti, to the governorship of Champagne. Condé also opposed the proposed marriage of Conti to Mademoiselle de Chevreuse (not least because the bride-to-be had been the mistress of de Retz). The whole Chevreuse family took this as an insult to their honour. Mazarin advised Anne to cultivate de Retz, who disliked Condé because the prince openly objected to his becoming a cardinal. De Retz might become a useful weapon with which Mazarin, through Anne, could attack Condé. The most effective way to acquire his allegiance, advised Mazarin, was to make sure that he achieved his much-coveted cardinal's hat. Anne took the appropriate steps. De Retz became a cardinal in February 1652. Other Frondeur divisions served Mazarin's purpose. Gaston d'Orléans made plans to call an Estates General. He was resisted by the Parlement of Paris, which regarded such a move as a threat to its own standing as the 'senior' legal body in the kingdom. Although arrangements reached an advanced stage, Gaston dropped his plan, but the damage had been done: his relations with the Parlement had been compromised.

As disputes between the princes and aristocrats multiplied, and the Parlement increasingly viewed them with suspicion, Mazarin established secret contact with de Retz and Mademoiselle de Chevreuse to discuss how to bring down Condé and perhaps readmit Mazarin to France. In mid-August 1651, Anne, prompted by Mazarin, struck against Condé. She published a list of grievances against the prince: he had ceased attending the *conseil d'en haut*; he kept his followers armed; the soldiers under his command in Champagne and Picardy had lost all sense of discipline and were committing appalling atrocities and damaging crops and property. Condé, accompanied by an armed guard, went in person to the Parlement of Paris to rebut the charges, but although the Parlement did not reject Anne's accusation, neither did it side with Condé. On 5 September the king had his thirteenth birthday; two days later the Parlement of Paris formally proclaimed his majority; the Regency was at an end. This changed the political landscape. The king would appoint a new *conseil d'en haut*, from which, probably, Condé would be excluded and perhaps even Gaston d'Orléans. The king might bring back Mazarin, as the exiled minister fervently hoped and expected. The Parlement of Paris had tried to forestall this eventuality by issuing a proclamation on 6 September confirming Mazarin's exclusion from France; but unless Louis XIV confirmed the declaration, it had no force of law. Most seriously of all, after the proclamation of the king's majority, Frondeurs could no longer maintain that resistance to the crown was directed at Mazarin or the Regent; henceforth, armed resistance would be rebellion.

Condé, who understood the adverse implications of the king's majority for his own position, decided on the drastic course of rebellion. It was a decision full of risks, but he calculated that armed resistance to the crown would achieve his purpose. His strategy was to create such military and political mayhem that the king would have to buy him off by readmitting him, and indeed other aristocrats of whom Condé approved, to the *conseil d'en haut*. Condé's career thus far had demonstrated that strong military action could produce desirable political results and personal advancement; he saw no reason to doubt that it would do so in future. His recent conduct had alienated many leading Frondeurs, but he still had the support of his brother Conti, their sister the Duchesse de Longueville, and some other aristocrats. Moreover, he was still in contact with Spanish representatives, and after his break with the king he accelerated the talks until, in November 1651, he signed an agreement whereby he would receive Spanish financial and military assistance. By this time, Condé had taken his army to Guyenne, of which he was now governor, and he intended making this province his stronghold.

Louis XIV and his mother personally accompanied a royal army which headed for Guyenne to counter Condé. Their aim was political as much as military: as they proceeded south-west and passed through towns *en route*, crowds turned out to welcome the king. When the royal procession reached Bourges in October, Louis XIV issued a declaration proclaiming Condé and his associates guilty of treason; anybody who gave assistance to them would be implicated in their guilt. The royal train moved on to Poitiers, which Louis XIV and his mother made their base. From there they sent an instruction to Mazarin to prepare to return to France. Relieved that the end of his exile was imminent, Mazarin began to raise an armed force, without which he dared not attempt to cross the frontier. Meanwhile, as the autumn advanced, both Condé and the royalist forces tried to take control of important ports and towns in the west and south-west. La Rochelle was especially important. Condé tried to occupy it, but it remained loyal to the king, whose forces moved in by the end of November 1651. The failure to take La Rochelle was a serious blow to Condé; on the other hand, Bordeaux had declared in his favour. Condé formally entered the city on 22 September, where the Parlement of Bordeaux pronounced itself committed to his cause. It refused to recognise the majority of the king and called for a form of government in which princes and Parlements would play their 'rightful' part.

The Return of Mazarin and the Fronde of the Princes

On 24 December, Mazarin entered France with a small military force. The Parlement of Paris reaffirmed its ban on him, but on 11 January 1652 Louis XIV issued a declaration stating that it was at his command that Mazarin had returned, and that all of his subjects must give every assistance to Mazarin. At the end of the month, Mazarin joined the king and Queen Mother at Poitiers. There were immediate and portentous political consequences. Just as the exile of Mazarin had led to the collapse of the unity of the Fronde of the Princes, his return to France restored that unity. Gaston d'Orléans, declaring that he would rather be a Turk than consent to the restoration of Mazarin, signed an accord with Condé, and the Duc de Rohan raised rebellion in Anjou. The crown once again faced the prospect of a hostile, united aristocratic front.

The forces of the crown, led by Turenne (who had changed sides again) and Henri de Lorraine, Comte d'Harcourt, soon restored royal control over Anjou, but a race set in to get to Paris. It was won by Condé, who entered the capital in April 1652 and prepared to defend it against the king. Meanwhile the Duc de Lorraine, serving the Spanish, invaded from the north-east and began to devastate the Paris basin; he was eventually bought off by Mazarin and he left France in June, much to the disappointment of the rebels. The next few months saw Paris and its region at the centre of a savage and destructive civil war. The court returned to Saint Germain, from where it directed its campaigns. From inside Paris it received reports from d'Aligre as to the temper of the city. After Condé's arrival, d'Aligre noted a marked heightening of tension as radicals in the Parlement and on the streets of Paris gained the initiative. People of royalist sympathies had to move about the city with caution, for there was a general sense of impending catastrophe that could easily turn into another 'August 1648'. D'Aligre was frank in informing the court that the one factor holding the Frondeurs together was Mazarin. His presence in France united otherwise disparate groups whose radicalism was bringing Paris to the verge of anarchy. On 4 July a rioting crowd attacked and burned down the town hall; later in the month a radical rump of the Parlement (most magistrates having fled the capital) in effect handed Paris over to Condé, who appointed his administration to run the city. After these events, d'Aligre informed the court:

> If his Excellency [Mazarin] would depart for two months it would change the face of affairs... the levies of money in Paris, the pillage committed by troops of the princes, and the imprisonment of citizens... disgusts the people... and if the Cardinal would withdraw for a certain time... I am convinced that everything would be restored, notwithstanding the opposition of the princes.[7]

Evidence from many sides corroborated d'Aligre's analysis, and Mazarin duly acted. On 19 August, Mazarin once again went into exile. This time he did not leave France (he went as far as Bouillon), but his departure from Saint-Germain had the desired effect. D'Aligre reported a dramatic change of mood in Paris and a growing, popular demand for peace. As the princes' soldiers continued to wreak havoc both inside and outside of Paris, the princes quickly lost any semblance of popular backing. On 23 September, city councillors met d'Aligre and asked him to arrange a meeting with Turenne to discuss the surrender of Paris. As those meetings went ahead, d'Aligre was instructed by the crown to hold secret talks with Gaston d'Orléans, the tactic being to divide him from Condé. Gaston saw that the Fronde of Princes was at an end; he reached terms with d'Aligre and was allowed to leave Paris. Condé fled, eventually reaching the Spanish Netherlands where he entered Spanish military service. On 21 October 1652, Louis XIV and the court entered Paris and were received amidst scenes of rapture. The fighting did not cease immediately, and Bordeaux held out for the time being; but when the rising there collapsed in 1653, the Frondes were over. Mazarin did not accompany the king into Paris, and indeed did not return to the city until February 1653. By then a new political climate was emerging, and he was able to do so without controversy.

The Frondes were, without question, a major juncture in the history of seventeenth-century France and as such have attracted much attention on the part of historians. No simple label can encapsulate the Frondes. At various stages they displayed elements of a constitutional struggle between crown and magistrates, attempts by some magistrates and aristocrats to overthrow Mazarin, efforts by aristocrats and princes to re-enter government, popular uprisings against socio-economic distress, and, beyond Paris, movements for the defence of provincial rights against the alleged 'illegal' incursions of crown agents over the preceding two decades.

Yet these elements rarely, and only briefly, coalesced; they lacked the binding agents which might have transformed the Frondes into full-blooded revolution. For one thing, they remained secular in character; they did not transmute into another War of Religion. Given the regularity with which religious tensions had exacerbated socio-political conflict in France as recently as the 1620s, the government was fortunate that Richelieu's strategy of separating the strictly religious clauses of the Edict of Nantes from the military and political, bore fruit. The Huguenots did not rise as a body during the Frondes; on the contrary, many proclaimed their loyalty to the crown. The ideological ferocity arising from dogmatic religious commitments, which had polarised wide sections of society in earlier civil conflicts, was absent from the Frondes. The Frondes proved susceptible to 'normal' political resolution in a way that the Wars of Religion had not; they were a very different class of risings from the Wars of Religion. Again, although radicals were to be found among the magistrates and some provincial rebels, such as those in Bordeaux, they were never in a position to impose their authority on the movement of events. Ironically, this is to be explained in part by the inability of the crown quickly to crush the Frondeurs. During the contemporaneous Civil War in England, radicals were able to organise and exercise an influence out of all proportion to their num-bers because at certain crucial stages they controlled the New Model Army, which had been formed at the instigation of Parliament. In France, the Frondeurs never felt the need for a 'New Model Army'; the various factions were confident that militarily they could hold their own against the crown and had no need to create a force based on new military principles and including political radicals who might divert the army to their own ends.

By contrast, whereas the Frondeurs lacked a religious or political ideology which might sustain and bind them together, the royalists possessed the supreme incarnation of ideology, the king. None of the Frondeurs admitted that they were fighting the king; all insisted on their loyalty. Their insistence that resistance to the Regent and Mazarin was consistent with loyalty to Louis XIV involved them in extravagant intellectual contortions; but even they became impossible after the proclamation of the king's majority in 1651. Thereafter, the Frondes were nothing other than rebellion; and since they lacked anything resembling an ideological infrangibility, it was only a matter of time before they disintegrated.

Turning to Mazarin's role in the Frondes, he may be counted among its causes to the extent that many Frondeurs saw him as the new embodiment of that ministerial absolutism which they loathed. This being so, his experiences during the Frondes were of more than personal significance, for they bore direct relevance to some of the wider constitutional issues in contention. Even so, he attracted an extraordinary amount of personal opprobrium. This might appear surprising given his reputation for gracious manners, his propensity for avoiding heated confrontation, and his shunning of the kind of rough-house tactics to which Richelieu had often resorted. Two possible explanations for the animosity which Mazarin provoked might be offered. First, he was an Italian. This in itself was no necessary impediment, but in the minds of many older *parlementaires* and aristocrats he recalled the hated Concini. Their memories of Concini, the influence he had exercised over Marie de' Medici and the honours and gifts he had wrung from her, were such that they saw in Mazarin yet another acquisitive Italian ready to manipulate an emotionally vulnerable woman. Secondly, and by a similar mental process of guilt-by-association, he was seen by his opponents as a reincarnation of Richelieu. There was, perhaps, more substance to this charge than to the first. Mazarin never disguised his admiration for Richelieu or his determination to continue the policies and strategies which his mentor had developed. Many of those in the Parlement of Paris or from the ranks of the aristocracy who were most offensive towards him, were retrospectively taking revenge on Richelieu. To many of his enemies Mazarin was a loathsome hybrid in which the most despicable features of Concini and Richelieu were united.

One of the principal media through which anti-Mazarin sentiments were disseminated were the Mazarinades, and although he and the Regent recognised the need to respond to the apparently endless stream of pamphlets attacking him, Mazarin was unable to put up much of a defence. To a certain extent he could blame only himself. Richelieu had paid close attention to the employment of propagandists working on his behalf, but Mazarin failed to muster anything like an adequate team of writers. The only figure to present a serious response to Mazarin's press critics was his librarian, Gabriel Naudé. Naudé published a defence of his protector in a work popularly known as the *Mascurat*.[8] It was almost 500 pages long and was first published in 1649; a second edition of 700 pages appeared in 1650. It took the form of a dialogue between two persons, Saint-Ange (who represents Naudé's views) and Mascurat. In their discussions they attack by name some of the Mazarinades which had appeared, and commend Mazarin as somebody rendering faithful service to the crown and willing to suffer public abuse in the cause of furthering the interests of the French state; instead of fulminating against him, the French public should give thanks that the king had such a disinterested and devoted servant advising him. It must be conceded that, whatever the merits of its arguments, the *Mascurat* was too long and littered with too many rambling Latin quotations to be effective as a weapon of propaganda. It lacked the pithy, hard-hitting qualities of the shorter, more concise Mazarinades. In the atmosphere of 1648 and the years following, what was needed was some equally brusque rebuttals of the charges against Mazarin, not a 500- or 700-page dissertation. Mazarin lost the propaganda war fought during the Frondes, and this was a lesson not lost either upon himself or upon the young Louis XIV. When Louis assumed personal responsibility for government after the death of Mazarin, he placed propaganda high on his list of priorities and ensured that never again would the crown and its ministers be at a disadvantage *vis-à-vis* their critics.[9]

The fact that Frondeurs, and indeed others who objected to certain policies of the Regency, turned their grievances into personalised attacks on Mazarin, too easily diverted attention from the question of whether or not they had serious points to make. Certain facts were beyond dispute: for many years the government's finances had been out of control; the government was excessively reliant on extraordinary sources of revenue; the procedures whereby it assessed and collected revenue would not stand too close a scrutiny; and the crown, through its agents, was circumventing the normal judicial procedures. One could continue the list, the point being that *officiers*, magistrates and others who supported the Frondes often did so for serious political and legal reasons. A similar comment may be made about the Fronde of the Princes. There can be no doubt that self-interest, ambition, rivalry and jealousy played their part, but they do not constitute the whole explanation for the movement. Since the days of Richelieu, aristocrats increasingly sensed that their 'traditional' and 'rightful' relationship with the crown had been eroded by the incursions of the principal minister. Mazarin, like Richelieu before him, allegedly had attempted to diminish the 'affection' and 'friendship' (*amitié*) that ought to exist between king and aristocracy, and insinuate himself into a position of political power which ought to be occupied by a Prince of the Blood or some other 'worthy' figure. Mazarin, like Richelieu, pleaded *raison d'état*: at a time when France was engaged in a long war, he had to resort to any measures necessary to preserve the state. In so far as the Frondes failed as movements of rebellion, it might be said that Mazarin's stance triumphed. However, as the political temperature dropped in the later 1650s, and even more so after Mazarin's death in 1661, Louis XIV and his advisers were able to make a cooler assessment of the expression of grievances during the Frondes. They tacitly conceded that many of these grievances were justified (especially those of a fiscal nature), and took the first steps towards placing fiscal, but also legal, practices on a more 'regular' footing.

Mazarin survived the Frondes, and this in itself was a major achievement given the opposition which confronted him. Louis XIV, after his majority, retained Mazarin as principal minister, and Mazarin devoted many hours of each week to educating the king in the practice of government, training him in the skills of administration, bringing him into councils of government, and instructing him in the nature of European international relations. Louis XIV later referred to 'the craft of kingship' (*le métier du roi*), and it was thanks in no small measure to Mazarin that he was such a gifted practitioner. We may infer that it was Mazarin himself, perhaps reflecting on the Frondes and the frequency with which Frondeurs drew a distinction between their loyalty to the king and their resistance to his principal minister, who advised Louis to dispense with a principal minister. Principal ministers could be invaluable under certain circumstances, but France would never be fully stable until it was ruled by a king who governed as well as reigned. This proposition arose also from a reflection on the Fronde of the Princes. In the light of that episode, it was evident that it was in the crown's interest to restore trust and harmony between king and aristocracy. This was a precondition of political stability in France, but it could not be achieved if the king ruled through a principal minister and his *créatures*. Direct government by the king must be restored; only a monarch who ruled personally could recreate that *amitié* which was the binding force between king and aristocracy. The Frondes, in short, helped to persuade Mazarin that henceforth he must work towards the redundancy of the very position he had held since the death of Richelieu.

Chapter 11: Mazarin, Foreign Policy and Domestic Tensions, 1653–61

Mazarin Triumphant

After the collapse of the Frondes, Mazarin felt the kind of triumphant confidence that Richelieu had experienced after the Day of Dupes. This is not to say that the country had been reduced to a state of unquestioning obedience. In April 1655 the Parlement of Paris announced its intention of discussing financial edicts which the crown had sent for registration. On 13 April, Louis XIV went in person to the Parlement and ordered the assembly to desist from discussion and restrict itself to registering edicts (this is the occasion when he is alleged to have said 'l'état, c'est moi' [I am the state]). However, Mazarin was sufficiently assured of his position to concentrate on the war against Spain. Since he expected to be absent from Paris for long periods, he followed the example of Richelieu and created in the central administration a team which he trusted to implement his policies. In finance, he retained the services of d'Aligre and Morangis, both of whom had remained loyal to him during the Frondes; above them he put Abel Servien, who had been a principal French representative at the negotiations in Münster, and Nicolas Fouquet, who since 1650 had been a senior figure in the Parlement of Paris. Fouquet also had stood by Mazarin during the Frondes, and Mazarin greatly admired his financial acumen. The principal minister advanced not only Nicolas himself, but also his brothers: François was made Archbishop of

Narbonne and Louis became Bishop of Agde. Gilles and Yves Fouquet had careers in the army and diplomacy, and the Abbé Basile Fouquet was appointed to serve in Mazarin's household.

The coronation of Louis XIV, held in Rheims on 7 June 1654, was a signal that royal authority was in the ascendancy. Mazarin would now be able to pursue the war relatively unhindered by internal political worries. The ceremony was notable for its absentees. The Bishop of Soissons officiated instead of the Archbishop of Rheims, although this was for technical reasons: a new archbishop had recently been appointed but not yet consecrated. Only two Princes of the Blood attended: the king's brother, Philippe, and Louis, Duc de Vendôme. The Prince de Condé was, of course, in exile, Gaston d'Orléans had retired to Blois just before Louis and his mother entered Paris in October 1652, and the Prince de Conti was given permission to absent himself.[1] Some former Frondeurs claimed that the coronation therefore was inferior to those of Louis's predecessors, but this was self-delusion. The ritual of the coronation proclaimed the majesty and supremacy of the king, and the obedience which even *les grands* owed to a monarch who stood in an allegedly unbroken line of succession going back perhaps a thousand years. The absence of Princes of the Blood, and indeed other aristocrats who normally would have attended, was not a mark of their independence, or a slight on the honour of the king; on the contrary, it signalled that they were excluded from the ranks of those close to the person who was the very embodiment of sovereignty, power and authority.

There was another 'absentee' from the coronation: the city of Paris. Normally, a king of France, after his coronation, proceeded to Paris, which he entered in magnificent procession. The city was decked in arches and bunting, church bells pealed, tens of thousands of people, their numbers swollen by visitors from many parts of the country, joined in the celebrations. Louis XIV, however, excluded Paris from his post-coronation celebrations. This was a form of 'punishment' for a city which had supported the Frondes and resisted the Regent, and in which he had suffered personal humiliation. Louis did not formally enter Paris until after his wedding in 1660, but nobody could misunderstand the implication of the decision taken in 1654. Paris had been unfaithful during the Frondes; it must pay the price for having earned the king's displeasure.

As he reflected on the Frondes, Mazarin was left with a profound suspicion of a particular religious movement within Catholicism: Jansenism. This was based on the teaching of Cornelius Jansen, former Professor of

Theology in the University of Louvain and Bishop of Ypres.[2] Jansen died in 1638, but his theology, known hitherto mainly in ecclesiastical and academic circles, attained a wider audience after the publication in 1640 of his *Augustinus*, a study of the thought of Saint Augustine. Jansen developed a theology of predestination that was close to that of Calvin. Inevitably, questions arose as to Jansen's orthodoxy, but he and his disciples – Jansenists – contended that not only was his orthodoxy beyond reproach, he was seeking to lead Calvinists, including Huguenots in France, back to the Catholic Church by demonstrating that the theology of Calvin himself indicated such a *rapprochement*. The *Augustinus* was read widely in Catholic Europe, and nowhere more than in France, where several leading aristocrats, intellectuals, prelates and members of religious orders adopted Jansen's views. In spite of protestations by Jansenists, however, Pope Urban VIII in 1643 issued a bull censuring the *Augustinus*; if not wholly heretical, it was at least of doubtful orthodoxy.

In the same year, one of France's leading Jansenists, Antoine Arnauld, published *De la Fréquente Communion*, which became one of the great texts of the movement in France; it attracted many devotees to the cause, including such intellectually prestigious figures as Blaise Pascal and Jean Racine. There were also aristocratic Jansenists who later were prominent in the Frondes: they included the Duc de Luynes, the Duchesse de Chevreuse and the Duc de la Rochefoucauld. Mazarin, after the Frondes, convinced himself that the rebellious conduct of such people was directly related to their Jansenist beliefs. The theological and doctrinal niceties of Jansenism did not particularly concern him (unlike Richelieu, he did not claim theological expertise); however, its socio-political implications did cause him concern. Whereas royal propaganda in France insisted that monarchy and the institutions of government were nothing less than instruments created by God to fulfil His purposes, Jansenists held that human institutions have no necessary divine sanction; they are created by fallible human beings and therefore contain imperfections; they might be used for good, but they can also be turned to the pursuit of degenerate ends if they fall into the hands of unscrupulous people. Herein, decided Mazarin, was an explanation for the treacherous behaviour of so many aristocrats during the Frondes: they had been drawn into the Frondes by Jansenist thought which afforded a spurious 'legitimation' of political resistance. During and after the Frondes, Jansenists themselves insisted that no link existed between the theology of Jansen and political dissidence; if Jansenist aristocrats did engage in resistance to the crown, it was for political, not religious, reasons. Their protestations failed to sway Mazarin, who remained resolute in his conviction that the Fronde of the Princes owed much to a Jansenist questioning of the legitimacy of regal institutions. He was convinced that Jansenism was a sinister religious movement and that Jansenists could not be trusted to remain loyal to the crown.

In the few years after the end of the Frondes, Mazarin was frequently on the move, chiefly between Paris and the northern provinces where most of the fighting against the Spanish took place. On several occasions he took Louis XIV with him. The king was now in his mid-teens, and Mazarin had persuaded the Queen Mother that the time had come to expand her son's preparation for kingship by giving him first-hand experience of the reality of military campaigns. The king attended the sieges of Mouzon and Sainte-Menehould in 1653, and was present at the siege of Montmédy in 1657. In 1658 Louis accompanied Mazarin to Flanders, but fell dangerously ill. This was an episode of intense political drama as well as a personal crisis for the king. In Paris, Mazarin was blamed for having exposed the king to experiences which threatened his life. Rumours spread that, if Louis XIV died, Mazarin would be dismissed and exiled. Mazarin sent orders to his household to prepare to gather his treasures for a departure from Paris, but Louis recovered and his principal minister survived. These expeditions to the war front stimulated and excited the young king, who acquired a taste for warfare which never left him. Later, during his personal reign, there were several occasions when he accompanied the army and personally directed the campaigns in which it was involved.

War against Spain

During the Frondes, Mazarin was reduced to defensive tactics in the war against Spain, and could aspire to do little more than hold the frontiers. The Spanish had won back some of the strongholds and regions that they had earlier lost either to France or to its 'clients'. The King of Spain recovered much of the rebellious province of Catalonia and drove out the French. In Italy, the fortress at Casale fell to the Spanish, and in Flanders so did Gravelines and Dunkirk. From 1653 onwards, however, Mazarin was able to bring greater military resources to bear on the war, and although he took up arms again in Italy and Catalonia (a French army under the command of the former Frondeur Conti invaded Catalonia in 1654), the frontier region between northern France and

Flanders was the main focus. Condé was prominent in the Spanish forces during this phase of the war, and on numerous occasions found himself pitted against former Frondeur colleagues; especially Turenne, who was now in command of the French armies in the north, and working closely with Mazarin in planning and coordinating the campaigns. In 1653, Condé was at the head of a Spanish force which besieged Rocroi, the scene of a famous French victory ten years before; a French relief force drove him into retreat. Meanwhile, as just mentioned, Mouzon and Sainte-Menehould fell to the French after sieges attended by Louis XIV.

It was in 1654 and 1655, however, that French armies enjoyed their principal successes. In July 1654, a combined army of Spanish and Lorraine troops, with Condé among the commanders, laid siege to Arras. Turenne was sent to relieve the city, which he did in August; and as the enemy went into retreat, Turenne seized the opportunity to take Quesnoy. The relief of Arras was celebrated in Paris and elsewhere in France as a major victory: it was widely seen as evidence that France was gaining the upper hand in the war. Sharing this mood of confidence, the Parlement of Paris passed the death penalty on Condé in the expectation that before long he would be in French hands. The successes continued in 1655. Turenne placed Landrecies under siege, and although the Spanish sent Condé against him, Turenne drove the enemy back and Landrecies capitulated. This too was celebrated in Paris, where a *Te Deum* was sung in Notre Dame and attended by the king and members of the government. Other frontier towns fell to the French in the summer of 1655, and there was even talk of pushing on towards Brussels. Mazarin was opposed to this plan, since he still regarded the security of northern France as the main priority. He was further disturbed when he received information that a former Frondeuse, the Duchesse de Châtillon, was trying to persuade the French governor of Péronne, the Marquis d'Hocquincourt, to hand it over to Condé. Mazarin had the duchesse arrested.

In 1655 Mazarin also made progress on the diplomatic front. England in the early 1650s was emerging not only from civil war but from a revolution which turned that country, as well as Scotland and Ireland, into a republican Commonwealth under Cromwell. Relations between England and France were uncertain. The exiled Stuarts – Charles I's widow the French princess Henriette, their son Charles II and their attendants – had taken refuge in France, and Mazarin allowed English 'royalist' ships which had followed them to use French ports as bases from which to attack English Commonwealth shipping. Ideologically, the two countries were poles apart, and trade barriers between them added to the sources of division and possible conflict. Mazarin concluded that it was in France's interest to improve relations with England, even though it was in many respects a pariah state. His guiding principle was the war against Spain. A re-emergent England was a potential major power in the North Sea, and given its proximity to the Flanders coast, it could not be ignored. Mazarin's desire to cultivate better relations with Cromwell was quickened when he heard that the Spanish were thinking in similar terms; if an Anglo-Spanish accord were signed, allowing easy passage of Spanish ships to Flanders, that could have serious implications for the war. Mazarin took the appropriate steps. In 1654 he persuaded and paid Henriette, Charles II and their court to leave France and take up residence in Cologne. In 1655 he approached Cromwell with a proposal for a treaty of commerce, which was signed at Westminster in November: their mutual trade embargoes were suspended, Mazarin ordered an end to attacks on English ships, and each side promised not to give refuge to enemies of the other (in effect, Mazarin promised not to allow the Stuarts back into France).

So pleased was Mazarin with progress in the war that in 1656 he contacted the Spanish government with proposals for peace. He was prepared to be generous, even to the point of restoring conquests in Flanders, if Spain would agree to his main proposal: that Louis XIV should marry Maria Teresa, the elder daughter of, and successor to, Philip IV of Spain. Maria Teresa was one of the most eligible princesses in Europe; the question of her marriage carried immense political and diplomatic implications. Emperor Ferdinand III was determined that she should marry one of his sons, thereby reinforcing Habsburg family solidarity and confirming the Vienna–Madrid axis in international affairs. The Emperor accordingly urged the Spanish to stand firm and resist the French offer, for if the marriage between Louis and Maria Teresa went ahead, Spain inevitably would be drawn into the French orbit and the French government would exploit the resources of Spain, both in Europe and in the Americas, to its own ends. It did not need the Emperor to point this out to the Spanish, who refused Mazarin's terms. They did so, not only because they found the marriage unacceptable, but because the war suddenly took a turn for the better from the Spanish point of view. In July 1656, Turenne laid siege to Valenciennes, which was defended by Condé. Had Turenne taken the town, the entire Spanish position in northern France would have been on the verge of collapse; but he failed. Condé held out and Turenne had to withdraw.

This reversal was one of the factors which persuaded Mazarin that he must strengthen the ties with England, whose fleet could be of invaluable help against Spanish-held ports on the Flanders coast. In 1655 an English fleet had taken Jamaica from the Spanish, and in 1656 another captured the Spanish treasure fleet as it headed for Spain. Such maritime power, if combined with the French navy and army, could prove decisive in the war. In 1657 Mazarin opened negotiations for an alliance with Cromwell, but faced in *dévot* circles the kinds of criticisms that Richelieu had encountered when he allied with Sweden: was it not shameful to commit France to an alliance with a state that had executed its king and humiliated its French-born queen? Nevertheless, Mazarin pressed ahead, and on 3 March 1657 signed the Treaty of Paris. The two states formed an alliance whose aim was to capture Gravelines and Dunkirk; the first would be retained by France, and Dunkirk by England. The military justification for Mazarin acquiring an ally was reinforced by other setbacks in the war, notably at Cambrai, another Spanish-held stronghold which Turenne besieged but failed to take. Montmédy was besieged by a French army, with Louis XIV present, but victory in the land war was still far from certain.

In 1657 an opportunity for Mazarin to strike at the Austrian Habsburgs presented itself. The Emperor Ferdinand III died, thereby necessitating a meeting of the Imperial Electors to choose his successor. The main candidate was Ferdinand's son Leopold, who was duly elected. French ambassadors – the Duc de Gramont and Hugues de Lionne – attended the election in Frankfurt, having been authorised by Mazarin to spend as much as they wished in buying the support of princes and their representatives who gathered for the occasion. They were also instructed to ensure that Leopold promised to abide by the terms of the Peace of Westphalia as they affected France. Leopold's commitment to the peace was a subject of deep concern also to the German princes. At his election, Leopold gave the necessary assurances, but princely apprehensions continued. The French ambassadors played on this fear, using it to persuade many of the Rhineland territories to form a League of the Rhine (August 1658), which France joined soon afterwards. 'Westphalia' had conferred upon France rights in Alsace, even though they were not clearly defined; now, long stretches of the Rhineland looked to France for protection should Leopold seek to overturn the agreements reached in 1648.

In 1658, the joint forces of France and England succeeded in making significant military headway. The key victory occurred at Dunkirk. Commanding an army which included English auxiliaries, Turenne fought and defeated Condé at the Battle of the Dunes, near Dunkirk, on 14 June. There followed the occupation of Dunkirk by Turenne (Mazarin abided by the Treaty of Paris, and transferred it to the English government), from which other successes flowed: Bergues, Furnes, Gravelines, Menin, Ypres and other places in Flanders were taken. Philip IV, desperately short of money and engaged also in trying to recover Portugal, which had declared its independence in 1640, accepted that the time had come to sue for peace. Receiving pessimistic reports from his commanders in Flanders and having lost control of the Channel and North Sea, he feared that if he continued fighting in Flanders, it was only a matter of time before his French and English enemies triumphed and created a position from which they could dictate terms. When Mazarin offered peace in 1656, the main sticking point had been the marriage of Louis XIV and Maria Teresa. Philip was now willing to reconsider. A Franco-Spanish marriage was not in itself an unusual occurrence. After all, Philip IV's first wife, Elisabeth, was French, and his sister Anne had married Louis XIII. A crucial difference now was that Philip had no son and, if things remained as they were, Maria Teresa one day would rule as Queen of Spain; but, of course, the family situation might change, as indeed it did in 1661 when Philip IV's son, the future Charles II, was born and took precedence in the succession over Maria Teresa. When Anne had married Louis XIII in 1615, she had renounced any claims she had to the throne of Spain; the French government, just as much as the Spanish, had accepted this as a legitimate and binding commitment. If peace with France were to be signed now and Maria Teresa were to marry Louis XIV, a necessary condition would be a similar renunciation on her part.

Mazarin knew that Philip IV was contemplating an offer of talks, and attempted to hurry him along by a bluff. He raised the possibility of a marriage between Louis XIV and Princess Margaret of Savoy, and in the summer of 1658 the French court travelled to Lyon, to which the princess and her mother came in good faith, supposedly to negotiate the match. The move had the desired effect. Philip IV wrote a private letter to his sister, Queen Anne, offering the hand of his daughter Maria Teresa, provided a satisfactory peace could be settled. Mazarin immediately agreed (his decision was kept from the Savoyards, who were detained in vague talks which led nowhere), and returned to Paris where he entered into secret negotiations with Spanish representatives. On 7 May 1659 a truce in the war was signed, and on 9 June the preliminaries of peace were agreed. Mazarin travelled to the south-west of France for formal negotiations, and in mid-August met his Spanish counterpart, Luis de Haro, on an island in the middle of the River Bidassoa. The talks were long and hard, but resulted in the Peace of the Pyrenees, which was signed on 7 November 1659. France made important territorial acquisitions: Roussillon and Cerdagne in the south, Artois and parts of Flanders, Hainault, Lorraine and Luxembourg in the north. It promised to withdraw assistance from the Portuguese, and lifted the death sentence on Condé, who would be allowed to return to France; an amnesty was extended to his followers. The Spanish consented to the marriage between Louis XIV and Maria Teresa, with the proviso that she renounce her claim to the throne of Spain.

In many respects the Peace of the Pyrenees was a retrospective vindication of the policy which Richelieu had adopted some thirty years before, and it completed the unfulfilled task undertaken in the peace talks at Münster. Indeed, France had dealt with Spain from a position of military dominance in 1659, and secured better terms than could have been hoped for in 1648. To this extent, Mazarin could justify having continued the war, although whether the improvement in the terms of 1659 over those available in 1648 warranted another eleven years of warfare was open to question. The Peace of the Pyrenees enhanced French security on the northern and southern frontiers and strengthened control of the 'gates' leading to Germany. When added to France's *de facto* protection of the League of the Rhine, the peace of 1659 placed France in its most advantageous international position for over a century.

The prestige of France and of Mazarin stood high in Europe, and helped Mazarin to achieve the last great diplomatic *coup* of his life: the Peace of Oliva (1660). He had first made his name back in the 1620s as a mediator with exceptional gifts, and it was this role that the French government played in 1660. Since 1655 an international war had been fought in the Baltic region, involving Sweden, Poland, Denmark, Brandenburg and Russia. France mediated at the peace talks which took place at Oliva, near Danzig (separate talks between Denmark and Sweden, mediated by the Dutch Republic, were held in Copenhagen), and oversaw the settlement reached there. In 1660, most of Europe was at peace, a rare condition to which Mazarin made a major contribution.

Internal Unrest in the Late 1650s

It has been suggested above that Mazarin negotiated peace with a Spanish government that felt itself under pressure on both the international and

...ts; but it must also be recognised that the French gov-
...as becoming concerned at a new upsurge of domestic dis-
...rebellion, which undoubtedly helped to impel Mazarin
...:ace. For a few years after 1653, France was relatively calm,
... isolated cases of riot and protest occurring. However, Fouquet,
now ı charge of government fiscal policy under the authority of
Mazarin, continued the kinds of practices which had run through the
1640s: high levels of taxation, an increasing reliance on extraordinary
sources of revenue, and borrowing at high rates of interest.[3] Between
1657 and 1660 in several parts of France, but mostly in the north-west
and south, elite and popular movements of protest and resistance began
to reappear, and although they did not occur on the scale of the late
1630s or the late 1640s, they portended further unrest unless remedial
action was taken by the government.

In Normandy in 1657 and 1658, groups of nobles gathered in assembly and drew up lists of grievances, which they sent to the government.
They called for the restoration of all the traditional rights and privileges
of the nobility, especially with regard to fiscal matters, and from some
assemblies came the proposal that an Estates General be called to review
the whole of royal policy, domestic and foreign. The example of the
Norman nobles inspired others; similar meetings took place in nearby
regions such as Anjou, Beauce and the area around Tours, and spread
down into Poitou. The nobility did not have resort to actual rebellion,
but their protests were significant straws in the wind, which Mazarin
would do well to heed. A 'traditional' popular rebellion did break out in
the Sologne region in 1658. The 'Sabotiers', as the rioters were known,
were mostly peasants objecting to the high rates of *taille* and other fiscal
charges. The government suppressed the rising by force, but did make
concessions on the *taille*.

More serious, given their geographical proximity to the peace talks,
were the risings in the south.[4] These too had a double aspect: they were
manifestations of resistance by the elites, in law and local government, to
the 'unjustifiable' incursions of royal authority into their traditions and
customs, but they also had a 'popular' dimension which drew in peasants
and townspeople from the lower social orders. The incident which triggered much of the protest was an instruction from the government
regarding the maintenance of troops in Provence, of which there was an
abundance in this frontier province. Normally, when fighting was
suspended during winter, troops were billeted on civilians, who had to
provide food and lodging. On 30 November 1657, the crown issued an

instruction whereby the king's subjects in Provence would now pay a fiscal charge, out of which soldiers would be paid. There were protests from all over the province, and when, in February 1658, the governor, the Duc de Mercoeur, tried to impose the charge on two towns where troops were based, Tarascon and Draguignan, he provoked violent resistance which soon spread to other parts of Provence, including Aix and Marseille. In the case of Marseille, commercial interests also were at stake. The war against Spain had weighed heavily on Marseille, whose activities as a port were constantly endangered by Spanish ships, not least privateers operating out of Majorca. In order to provide for the defence of their shipping, merchants from Marseille had equipped a war galley from their own resources and placed it under a commander of their choice. The crown ordered them to hand over the galley and place it under the command of a royal nominee.

The status of the galley and its commander became a *cause célèbre* among the merchant communities of Marseille, who interpreted the royal instructions as yet another instance wherein local opinion and rights were over-ridden by an insensitive government. The contending political factions in Marseille took different sides on the question of the galley, and when, on 13 July 1658, a violent demonstration against concessions on the question of the galley took place, the governor prepared to intervene by sending in troops. This provoked even larger demonstrations on 19 July, and barricades went up in the city to keep out the troops. Mazarin and Louis XIV were at Lyon, supposedly negotiating the Savoyard marriage. They called some of the consuls (leading city councillors) from Marseille to Lyon, and instructed them to restore calm in the city. In spite of the royal command, political deadlock remained in Marseille and the king's authority in effect was null and void. On 16 October 1659, an order from the king was even publicly torn in two in the Hôtel de Ville. Mazarin decided that direct royal intervention was necessary. After signing the Peace of the Pyrenees, Mazarin, the Queen Mother and the court proceeded to Toulouse, Beaucaire, Tarascon, Arles and Aix, which they reached on 18 January 1660. From there the court proceeded towards Marseille, while announcing decisions affecting the city. First there would be a military occupation (on 20 January, 6000 soldiers marched into the city). Secondly, a special judicial tribunal, composed of lawyers from Aix, would investigate the recent troubles and pass sentence on any whom they considered guilty of law-breaking. Thirdly, the walls and other military defences of the city were to be lowered, thereby reducing the ability of the city to resist royal troops.

Fourthly, a citadel would be constructed to ensure the obedience of the city in future. On 2 March 1660, Louis XIV personally entered Marseille and three days later announced changes to the municipal institutions and administration of the city. Henceforth the title of *consul* was abolished; the city would be run by two senior councillors (*échevins*) elected by a body of sixty ordinary councillors. The responsibilities of the *échevins* specifically excluded their defence of the rights and privileges of Marseille; any appointments they might make to administrative positions had to receive the consent of the governor. The changes announced in 1660 effectively ended the autonomy of the city, and placed Marseille firmly under the control of the crown.

The subjection of Marseille was of more than local significance. It proclaimed that, now that the kingdom was at peace, the crown was resolved to impose its authority even if this meant a radical examination and restructuring of France's political, provincial and municipal institutions. However, the subjugation of Marseille did not mark the end of movements of protest. In the early 1660s, further resistance, both popular and elite, was forthcoming from the region around Boulogne, only to be repressed with the utmost severity. The Peace of the Pyrenees did not bring an immediate end to the cluster of rebellions which began in the late 1650s, but it placed the crown in an unassailable position from which to counter them.

The Final Months of Mazarin

The court, including Mazarin, remained in the south of France and visited several towns, so allowing the king to see and be seen by his subjects. It then proceeded across-country towards Bayonne, via Montpellier, Narbonne, Perpignan and Toulouse. From Bayonne it went the short distance to Saint-Jean-de Luz, which it reached on 8 May 1660 to await the arrival of Philip IV with his daughter Maria Teresa. Philip and Maria Teresa, with an appropriately numerous and splendid train of courtiers, arrived on 11 May, and for the next few weeks festivities took place. On 7 June, Philip IV formally handed over his daughter to Louis; the marriage took place in Saint-Jean-de-Luz on 9 June 1660.[5] Louis and his bride then proceeded towards Paris, being received with spontaneous as well as organised acclamation along the route. Their entry into Paris, which confirmed the reconciliation between Louis XIV and the city, took place on 26 August. The roads, streets and bridges were decorated, triumphal arches were constructed, and barges filled with musicians and other celebrants sailed along the Seine. The royal procession included Mazarin, who had a place of honour and prominence in the parade. The minister's health had been giving concern for some months. He had been in frequent touch with Colbert, who managed his personal affairs, to ensure that they were as orderly as possible. As will be seen shortly, Mazarin had acquired a large fortune, and was anxious that it should be preserved after his death. He was especially concerned that the duchies and benefices which he had amassed should be retained by his family: the former comprised the duchies of Mayenne and Nevers, and the latter included the great abbey of Cluny and its sister houses, Saint-Denis and Saint-Pierre de Corbie, all extremely wealthy foundations. Through the winter of 1660–1, his health declined further and he sensed that his life was nearing its end. On his last visit to his palace in Paris early in February 1661, he was heard to murmur: 'I will soon be gone from all of this.' Soon afterwards he was taken to the royal palace at Vincennes, where the air was thought to be healthier than in Paris. Louis XIV visited him there, and they discussed state affairs at length. It is thought that Mazarin urged Louis now to rule alone; he also commended Colbert to the king's service, advising Louis to make use of this gifted administrator. Mazarin signed his last will and testament on 7 March 1661. In the document he thanked the king for his support and bequeathed his finest jewels to the king, the queen and the king's brother Philippe. Other bequests went to his own family, numerous other individuals and institutions (including monasteries, convents and hospitals), and he provided for the foundation of a new college to be attached to the University of Paris; when completed it was known as the Collège des Quatre Nations. He died at Vincennes on 9 March 1661. After lying in state in the Sainte Chapelle in Paris, he was buried there until the Collège des Quatre Nations was completed. On 9 September 1684, in grand and solemn ceremony, he was reburied in the chapel of the college.

Chapter 12: Mazarin as Patron and Collector

Mazarin and Patronage

The discussion of Mazarin so far has dealt with him mainly as principal minister, and the subject matter has been drawn from the policies that he pursued and the services he rendered to the crown. As with Richelieu, however, a more rounded assessment of him as a statesman must take account of the patronage which he exercised and the wealth he accumulated while in France. Richelieu undoubtedly served as a model which inspired Mazarin, but so did the Barberinis. As a young man growing up in Rome and later entering the papal diplomatic service, Mazarin studied techniques of patronage as exercised by this powerful family, especially Pope Urban VIII. He reached conclusions which he later applied to his own strategies of patronage in France; first among them was the conviction that patronage was of inestimable importance to the creation and preservation of political power. This proposition was not, in itself, remarkable; after all, popes, kings, prelates, aristocrats and others had linked patronage and power for centuries. In Mazarin's mind, however, the principle extended beyond the conventional practices whereby ecclesiastical and political appointments were made, to the spheres of the visual arts.

In Rome, the Barberinis, sensitive to the pre-eminence of their religious and political status, had used the architectural and visual arts to evince their standing in the city and the Church. They persevered with the work of Sixtus V, who, during his brief pontificate from 1585 to 1590, had begun an ambitious programme to modernise Rome by building squares, boulevards, fountains, churches and other fine public buildings.[1]

Sixtus had contended that if Rome were to be equal to its unique religious mission, it must be planned so as to meet the needs of the tens of thousands of pilgrims and other visitors who came each year; it must have buildings whose majesty and splendour proclaimed the primacy of the bishop and the city. Urban VIII upheld this tradition as Rome was expanded and beautified further by the masterpieces of those supreme practitioners of Roman Baroque architecture, Giovanni Bernini and Francesco Borromini. The Rome of the Barberinis was a triumph of modern architecture – the basilica of Saint Peter's was completed – and of town planning which, at one and the same time, expounded a religious and a political message. It inspired Mazarin to think in similarly grandiose terms, but it also convinced him that the Roman Baroque architectural style, with its emphasis on the theatrical, the colourful and the dramatic, was best suited to his purposes. Baroque stood for everything that was new and innovative in the visual arts; it implied a regime which was committed to change and modernity. It was a style that corresponded to his own temperament and which, he believed, expressed the forward-looking ideals which guided him in politics.

When he moved to Paris, Mazarin took it almost as axiomatic that, like the Barberinis in Rome and Richelieu in Paris, he must build on a grand scale. More than that, he felt what can only be described as a sense of mission to transform the French elites into lovers of Roman Baroque.[2] His enthusiasm also arose from a concern that the reputation of Italy and things Italian was in decline in Paris, and that in so far as he championed Baroque architecture and painting, by so much would he help to restore respect for Italy. In the early decades of the seventeenth century, Italian literary, theatrical and musical fashions had ruled Paris, and did so thanks, in no small measure, to the patronage shown by the queen, Marie de' Medici, to artists, actors, musicians and others from her homeland. By the mid-1630s, however, a reaction had set in, caused in part by the popular detestation shown towards Concino Concini. His political misconduct, leading to his eventual assassination, brought Italian artistic fashions into disrepute and contributed to the spread of a popular phobia against Italians which was still in evidence when Mazarin settled in France. On the other hand, Richelieu had no qualms about employing the Roman-influenced architect Lemercier, and the church of the Sorbonne which Lemercier designed was an unashamed exercise in Roman Baroque.[3] Nevertheless, Mazarin proceeded with caution, advocating Roman Baroque artistic and architectural styles discreetly and without displays of show or ostentation. He made private gifts of

Italian paintings or statues to aristocrats and other notabilities, hoping to persuade the recipients of the virtues of *avant-garde* works of art. He also invited Italian artists such as Giovanni Grimaldi and Pietro da Cortona either to come to Paris or to send examples of their work; and his greatest ambition was to persuade Bernini, whom he revered as the supreme master of Baroque sculpture and architecture, to undertake projected extensions to the Louvre. Bernini did eventually make the journey to Paris, but only after Mazarin's death, and the episode was far from being a success.[4]

The Palais Mazarin

To somebody of Mazarin's mentality and status, it was natural that he should desire a large property in Paris. It would be not only a residence but a showcase for his tastes as a collector and patron. The royal court often stayed in Richelieu's former palace, and Mazarin, knowing the political importance of being physically close to the king, determined to buy something nearby. He fixed on three houses adjacent to the Palais Royal and belonging to Jacques Tubeuf, a senior financial officer in the government. Mazarin occupied the property in the mid-1640s, although the transfer of legal ownership was not completed until 1649. He employed the architect François Mansart to link the houses and turn them into a single residence, but also add extensions including galleries suitable for the display of sculpture, paintings, tapestries, fine furniture and so on. Other extensions were undertaken by Pierre le Muet, including part of a gallery intended as the library.

Mazarin's choice of a residence and the execution of the alterations and extensions coincided with the arrival in Paris of members of the Barberini family in exile. A political struggle had broken out in Rome when the new pope, Innocent X, was elected in 1644. Innocent instituted proceedings against the Barberinis, charging them with having embezzled public funds. Antonio and Francesco Barberini fled and sought refuge with their former protégé, Mazarin. He welcomed them, not only because of his long-standing links with the Barberini family, but also because he took it as a mark of personal honour that they turned to him for assistance. Within the entourage that accompanied them to Paris were artists whom they had patronised, but who now shared their disgrace. Their arrival was timely, for Mazarin needed artists who could decorate the walls and ceilings of his palace in the Roman manner. He also required a major figure who could direct this commission and impose on it a general thematic unity. The Barberinis recommended, and brought from Rome, one of the finest decorative painters of the period, Giovanni Romanelli. Assisted mainly by Paolo Gismondi, Romanelli executed the painting of the ceiling and walls of the main gallery in the palace. At first he intended depicting themes from Roman history, but after discussions with Mazarin he decided that this might lay undue stress on the principal minister's Italian origins. He did retain some Roman subjects – Romulus and Remus, or Jupiter fighting the giants – but mostly he chose scenes from the *Metamorphoses* of Ovid, which were more light-hearted and, so he was advised, more to the French taste. When Romanelli left France in 1647, Giovanni Grimaldi took over and directed the cycle of painting until 1651. Grimaldi faced considerable difficulties and interruptions for, of course, these were the years of the Frondes. Work in the palace sometimes had to be suspended because of civil disorder in the city, but when they were finished, the galleries, hallways and other rooms were a wonderful and coherent architectural and artistic ensemble.

Mazarin stocked the palace with a magnificent collection of statues, paintings, engravings, tapestries, furniture, mirrors, ceramics, medallions, precious stones and other ornaments. It was an exhibition centre as much as a residence or place of work. The collection included about 350 busts and statues, almost all of which were antiquities (he had surprisingly few modern pieces), and over 540 paintings. Among the latter were works by Titian, Raphael, Correggio, Veronese and other Italian masters. Italian artists accounted for some 285 of the paintings, Germans, Flemings and French for about 80 each, with the remainder coming from various other sources. The *galérie Mansart* in the palace housed Mazarin's library of books and manuscripts. He appointed Gabriel Naudé as his librarian. Working through the principal minister's agents in France and abroad, Naudé built up the stock to some 40,000 volumes by 1648. The library was made available to scholars, but during the Frondes it had a che-quered history. In 1651 the Parlement of Paris confiscated the library and sold it off. After the Frondes, Naudé set about tracking down the buyers and reconstituting the collection, which was back to something like its former glory by the late 1650s.

The Académie Royale de Peinture and the Collège des Quatre Nations

The construction of Mazarin's palace occurred at a sensitive time in the corporate history of Parisian artists, sculptors, goldsmiths and other artisans. Although traditionally there were no restrictions on foreign painters operating in the city, those arts and crafts which were organised into guilds (goldsmiths or silversmiths, for example) protected themselves by excluding outsiders and even by appealing to the Parlement of Paris to support them. Within the artistic community (Charles le Brun was a leading activist) there arose a movement to transcend this defensive stance by imitating their Florentine and Roman counterparts: they would form a society or academy to enhance the competitiveness of young French painters by giving them a formal, rigorous training. Le Brun was instrumental in helping to found the Académie de Peinture in 1648. At first it struggled because of the political situation in Paris, but in 1651, even though the Frondes were at their height, the crown extended recognition to the academy and allowed it the title 'Royal'. Mazarin, whose ideas on the utility of the visual arts to the crown corresponded with the aims of the academy, accepted the position of its protector. The academy became, among other things, a teaching institution with twelve professors and six assistants (*conseillers*); it had a modern curriculum requiring the students to study architecture, geometry, perspective, anatomy and history, as well as drawing and painting. It was reformed in 1663, but from the start it reflected Mazarin's conviction that great reigns were so designated, not just because of success in warfare, but because they patronised the arts and created a rich artistic heritage.

The Palais Mazarin was the principal architectural enterprise which Mazarin undertook during his lifetime, but it should also be remembered that the Collège des Quatre Nations, which he posthumously founded, also expressed his liking for Baroque. There was a certain appositeness about his decision to found a university college, for it complemented Richelieu's donation of a new chapel to the Sorbonne. It also reflected the perspective which he brought to French affairs as a foreigner. His intention was to create this college mainly for the sons of noblemen from frontier regions which France had conquered or annexed – hence the reference to the 'four nations'[5] – and to provide them with an education which would reconcile them to being ruled by the King of France. When they returned to their homes and in due course assumed positions of political leadership, they would, so he hoped, work to integrate their provinces into the kingdom. There was, in other words, an element of socio-political engineering in the foundation of the college. He left instructions as to its administration and teaching. He also ensured that the college was well provided for financially, and bequeathed to it his library. Shortly after his death a committee, which included Colbert, was charged by the king to oversee the building of the college. A site of considerable symbolic significance was chosen on the opposite bank of the Seine from the Louvre; when it was completed in 1668 the college faced the Louvre, thereby testifying to the close relationship that had existed between Mazarin and Louis XIV. The task of constructing the college was conferred on Louis le Vau, who had already undertaken several prestigious projects. The design embodied Mazarin's Baroque tastes: the central feature was the chapel crowned by a large dome, and from the façade at the front projected two curved arms which reached towards the river.

The Collège des Quatre Nations (now the Institut de France) still stands as one of the finest Baroque buildings in Paris, but its near-uniqueness is also an admission that Mazarin ultimately failed in his mission to convert the French. French architecture in the second half of the seventeenth century did retain some elements of Baroque (especially in the sheer scale on which buildings were constructed, Versailles being the supreme example), but it adapted Baroque to 'native' traditions and forms, so that even though one might still, in some cases, attach the appellation 'Baroque', one would not refer to it as 'Roman'.

Mazarin, so sensitive to the political possibilities inherent in the patronage of the visual arts, showed nothing like the same enthusiasm for the world of literature, even though he accumulated a large library. It was significant that, whereas he accepted the role of protector of the Académie Royale de Peinture, he was never protector of the Académie Française. Mazarin had no objection to literary patronage as such, and he certainly had no inherent objection to writers (even though many had attacked him in the Mazarinades). The main problem was one of finance. Richelieu had distributed financial gifts and pensions, from government funds, to selected writers, but in the late 1640s and early 1650s, the government was in a permanent state of near-bankruptcy. It was in such desperate straits that Mazarin cut back on official literary patronage. He tried to improve the situation towards the end of the 1650s, but it was only in the following decades that the crown once again made the patronage of writers and scholars a high priority.

Mazarin's Family and his Wealth

Mazarin would not have been a man of his times had he not used his position in government to further the careers and interests of other members of his family. As in so many other respects, he could look to the example of Richelieu in France and the Barberinis in Rome. Richelieu, as we have seen, conferred largesse on his nephews, nieces and other relations. Urban VIII had been a blatant nepotist in Rome, promoting and rewarding his nephews to an extent that brought retribution from Innocent X; but Urban's alleged misbehaviour was a matter of scale, not of principle. Mazarin regarded it as natural that he too should extend protection to his nephews and nieces. He did so by bringing them to France.[6] Mazarin had two sisters: one, Girolama, married Lorenzo Mancini, a Roman nobleman, and the other, Margarita, married Vincenzo Martinozzi. Between them they had nine children (Girolama seven and Margarita two), who travelled to France to be educated and then 'placed' by their uncle.[7]

The first batch arrived in 1647, and the others followed after the Frondes. Mazarin negotiated several spectacular marriages for his nieces, upon whom he conferred large dowries. While these matches unquestionably enhanced the standing and prosperity of the family, they also advanced Mazarin's political interests, for some were arranged with former Frondeurs and served to effect reconciliation between Mazarin and some of his earlier enemies. Such was the case, for example, with Anne-Marie Martinozzi, elder daughter of Margarita and Vincenzo Martinozzi, who in 1654 married no less a notability than Armand de Bourbon, Prince de Conti. In view of the fact that Mazarin had imprisoned him during the Frondes, and that Conti had been one of the principal minister's most obdurate opponents, this looks a surprising match; but it conferred prestige on the Mazarin clan and Conti was rewarded with command of the army in Catalonia, the presidency of the Estates of Languedoc and the governorship of Guyenne. Simply to list the marriages of the other nieces tells the story of their social ascension. Laure Mancini married Louis de Vendôme, Duc de Mercoeur; Olympe became Comtesse de Soissons; Hortense married Armand Charles de la Porte de la Meilleraye, Duc de Mazarin; and Marianne married Maurice-Godefroy de la Tour d'Auvergne, Duc de Bouillon. Two nieces entered into distinguished Italian matches: Laura Martinozzi with Alfonso IV, Duke of Modena, and Marie Mancini, who had a passionate love affair with the young Louis XIV, with Lorenzo Colonna, Duke of Talliaco and Constable of the kingdom of Naples (Mazarin doubtless felt satisfaction that this niece should join the family that had been served by Mazarin's father). The title of 'Duc de Nevers' was conferred upon Mazarin's nephew Philippe Mancini. Most of these marriages occurred towards the end of Mazarin's life, by which time his political standing was beyond question and he was in a position to back them with ample financial allurements. The extended family of Mazarin, like that of Richelieu, entered the ranks of the aristocratic elites of French society.

All of his nieces and nephews received bequests in Mazarin's will, although the principal legatees were Hortense and her husband La Meilleraye (who received the title of Duc de Mazarin). There was much confusion surrounding his succession, for his will expressly forbade the drawing up of an inventory of his possessions. The official explanation was that the interests of the state thereby would be served, but in fact it was to prevent a scandal: he was so wealthy that an outcry, and possible legal proceedings, would have followed.[8] Modern estimates put the value of the Mazarin inheritance between 35 million and 40 million livres, of which just over a half was in cash. The remainder was composed of estates (about 5,250,000 livres), residences (almost 1,500,000 livres), payments on his ministerial responsibilities (over 2,600,000 livres), the paintings, statues, tapestries and other adornments of his properties (over 4,400,000 livres), and other possessions including his books and manuscripts (about 325,000 livres). Mazarin's fortune was far in excess of the 20 million left by Richelieu, which in itself was considered an enormous sum; that of Mazarin was equal to about half of the government's budget for 1661.

Herein lies one of the paradoxes of the 1640s and 1650s: there was an invidious contrast between the crown's inability to fund its policies efficiently (as testified by the bankruptcy of 1648), and Mazarin's accumulation of wealth on a gargantuan scale. He does not seem to have been troubled in his conscience by the extravagant scale of his acquisition and expenditure, any more than by his 'selling' of his nieces in the aristocratic marriage mart. In the post-Fronde years he behaved in Paris much as the Barberinis had done in Rome, augmenting his fortune and audaciously promoting the interests of his family. It is not too much of an exaggeration to say that, in his latter years, he was the 'Urban VIII' of Paris.

If anybody knew the details of how Mazarin had built up his fortune it was Colbert and Fouquet. In 1661, Louis XIV retained these two figures in his service, but later in the year Fouquet was arrested on a charge of plotting insurrection and of having engaged in financial peculation. The former *surintendant des finances* was found guilty and incarcerated until the end of his life (Colbert being heavily implicated in Fouquet's downfall), but there is much evidence that his real 'crime' was that he knew too much about Mazarin's fortune, its size and the means whereby it had been amassed. Since neither Louis XIV nor Colbert trusted him to remain silent, he had to be removed from the political scene.[9]

When Mazarin died in 1661, there was no sense of political excitement or relief reminiscent of that occasioned by Richelieu's demise in 1642. The very ease with which Louis XIV took over personal control of government was perhaps a tribute to Mazarin's success in bringing the regime and the kingdom through the trials and tribulations of the 1640s and 1650s. The competence and efficiency with which Louis XIV handled government, even though he was still in his early twenties, also was testimony to Mazarin who, in earlier years, had taken the young king into council meetings, educated him in the ways of domestic politics and international relations, and ensured that he had a good grasp of the history of France (or at least of the actions of his predecessors, and of their strengths and weaknesses), and knew about rulers in other parts of Europe, the problems they faced and the measures they took to overcome them. In 1661 Louis XIV came to government well prepared, both in techniques of governing and administration and in the understanding which he had of the great issues of the day. The transfer of political power in 1661 ran smoothly, the disposal of Fouquet being the only serious rupture in the ministerial team which Mazarin bequeathed. Louis XIV began his personal reign under favourable political circumstances and over later years naturally acquired greater experience until he became probably the best informed and most competent ruler in Europe. It was Mazarin who prepared him for rulership and in so far as Louis deserved the epithet 'le Grand', it was in no small measure a retrospective recognition of the preparatory work of Mazarin.

Chapter 13: Conclusion: the Cardinals in Retrospect

The public careers of Richelieu and Mazarin are integral to the political history of France from the early 1620s to the beginning of the 1660s. The two cardinal-ministers, more than any other individuals, shaped and manipulated the historical forces which have provided much of the subject matter of this book. How may we summarise and assess the historical significance of their careers? One comment must be that Richelieu and Mazarin were central to the evolution of Bourbon monarchy in France during its first few decades. The last Valois king, Henri III, was assassinated in 1589. Henri IV, the first Bourbon King of France, faced formidable difficulties in the immediate aftermath of that tragedy, but as he brought the Wars of Religion to an end and began the daunting task of national recovery, he relied heavily on the assistance and guidance of Maximilien de Béthune, Duc de Sully[1]. Sully may even be seen as a prototype of the new-style ministers; the close collaboration in which Sully, Richelieu and Mazarin engaged with their respective monarchs was instrumental to the shaping of an early Bourbon pattern of government, which paved the way to the personal rule which the mature Louis XIV assumed in 1661.[2]

The era of the principal ministers lasted about sixty years. It was the product of a particular historical context in which a new ruling dynasty, two of whose members succeeded to the throne as minors, had to contend with a complex admixture of social, religious and political problems bequeathed by the Wars of Religion and perpetuated by more immediate

149

controversies and struggles; moreover, these domestic questions had to be confronted against a background of a rapidly deteriorating international situation which, by the late 1620s, was having direct implications for the internal affairs of France. The Bourbon response deemed principal ministers to be indispensable to the process of wrestling with those problems, but by 1661 sufficient progress had been made for Louis XIV to terminate the system. In this regard, the arrest, trial and imprisonment of Fouquet was of paramount significance: in formal terms, he was punished for financial offences, but in Louis XIV's eyes he had committed the political 'crime' of aspiring to become the new 'Richelieu' or 'Mazarin'. The condemnation of Fouquet was an emphatic proclamation that the era of principal ministers had ended; they had served their purpose, had rendered exceptional services to the crown and had been richly rewarded for doing so; but times had changed and they had no place in the political order which Louis XIV was constructing.

The 'system' of the principal ministers depended ultimately on political trust between monarch and minister, especially during periods of adversity. French monarchic rule during this period was intensely personal. For all the talk by Richelieu, Mazarin and others of 'the state' and '*raison d'état*', the structure of politics at the highest levels in France was governed mainly by personal liaisons and mutual obligation. This personal element meant that the political and courtly circles around the king were composed of contending and mutually suspicious groups driven as much by self-interest as by alternative ideological principles. If Richelieu and Mazarin were to preserve their political standing, it was essential to defend the trust that the king had in them. It was not always easy to do so, for enemies and rivals for the king's affection existed in abundance. In their different ways, Richelieu and Mazarin experienced episodes of potential crisis in their relationship with the king; that they survived was, in the final resort, thanks to the resolution of Louis XIII and Louis XIV, or at least the latter's mother until his majority in 1651. The two kings were persuaded of the imperatives of the *bon Français* policies which their principal ministers pursued; they were convinced that the well-being of crown and kingdom was more assured by them than it would have been by the *dévot* programme of association with the Habsburgs in a grand anti-Protestant alliance, which some opponents of the cardinal-ministers advocated. When serious attempts were made to unseat Richelieu or Mazarin, Louis XIII and Louis XIV stood by their ministers, shielding them against members of the royal family, aristocrats, magistrates and others who attempted to overthrow them.

The personalised character of French government extended to the dealings between Richelieu and Mazarin and the central administrative councils. If the principal ministers were to function efficiently they had to establish mastery over the *conseil d'état* (or *conseil d'en haut*), the *conseil des dépêches* and other bodies by building up teams of *créatures* upon whom they could rely. The enactment of government business depended in no small measure on loyalty or fidelity towards the principal ministers by senior administrators and officers; and the most effective way to guarantee this fidelity was for Richelieu and Mazarin to ensure that their *créatures* were well represented at these elevated levels.

The relative brevity of the period of government through principal ministers, and the dependence of that system on personal relations and networks, suggests another observation: that as far as central government was concerned, the so-called 'ministerial absolutism' of Richelieu and Mazarin was essentially conservative, perhaps even reactionary, both in nature and intent. The principal aim of the ministers was to restore royal authority to the point at which the king could rule alone; they did not have a 'ministerial revolution' or 'bureaucratic government' in view. If anything, they aspired to restore an idealised past in which the king's authority supposedly was acknowledged and obeyed throughout the kingdom.

Does this mean, then, that no credence can be extended to claims that the principal ministers were political innovators or that their careers implied new forms of 'absolutist' government? Not entirely, for it is a common historical experience that conservative or reactionary purposes inadvertently can lead to new and radical consequences. It might be pointed out, for example, that the unspectacular social origins of Richelieu and Mazarin made them unlikely candidates for the eminent position which they reached, and that their political ascension involved the exclusion from high office of great aristocrats and princes of the blood (although an exception to this latter trend can be found during the Regency of Anne of Austria, when Gaston d'Orléans served in the *conseil d'état*). It might also be added that, in so far as Louis XIV himself continued to employ ministers from relatively humble backgrounds and to exclude princes of the blood from his *conseil d'en haut*, he preserved novel features of the ministries of Richelieu and Mazarin. However, the significance even of this observation should not be exaggerated. Richelieu's father had served Henri III, and both he and Mazarin were cardinals, an ecclesiastical rank which placed them on a level with princes of the blood in France. Members of the Richelieu and Mazarin families rapidly joined the ranks of the aristocracy either through personal elevation or by marriage; and the same may be said of families of the ministers of Louis XIV after 1661. French government remained 'aristocratic' in ethos, even though the titles of ministers or their relations were of recent creation. When their whole careers are taken into account, it remains difficult to conclude that Richelieu and Mazarin were conscious instruments of a governmental revolution; they sought to control and manipulate time-honoured practices rather than construct a new system.

Their handling of the great law courts, provincial estates, *officiers*, financiers and municipalities likewise cautions against any simple labelling of Richelieu and Mazarin as 'absolutist'. Lacking anything approximating to a modern bureaucracy through which the royal will could be implemented throughout the kingdom, the two ministers had no option but to use a combination of persuasion, negotiation, bribes and threats. Knowing that legal bodies and provincial assemblies would only comply with the royal will in return for concessions (for example, the revision of financial demands downwards), Richelieu and Mazarin had frequent resort to compromise. They were especially cautious in their dealing with frontier provinces, where excessively energetic attempts to impose royal authority could endanger socio-political stability and perhaps even provoke rebellion.

The meeting of the provincial Estates of Languedoc in 1645–6 was characteristic of relations between crown and Estates. Royal commissioners attended the assembly and, after expressing the esteem of the Regent for the province, called on the Estates to vote an extraordinary sum of 1.5 million livres. After proclaiming their loyalty to the king, the Estates pleaded extreme poverty and offered only 600,000; the commissioners responded by proposing to reduce regular taxation in the province over the next few years by 3 million livres if the Estates would agree to the 1.5 million now; even payment over two years would be acceptable; but the Estates dug in their heels: they were respectful of the king, but were in no position to raise the extraordinary levy. When they disbanded in March 1646, agreement with the commissioners had not been reached, and the matter was left for another day.[3] On the other hand, provincial Estates and other bodies did recognise that their resistance to the crown should have limits; if not, the crown would, if necessary, impose punitive measures. The province of Normandy discovered this after the revolt of the *Nu-Pieds* in 1639 and so did the city of Marseille in 1660.

Are there grounds for presenting the *intendants* as evidence of 'absolutist' intentions on the part of Richelieu and Mazarin? Here again a distinction must be drawn between intent and outcome. The *intendants* were the cause of many grievances and much opposition from provincial bodies, legal as well as financial. Legal and financial *officiers* regarded them as interlopers who usurped the legitimate functions of *officiers*; and it is significant that one of the chief demands of the Chambre Saint Louis in 1648 was that the *intendants* should be disbanded: they had no place in the regular or traditional exercise of financial and legal administration. They were regarded as instruments through which Richelieu and Mazarin usurped legal and financial powers. This 'constitutional' objection had a certain point and cannot be dismissed simply as self-interest posing as principle. It was not so much the existence of the *intendants* which caused offence – there was a long history of the crown employing special commissioners to fulfil specific missions – as their increasing tendency to assume the functions of magistrates and financial *officiers*. This was a difficult issue to resolve at the theoretical level. The crown could argue that all law and administration was administered on behalf of the king; that normally the king delegated these functions to the law courts and ordinary financial bodies, but that he could confer them on others if he wished. In reply, *officiers* could contend that tradition conferred legitimacy on the normal judicial and financial procedures; that procedures were 'normal' precisely because the king's predecessors had found them to be effective and equitable; that the present king was being misled by his principal minister into thinking that an increasing use of *intendants* was politically necessary; and that the *intendants* in reality were a recipe for political and administrative chaos.

During the Frondes, the crown apparently gave in on the matter of the *intendants* and abolished most of them as the Chambre Saint Louis had insisted. Nevertheless, they were gradually reintroduced in the 1650s, and during Louis XIV's personal reign became a permanent feature of provincial administration. Whether Richelieu and Mazarin themselves were aiming at this outcome is another matter. The two ministers considered them essential to the government of France during the war-torn 1620s, 1630s and 1640s, but it is conceivable that they regarded them as temporary expedients, to be scaled down when peaceful conditions had been achieved. It was Louis XIV's choice to expand the use of *intendants*, although even then he and his ministers constantly urged the *intendants* to cooperate with local authorities, avoid confrontation and take every opportunity to emphasise their role as agents of liaison between a benevolent king and his obedient subjects.[4]

Richelieu and Mazarin helped to lay the foundations of absolute monarchy in France in so far as they imposed the effective authority of the king over his subjects; nevertheless they considered this to be a task of restoration, not innovation. Neither of them was a radical reformer of institutions. They both manipulated institutions to the limit, and it might even be argued that one reason for the Frondes was that the relatively inexperienced Mazarin overstepped the mark. He went too far in his 'absolutist' dealings with the *parlements* and other bodies and turned what had only been a potential conflict under Richelieu – this minister being sufficiently skilled to hold it in check – into the actual crisis of 1648. After 1653, Mazarin worked to create a spirit of accommodation with the Parlement of Paris.[5] He refrained from attempting to infiltrate his own *créatures* into the Parlement, and the crown also cut back on its interventions into the regular judicial processes. On its side the Parlement, as it saw its judicial functions increasingly being respected by the crown, had fewer occasions to have recourse to remonstrance or otherwise resist the royal will. By the 1660s, crown and Parlement were carefully refraining from trespassing on each other's territory, and when Louis XIV issued his famous instruction in 1673 that in future, the Parlement of Paris should remonstrate only after having registered legislation, this was not the explosive issue that it would have been thirty years before.

One realm in which Richelieu and Mazarin failed to provide Louis XIV with a significantly improved inheritance was public finance. The pressures of circumstance, especially warfare, had prevented them from making any notable headway towards the structural reforms which were so desperately needed. They had become so dependent on extraordinary revenues, that the 'extraordinary' was in danger of becoming the ordinary. The problem of how to fund government and its policies, especially in time of warfare, was just as intractable after 1661 as it had been in the 1620s. After the overthrow of Fouquet, Jean-Baptiste Colbert assumed direction of finances, and in the 1660s he not only made commendable progress towards reducing the crown's debt, but began to work towards precisely the kinds of fiscal reforms which might provide the king with a more reliable tax base. Unfortunately for Colbert's plans, Louis XIV engaged in war against Spain again from 1666 to 1668 and against the Dutch Republic and its allies from 1672 to 1678. Colbert's reforms probably could have withstood the effects of the short war against Spain, but the Dutch War wrecked his plans. He was driven back to the old fiscal devices, and found himself resorting to the discredited practices of Richelieu and Mazarin. The financial demands of government revived the power and influence of *traitants*, whose loans became essential to the funding of policy; the condition of French governmental finances by the 1690s was little different from what it had been fifty or sixty years before.

The preceding pages have employed such terms as 'absolutist' and 'absolute monarchy', but in this concluding discussion the question of 'absolutism' and the significance of Richelieu and Mazarin for this supposed historical phenomenon should be considered, albeit briefly.[6] 'Absolutism' and 'absolute monarchy' were derogatory phrases invented by French revolutionaries of 1789 to discredit the *ancien régime* (another label concocted by revolutionaries); in place of 'absolute monarchy', revolutionaries claimed to be creating 'constitutional monarchy'. By the second half of the nineteenth century, when the specific historical conditions which generated the term 'absolute monarchy' had disappeared, the phrase nevertheless had passed into common historical vocabulary, and may be considered to have acquired both a chronological meaning and a meaning signifying a system of government. As regards chronology, 'absolute monarchy' in France allegedly was coterminous with Bourbon rule: it was supposedly created, developed and perfected during the reigns of Louis XIII through to Louis XVI; then it was terminated by the Revolution. With regard to content, 'absolutism' was viewed by later historians as a system of government in which the king and his ministers consciously aspired to surround the king with a monarchic theory which not only placed all sovereignty in his hands, but all power as well, and which denied his subjects any right of legal resistance; as power increasingly was concentrated in the king, the 'rights and liberties' of provincial bodies, be they legal, financial or administrative, were systematically diminished, the functions of provincial bodies steadily being assumed by royal agents, the *intendants*: in short, 'absolutism' led to 'centralisation'. As French monarchy became ever more 'absolute', it supposedly alienated large segments of French society and its exploitation of the resources of the country in pursuit of a grandiose foreign policy turned it into a parasitic institution which, in the end, could not be reformed, but had to be dispensed with through revolution.

This programmatic view of 'absolute monarchy' has the attraction of concision, and it is one which affords Richelieu and Mazarin crucial roles in its early phases; indeed, as recently as 1992 the historian Yves-Marie Bercé could write a book entitled *La Naissance Dramatique de l'Absolutisme (1598–1661)*, in which the reality of absolutism was taken for granted, and in which Richelieu and Mazarin were key figures. It is fair to say that over the last twenty years or so, other historians, especially from the

English-speaking world, have challenged this traditional view of absolutism. Quite apart from the question of anachronism whereby eighteenth-century revolutionaries and nineteenth-century historians imposed upon the seventeenth century a concept of which Richelieu, Mazarin and their contemporaries were unaware, it seems to most present-day scholars that, as this study has contended, Louis XIII and even Louis XIV and their ministers saw themselves less as innovators than as restorers. Of course, they had an eye to the future; all governments do so. But they understood the future, not in terms of a 'new monarchy', but of a traditional monarchy which in the recent past, most notably because of the Wars of Religion, had been seriously undermined. The phrase 'absolute monarchy' has passed into common usage and doubtless will continue to be employed; but as many of the pages of this present study have attempted to demonstrate, it needs to be understood in its historical context and shorn of the tendentious meanings which so often have been attached to it.

If the two principal ministers can be attributed with making progress towards the restoration of royal authority and with having bequeathed Louis XIV a France which, while not entirely stable in socio-political terms, was less turbulent than for many decades, what may be said about their record in international relations? Had France's international standing been notably improved as a result of their policies? There are some obvious senses in which an answer must be in the affirmative. By 1659, France's frontiers were more secure than ever before. Territorial acquisitions along the frontier with the Spanish Netherlands, and in the north-east and the south, had given Louis XIV control of most of the 'gates' between France and its neighbours. France had also become pro-tector to several imperial territories in the western marches of the Holy Roman Empire; and the Peace of the Pyrenees had created a satisfactory *modus vivendi* with Spain. The Peace of Oliva (1660) enhanced France's international prestige: that France had successfully mediated the peace was a tribute to its standing and influence.

The foreign policies of Richelieu and Mazarin had borne fruit in another sense: they placed beyond serious question the proposition that *bon Français* imperatives must govern France's relations with other states. Both ministers signed alliances with Protestant states – Sweden, the Dutch Republic, England (even the Commonwealth) – and justified them in *bon Français* terms. To all intents and purposes this phrase had a similar meaning to that of *raison d'état*, except that it avoided the taint of Machiavellianism. It appealed to a nascent patriotism, a sense that it was the visible, tangible kingdom of France with its land and people, not some abstract concept of 'the state', whose interests determined foreign policy. By the time of Louis XIV's personal reign, the claims that foreign policy should be shaped according to religious criteria had lost their appeal and he was able to calculate his actions in the light of purely dynastic, political or diplomatic considerations. Yet wherein lay France's true interests after 1661?

Under Richelieu and Mazarin, foreign policy was conditioned by powerful, external factors, of which Habsburg hegemony in western Europe was by far the most exacting. In 1661, Spain remained a major power (it is a mistake to assume that its later decline was self-evident in 1661), but Richelieu and Mazarin had placed Louis XIV in an advantageous position, allowing him to make strategic choices rather than be restricted to the constant necessity of reacting to others. The character of French foreign policy changed after 1661. It became a search for new long-term strategies, which were not easy to decide. Should Louis XIV aim to replace Habsburg hegemony with that of France, or should he aim at a 'balance of power' in Europe; what emphasis should be placed on maritime affairs as against commitments on mainland Europe; and how important were the colonies to France's international standing: were they useful but disposable assets, or were they in any sense essential to French interests? To one historian, no French government after 1661, let alone that of Louis XIV, resolved these questions satisfactorily. Louis XIV, Louis XV, Louis XVI and even Napoleon oscillated between contending options to the ultimate detriment of French interests. Foreign policy after 1661 may be characterised as a failure by this great power to develop a consistent and coherent set of priorities;[7] but this is to take the discussion well beyond the careers of Richelieu and Mazarin, and later failures of policy cannot be laid at their door. What should be confirmed, however, is the judgement that the two cardinal-ministers left France at a strategic juncture in the history of its international relations.

So much may be said regarding consequences for France of the combined careers of Richelieu and Mazarin, but how do they compare with each other? Were there any significant differences between them, or should Mazarin be seen in all essential points simply as the continuation of Richelieu? The broad character and purposes of foreign and domestic policy demonstrate obvious respects in which Mazarin was the perpetuation of his predecessor; nevertheless there are certain topics on which speculation is justified as to whether Richelieu, had he lived, would have followed the same course as Mazarin. In domestic affairs, for example, one might ask whether Richelieu would have allowed the Frondes to occur? Since his experience of government and his knowledge of the French social, legal and financial elites was so much greater than that of Mazarin, would he have seen the coming crisis and taken preventive action, be it coercive or concessionary? Even if he had faced a Fronde, would he have handled it in the same way as Mazarin, or would he have succeeded in snuffing it out quickly? The Frondes with which Mazarin contended lasted five years; would they have done so under Richelieu? Although these questions take us into the realm of counter-factual speculation and therefore do not admit of other than hypothetical answers, they testify to possible divergences between Richelieu and Mazarin, and suggest that Mazarin's response to the internal crisis of the late 1640s and early 1650s bore his personal stamp.

Similarly in foreign affairs, the principal question attaches to the peace negotiations in Westphalia. Could Richelieu, had he been alive, have reached peace with Spain; and if so, on what terms? Any answer to these questions must depend upon certain assumptions, notably that the military situation in 1648 would have been the same under Richelieu as it was under Mazarin. If that supposition is made, then two other issues arise: first, would Richelieu have made the marriage between Louis XIV and Maria Teresa a condition of peace (this was a major stumbling block in the actual negotiations in 1648) or would he have withdrawn the demand; secondly – and this repeats what has just been said about the Frondes – would he have avoided the internal crisis of that year, a crisis which in reality encouraged the Spanish to continue the war; if so, would the Spanish, whose own internal problems were formidable, have cut their losses and signed a peace?

Returning to domestic politics, there is one subject on which Richelieu and Mazarin possibly held somewhat different views: religion in its socio-political context. In his treatment of the Huguenots, Richelieu was guided by *bon Français* principles: he severely curtailed their military independence, but left them their rights of worship as stated in the Edict of Nantes. Mazarin's difficulties were not with the Huguenots, whom he continued to treat as Richelieu had done, but with the Jansenists. As stated in an earlier chapter,[8] Mazarin emerged from the Frondes with a strong distaste for Jansenism and its acolytes. Jansenists, in his view, were not only suspect in their religious orthodoxy, but untrustworthy in their political commitments; and the fact that many aristocrats were Jansenists made the movement potentially all the more dangerous. He conveyed these fears to Louis XIV, and advised the king to root out Jansenism when circumstances were propitious. Jansenism, he argued, was not just a religious phenomenon; it carried dangerous political implications and therefore must be eliminated. Louis XIV heeded the warning and in due course did turn on the Jansenists; with the support of Rome, albeit sometimes reluctant, he subjected them to fierce persecution and, at least to his own satisfaction, eliminated them as a source of possible political opposition. Jansenism nevertheless survived in France; it turned into a movement of underground criticism of the Bourbon regime and made its own distinctive contribution to the complex tenor of French legal and intellectual debate in the eighteenth century.

In other respects Richelieu and Mazarin were of a piece. In part this might be explained through their personal acquaintance, and the reverence in which the latter held the former; but their similarity also arose out of the assumptions of the day as their conduct conformed to that of most great ministers of the period. They accumulated wealth systematically and left colossal fortunes; they patronised learning and the visual arts and left a fine architectural heritage. Their Parisian palaces have been transformed, but one can still acquire an impression of their size and splendour: the present-day Palais Royal retains the scale of Richelieu's palace, and the premises of the Bibliothèque Nationale in the rue de Richelieu are still redolent of the Palais Mazarin (not least in that they contain original paintings on some of the ceilings). Richelieu and Mazarin paid close attention to the social ascension of their nieces and nephews by marrying them into some of the most prestigious families in France. The personalities of Richelieu and Mazarin were somewhat different, for although they generated extreme sentiments in others, whether of esteem or of detestation, it is fair to say that Mazarin occasioned nothing like the fear that Richelieu struck into his opponents. Mazarin, to many of his enemies, was just another charming but devious Italian who took his chances in France, but Richelieu, even to his fiercest opponents, was a figure of outstanding political stature and domineering will, whom one crossed at one's peril.

Their contrasts notwithstanding, Richelieu and Mazarin jointly made contributions of lasting importance to the evolution of the French kingdom and with justification are numbered among the political giants of that century. History is much more than the sum of the actions of exceptional men and women, but equally does it transcend the mechanical operation of geographic, climatic, economic or any other deterministic forces. Richelieu and Mazarin, like their contemporaries, were faced with forces often beyond their control, but what is of interest to the historian is the response these ministers made to their particular historical contexts, and the measures they took to achieve their policy objectives. Therein lies their abiding attraction to scholars in the past and the present; and there is every reason to suppose that Richelieu and Mazarin will prove equally compelling to historians in the future.

Significant Dates

1585	9 September: birth of Richelieu.
1601	27 September: birth of Louis XIII.
1602	14 July: birth of Mazarin.
1606	17 April: in Rome, Richelieu inaugurated as Bishop of Luçon.
1610	14 May: Henri IV assassinated; Louis XIII becomes king. 15 May: Marie de' Medici becomes Regent. 26 July: Concino Concini enters the *conseil d'état*. 17 October: coronation of Louis XIII.
1614	2 October: majority of Louis XIII declared. 27 October: Estates General opens; Richelieu attends as member of First Estate (the Clergy).
1615	23 February: Richelieu addresses Estates General before its closure. August: Condé leads rebellion. 28 November: marriage of Louis XIII and Anne of Austria.
1616	1 September: arrest of Condé. 25 November: Richelieu enters *conseil d'état* for the first time.
1617	24 April: Concini assassinated. 3 May: Marie de' Medici retires to Blois, accompanied by Richelieu. 15 June: Richelieu leaves Blois and returns to his diocese. 8 July: Leonora Galigaï, widow of Concini, executed.

1618   Luynes presides over *conseil d'état*.
        7 April: Richelieu exiled to Avignon.

1619   21–2 February: Marie de' Medici escapes from Blois and joins
        Épernon at Angoulême.
        7 March: Richelieu receives instructions to leave Avignon and
        negotiate peace between Louis XIII and Marie de' Medici.
        30 April: Treaty of Angoulême between king and his mother.

1620   June: new phase of aristocratic rebellion begins.
        10 August: Treaty of Angers restores peace.
        September–19 October: Louis XIII occupies Béarn and unites
        it with France.
        25 December: Huguenot assembly at La Rochelle decides upon
        armed resistance to crown.

1621   April: Louis XIII and Luynes march against the Huguenots;
        Saumur taken, but siege of Montauban fails (August–November).
        15 December: death of Luynes.

1622   Royal campaigns against Huguenots continue.
        10 June: massacre at Nègrepelisse.
        5 September: Richelieu becomes Cardinal.
        18 October: Treaty of Montpellier between crown and Hugue-
        nots.

1623   7 February: Treaty of Paris.
        France forms league with Venice, Savoy and Grisons to resist
        Spain in Valtelline.

1624   January–February: dismissal of Brûlart de Sillery and his sup-
        porters.
        29 April: Richelieu brought into *conseil d'état* for second time.
        13 August: Richelieu becomes head of *conseil d'état* and principal
        minister.

1625   January: Rohan and Soubise engage in rebellion.
        11 May: marriage of Henriette de France and Charles I of
        England.

1626   5 March: Treaty of Monzón between France and Spain.
        19 August: execution of Chalais for plotting against Richelieu.
        July–August: creation of Compagnie du Morbihan.
        October: Richelieu becomes Grand Maître de la Navigation.

1627 20 March: France breaks with England and signs alliance with Spain.
22 June: execution of Montmorency-Boutteville and Chapelles for having fought a duel.
30 June: English fleet appears before La Rochelle.
25 July: Buckingham lands on île de Ré.
10 September: siege of La Rochelle by royal forces begins.
25 December: death of Vincent II, Duke of Mantua.

1628 28 October: La Rochelle surrenders.
1 November: Louis XIII and Richelieu enter La Rochelle.

1629 15 January: Code Michau published.
Spring–Summer: Louis XIII campaigns against Huguenots.
28 June: Peace of Alès redefines place of Huguenots in society.
21 November: Richelieu officially designated as 'principal minister of state'.
26 November: Richelieu created a Duke.

1630 29 January: first meeting between Richelieu and Mazarin.
31 March: French army takes Pinerolo.
27 February: revolt begins in Dijon.
25 July: Louis XIII arrives in Lyon and remains until autumn;
September: Louis XIII suffers severe illness.
26 October: Mazarin secures truce at Casale between French and Imperial forces.
10 November: Marie de' Medici breaks with Richelieu.
11 November: Day of Dupes leads to confirmation of Richelieu in office.

1631 18 January: Mazarin arrives in Paris for first time, to negotiate peace in Italy.
23 January: Treaty of Barwälde creates alliance between France and Sweden.
30 January: Gaston d'Orléans leaves the royal court.
3 February: anti-fiscal riots in Paris begin.
31 May: alliance between France and Bavaria.
19 June: Treaty of Cherasco; France retains Pinerolo and Casale, and the Duc de Nevers is recognised as Duke of Mantua.
18 July: Marie de' Medici escapes from France to the Spanish Netherlands and is joined by Gaston d'Orléans.

1632   3 January: secret marriage between Gaston d'Orléans and Marguerite de Lorraine.
26 June: Louis XIII imposes treaty of Liverdun on Charles IV of Lorraine.
June–August: Henri de Montmorency, assisted by Gaston d'Orléans, raises rebellion in south-west.
September–October: rebellion suppressed and Gaston flees again.
16 November: Gustavus Adolphus of Sweden killed at battle of Lützen.

1633   September: Louis XIII occupies Lorraine.

1634   25 August: Mazarin sent by Urban VIII on diplomatic mission to France.
20 September: France enters into accord with Sweden and German princes to protect Rhineland.

1635   25 January: creation of Académie Française.
8 February: alliance between France and United Provinces.
May–June: riots in Bordeaux.
19 May: France declares war on Spain.
27 October: alliance between Luis XIII and Prince Bernard de Saxe-Weimar.

1636   January: Mazarin recalled to Rome.
April–May: risings of Croquants in Angoumois.
15 August: Spanish seize Corbie and cause panic in Paris.
10 November: Corbie recaptured by French.

1637   April: risings of Croquants spread to Périgord.
11 December: the 'Vow' of Louis XIII, who devotes his kingdom to the Virgin Mary.

1638   16 March: France and Sweden renew alliance.
March: victories of Bernard of Saxe-Weimar in Rhineland.
5 September: birth of Louis XIV.
7 September: defeat of French at Fuenterrabia.
19 December: Bernard of Saxe-Weimar takes Breisach.

1639   7 June: French army defeated at Thionville.
16 July: rising of the Nu-Pieds begins at Avranches and spreads to other parts of Normandy.

18 July: death of Bernard of Saxe-Weimar.
21 October: victory of the Dutch over the Spanish fleet at the Battle of the Downs.
14 December: Mazarin leaves Rome for the last time and goes to France.

1640   March: revolt of the Nu-Pieds finally suppressed.
7 June: beginning of revolt in Barcelona against Philip IV of Spain, which spreads to rest of Catalonia.
13 June–8 August: French besiege and take Arras.
21 September: birth of Philippe, brother of Louis XIV and future Duc d'Orléans.
December: rising in Portugal against Philip IV of Spain.

1641   1 February: alliance between France and Portugal.
1 August: Pope Urban VIII condemns Jansen's *Augustinus*.
19 September: Louis XIII agrees to become 'Count of Barcelona'.
15 December: Mazarin created a cardinal.

1642   13 June: arrest of Cinq-Mars and De Thou.
3 July: Marie de' Medici dies at Cologne.
12 September: execution of Cinq-Mars and De Thou.
4 December: death of Richelieu.
5 December: Mazarin enters *conseil d'état*.

1643   19 January: papal bull *In Eminente* denounces Jansenism.
21 April: baptism of Louis XIV; Mazarin is godfather.
14 May: death of Louis XIII, succession of Louis XIV.
18 May: Anne of Austria assumes regency; Mazarin retained as principal minister.
19 May: French victory at battle of Rocroi.
July–September: rise and fall of 'Cabale des Importants'; rising of Croquants of Rouergue.
September–December: preliminary peace talks in Westphalia.

1644   3–8 August: French victory at battle of Fribourg.
12 September: Turenne takes Philippsburg.
December: formal peace talks begin in Westphalia.

1645   13 August: Treaty of Brömsebro between Sweden and Denmark, mediated by Mazarin.

1646   June–October: French successes in Spanish Netherlands:
            Courtrai (29 June), Furnes (7 September), Dunkirk (11 October)
            taken.
            8 October: French take Piombino.
            26 December: death of Duc de Condé.

1647   13 March: armistice signed at Ulm between France, Sweden,
            Bavaria and other German territories; Bavaria breaks the
            truce in the autumn.
            18 July: Particelli d'Emery appointed *surintendant des finances*.

1648   15–16 January: Parlement forced to register creation of new
            offices; then annuls registration; Fronde of the Parlement
            begins.
            30 January: peace between Spain and Dutch Republic.
            13 May: Arrêt d'Union, Parlement of Paris joins forces with
            other courts in Chambre Saint Louis.
            2 July: Chambre Saint Louis presents charter for reform.
            9 July: dismissal of Particelli.
            13 July: abolition of *intendants* (except in frontier provinces).
            26 August: arrest of Broussel and other *parlementaires*.
            27–8 August: barricades erected in Paris; Broussel released.
            22 October: crown concedes demands of Chambre Saint Louis.
            24 October: treaties of peace signed in Westphalia.

1649   5–6 January: royal family leaves Paris and goes to Saint-
            Germain.
            29 March: Bordeaux declares solidarity with Fronde of Paris.
            1 April: Peace of Rueil between crown and Fronde of the
            Parlement.
            18 August: royal court returns to Paris.

1650   18 January: arrest of Condé, Conti and Longueville; their
            supporters in provinces raise rebellion.
            February–April: court travels to Normandy and Burgundy to
            pacify country.
            22 June: 'Ormée' movement founded in Bordeaux.
            5 October: king and Queen Mother enter Bordeaux.

1651   February: union of Frondes of Princes and the Parlement.
            6–7 February: Mazarin leaves Paris and goes to Germany.
            13 February: Condé, Conti, Longueville released from prison.

16 February: triumphant return of these princes to Paris.
7 September: majority of Louis XIV proclaimed in Parlement of Paris.
22 September: Condé arrives in Bordeaux, which declares in his favour.

1652　28 January: Mazarin returns and joins royal court at Poitiers.
18 May: Spanish retake Gravelines.
2 July: after several defeats by crown forces Condé retreats into Paris.
4 July: attack on Paris Hôtel de Ville by supporters of princes; princes impose their regime over the city.
19 August: Mazarin goes into exile for second time.
16 September: Spanish retake Dunkirk.
13 October: Condé leaves Paris and flees to Spanish Netherlands.
21 October: Louis XIV and royal court re-enter Paris; Spanish retake Casale.

1653　3 February: Mazarin returns to Paris.
July: end of Ormée of Bordeaux.
9–26 September: Louis XIV present at siege and capture of Mouzon.
27 November: Louis XIV present at surrender of Sainte-Menehould.

1654　7 June: coronation of Louis XIV at Rheims.
6 August: Louis XIV present at capture of Stenay.

1655　14 July: capture of Landrecies by French.
3 November: commercial accord between France and England by Treaty of Westminster.

1656　23 January: Pascal publishes the first of his pro-Jansenist *Lettres Provinciales*.
July: Turenne fails to take Valenciennes.

1657　3 March: Anglo-French alliance formed by treaty of Paris.
6 August: Louis XIV present at capture of Montmédy.

1658　April–August: revolt of Sabotiers in Sologne.
June–July: Louis XIV seriously ill, but recovers.
14 June: French victory at Battle of the Dunes near Dunkirk.

23 June: French take Dunkirk and hand it to the English.

14 August: League of the Rhine formed, joined by France.

December: Louis XIV meets Marguerite of Savoy and marriage discussions take place; Spanish approach with offer of marriage between Louis XIV and Maria Teresa.

1659   7 May: France and Spain cease fighting.

16 October: Marseille in rebellion, royal orders publicly torn up.

7 November: Peace of the Pyrenees between France and Spain.

1660   2 March: Louis XIV enters Marseille.

3 May: France mediates Peace of Oliva between Sweden, Poland and Brandenburg.

5 June: Treaty of Copenhagen between Sweden and Denmark.

9 June: marriage of Louis XIV and Maria Teresa in Saint-Jean-de-Luz.

1661   9 March: death of Mazarin.

10 March: Louis XIV announces that he will govern personally.

1 April: marriage of Philippe d'Orléans (brother of Louis XIV) and Henrietta of England (sister of Charles II).

Glossary

aides	duties on wine and other commodities
conseil d'en haut	see *conseil d'état*
conseil d'état	the king's inner council
don gratuit	money voted to the crown by a provincial Estate or some other body, usually in lieu of taxes
élections	areas of royal fiscal administration; subdivisions of *généralités*
fermiers	tax farmers who bought from the government the right to collect certain taxes
gabelle	a tax on salt
généralités	main areas of royal financial administration (sub-divided into *élections*)
gouvernements	areas of military importance created mostly in the 16th and 17th centuries and administered by governors
lit de justice	ceremony wherein the king personally attended the Parlement of Paris and registered edicts
officiers	the holders of posts in public administration (usually in law and finance)
parlements	senior law courts, of which the Parlement of Paris was the most important
paulette	an annual charge paid by *officiers* and conferring on them *de facto* ownership of their posts
pays d'élections	parts of the country in which taxes were assessed and raised through *élections*
pays d'états	provinces with their own Estates or assemblies
rentes	government bonds

taille   the main direct tax, assessed sometimes on individuals
                         (*taille personnelle*), sometimes on property (*taille réelle*)
traites   customs duties on goods entering France, and also
                         on goods passing between some provinces
vénalité d'offices   the sale, by the crown, of public offices

Notes

Chapter 1: The Government of France

1. The notion of France in crisis is examined in the essays in P. J. Coveney (ed.), *France in Crisis, 1620–1675* (London, 1977).
2. The king's inner council had no formal title; that of *conseil d'état* was common, but it was also referred to as the *conseil secret* or, later in the century, the *conseil d'en haut*; in this book it will be referred to as the *conseil d'état*.
3. Henri III, father of Francis II, Charles IX and Henri III, was killed while taking part in a tournament in 1559.
4. The *gouvernements* in the early 1600s were Brittany, Burgundy, Champagne, Dauphiné, Guyenne, Île-de-France, Languedoc, Lyonnais, Normandy, Orléanais, Picardy, Provence.
5. They were at Paris, Toulouse, Grenoble, Bordeaux, Dijon, Aix, Rouen, Dombes and Rennes.
6. J. Russell Major, *From Renaissance to Absolute Monarchy: French Kings, Nobles and Estates* (Baltimore, 1994), pp. 237–8.
7. W. Doyle, 'Colbert et les Offices', in *Histoire, Économie et Société*, no. 4 (2000), 469–70.

Chapter 2: Richelieu: Bishop and Emerging Political Leader

1. Details are in J. Bergin, *Cardinal Richelieu: Power and the Pursuit of Wealth* (London, 1985), pp. 23–32.

2. The following information is from ibid., pp. 32–4.

3. In the early seventeenth century the diocese generated about 8000 livres in revenues, a figure which put it among the poorer dioceses (J. Bergin, *The Making of the French Episcopate, 1689–1661* (London, 1996), p. 111).

4. Formally, French bishops had to be at least 26 years old at the time of nomination (30 in other parts of Europe), but between 1601 and 1620, twenty-six under-age bishops were nominated in France; thereafter the incidence declined and the norms were almost always respected. Richelieu's nomination, while unusual, occurred at a time when Rome was willing to tolerate such exceptions (Bergin, *The Making of the French Episcopate*, pp. 298–301).

5. Richelieu wrote theology himself, his best known works being *Les Principaux Poincts de la Foy de l'Église Catholique* (1618) and the *Instruction du Chrétien* (1621); for a discussion of Richelieu as a theologian, see J. de Viguerie, 'Richelieu Théologien', in R. Mousnier (ed.), *Richelieu et la Culture* (Paris, 1987), pp. 29–42.

6. Although he had not yet adopted the name of this family estate, the term henceforth will be used since this is the name by which Armand-Jean is best known.

7. The Oratory, in its 'modern' form, was a movement founded in Italy around the middle of the sixteenth century by St Philip Neri. Its aim was to revitalise the priesthood and laity alike, especially, although not exclusively, through pastoral work, prayer and education. Neri's movement inspired Pierre Bérulle to establish the French Oratory.

8. They can be followed in J. M. Hayden, *France and the Estates General of 1614* (Cambridge, 1974).

9. It was there Richelieu wrote *Les Principaux Poincts de la Foy de l'Église Catholique*.

10. A more detailed account is in A. D. Lublinskaya, *French Absolutism: The Crucial Phase, 1620–1629* (Cambridge, 1968), pp. 243–71.

11. D. J. Sturdy, *The d'Aligres de la Rivière: Servants of the Bourbon State in the Seventeenth Century* (Woodbridge, 1986), pp. 31–3.

12. They were Phélypeaux d'Herbault (for Spain, Italy, Switzerland and the Valtelline), Potier d'Ocquerre (for Germany, Poland, the Dutch Republic and the Spanish Netherlands) and La Ville-sux-Clercs (for England, Turkey and the Levant), see Lublinskaya, *French Absolutism*, p. 259.

Chapter 3: Richelieu as Minister

1. See below, pp. 54, 62–3, 150. Key works on this subject include W. F. Church, *Richelieu and Reason of State* (Princeton, 1972), and E. Thuau, *Raison d'État et pensée politique à l'Époque de Richelieu* (Paris, 1966).

2. Niccolò Machiavelli (1469–1527), Italian statesman and author of, among many other works, *Il Principe* [*The Prince*] (first published 1532), which was condemned by Pope Clement VIII.

3. P. Grillon (ed.), *Les Papiers de Richelieu*, vol. i (Paris, 1975), p. 207.

4. L. Moote, *Louis XIII, the Just* (Berkeley, CA, 1989), pp. 165–6.

5. Marie de Montpensier died the following year giving birth to a daughter, Anne-Marie-Louise (known under Louis XIV as 'La Grande Mademoiselle').

6. On duels, see F. Billacois, *The Duel: Its Rise and Fall in Early Modern France* (London, 1990).

Chapter 4: The First Years of Richelieu's Ministry, 1624–30

1. The Holy Roman Emperor was elected by seven Electors: three prelates, the archbishops of Mainz, Trier and Cologne, and four secular rulers, the King of Bohemia, the Margrave of Brandenburg, the Count Palatine of the Rhine and the Duke of Saxony. By the seventeenth century the custom had grown whereby the Electors signalled their intention, eventually, to elect the heir apparent as Emperor, by first choosing him King of the Romans (an honorific title); before doing so, the Electors normally secured concessions from the existing Emperor, and promises from the heir apparent.

2. In fact the Electors still refused to do so.

3. P. Grillon (ed.), *Papiers de Richelieu*, vol. i (Paris, 1975), pp. 243–4.

4. Ibid., vol. ii, pp. 650–1.

5. The progress of the siege and the treatment of the defeated rebels can be followed in ibid., vol. iv (1980), pp. 322–63, 408–9.

6. On the *chambre* and its work, see R. Bonney, *The King's Debts: Finance and Politics in France, 1589–1661* (Oxford, 1981), pp. 117–21.

7. Ibid., p. 121.

8. On these figures see O. Ranum, *Richelieu and the Councillors of Louis XIII: A Study of the Secretaries of State and Superintendents of Finance in the Ministry of Richelieu, 1635–1642* (Oxford, 1963).

9. See above, p. 13.

10. R. and S. Pillorget, *France Baroque, France Classique, 1589–1715* (2 vols, Paris, 1995), vol. i, pp. 267–9.

Chapter 5: Richelieu and French Foreign Policy, 1630–42

1. Gaston was allowed to return to France in October 1634 on condition that he acknowledge that his marriage was invalid. However, after the birth of Louis XIV in 1638 Louis XIII withdrew his objection and recognised Marguerite as Duchesse d'Orléans.
2. For an assessment of the imperial position in 1630, see R. G. Asch, *The Thirty Years War: The Holy Roman Empire and Europe, 1618–48* (London, 1997), pp. 92–3.
3. A summary of the treaty and extracts from its terms are in M. Roberts (ed.), *Sweden as a Great Power, 1611–1697* (London, 1968), pp. 136–7.
4. Gustavus had been succeeded by his infant daughter Christina.
5. For a discussion of these arguments, see Asch, *Thirty Years War*, pp. 120–5.
6. J. A. Lynn, *Giant of the Grand Siècle: The French Army, 1610–1715* (Cambridge, 1997), pp. 42–4.
7. Ibid., pp. 477–8.
8. On this subject, see P. Castagnos, *Richelieu face à la mer* (Rennes, 1989).
9. Outlines are in R. J. Knecht, *Richelieu* (London, 1991), chap. 7; Asch, *Thirty Years War*, pp. 117–33; G. Parker, *The Thirty Years War* (London, 1984), pp. 144–53, 162–70.
10. J. I. Israel, *The Dutch Republic: Its Rise, Greatness, and Fall, 1477–1806* (Oxford, 1995), pp. 528–31.
11. Contemporary opinions for and against Richelieu's foreign policy are discussed in W. F. Church, *Richelieu and Reason of State* (Princeton, 1972), pp. 372–415.
12. See above, pp. 28–9.
13. A concise outline of modern interpretations for and against Richelieu is in Asch, *Thirty Years War*, pp. 117–25.

Chapter 6: Richelieu and the Internal Government of France

1. The principal *surintendants* during Richelieu's ministry were Effiat (1626–32), Bullion (1632–40) and Bouthillier (1640–3).
2. These figures (rounded up and down) are from R. Bonney, *The King's Debts: Finance and Politics in France, 1589–1661* (Oxford, 1981),

pp. 304–5. They must be used with care, for they represent estimates of what was raised, and not of amounts that actually reached
the government.

3. J. Russell Major, *From Renaissance to Absolute Monarchy: French Kings, Nobles and Estates* (Baltimore, 1994), pp. 268–82.

4. On the origins and development of the *intendants*, see B. Barbiche, *Les Institutions de la Monarchie Française à l'Époque Moderne* (Paris, 1999), pp. 382–9, and R. Bonney, *Political Change in France under Richelieu and Mazarin, 1624–1661* (Oxford, 1978), pp. 29–56.

5. Bonney, *Political Change in France*, p. 30.

6. Ibid.

7. These instructions are printed in L. du Crot, *Le Nouveau Traité des Aydes, Tailles et Gabelles* (Paris, 1636).

8. D. J. Sturdy, 'Tax Evasion, the *Faux Nobles*, and State Fiscalism: the Example of the *Généralité* of Caen, 1634–35', in *French Historical Studies*, IX, no. 4 (1976), pp. 549–72.

9. A. Guéry, 'Les Finances de la Monarchie Française sous l'Ancien Régime', in *Annales ESC*, no. 2 (1978), p. 236.

10. This term of abuse was first used against them by an artisan in 1636; the standard work on the rising is Y.-M. Bercé, *Histoire des Croquants. Études des Soulèvements populaires dans le sud-ouest de la France* (2 vols, Geneva, 1974).

11. On the Nu-pieds, see, M. Foisil, *La Révolte des Nu-Pieds et les Révoltes Normandes de 1639* (Paris, 1970).

12. E. Thuau, *Raison d'État et Pensée Politique à l'époque de Richelieu* (Paris, 1966), p. 169.

13. J. Klaits, *Printed Propaganda under Louis XIV: Absolute Monarchy and Public Opinion* (Princeton, NJ, 1976), pp. 7–8.

14. On Renaudot and the *Gazette*, see H. M. Solomon, *Public Welfare, Science and Propaganda in Seventeenth-Century France* (Princeton, NJ, 1972).

15. An assessment of Lemercier is in A. Blunt, *Art and Architecture in France, 1500–1700* (London, 1953), pp. 117–21.

Chapter 7: Richelieu: an Assessment

1. Parrott, *Richelieu's Army*.

2. Bergin, *Cardinal Richelieu: Power and the Pursuit of Wealth* (London, 1985); the author's conclusions are summarised in chapter 7, on which the following comments are based.

3. An interesting analysis of Richelieu's personality (compared, in this case, with his Spanish equivalent and rival, Olivares) is in J. H. Elliott, *Richelieu and Olivares* (Cambridge, 1984), chapter 1, and J. H. Elliott, 'Richelieu, l'homme', in R. Mousnier (ed.), *Richelieu et la Culture* (Paris, 1987), pp. 187–98.

Chapter 8: Mazarin: Origins and Early Career

1. In the seventeenth century, this did not mean that he lost his status as a Roman; its principal significance was that he could bequeath property in France and hold benefices there, see G. Dethan, *Mazarin et ses Amis* (Paris, 1968), pp. 169–70.
2. On the international context at this time, see D. J. Sturdy, *Fractured Europe, 1600–1721* (Oxford, 2002), pp. 66–75.
3. See above, p. 34.
4. Dethan, *Mazarin et ses Amis*, p. 180.

Chapter 9: Mazarin in Government and the Conduct of War

1. For an analysis of the French negotiating position and its evolution between 1645 and 1648, see A. Osiander, *The States System of Europe, 1640–1990: Peacemaking and the Conditions of International Stability* (Oxford, 1994), pp. 26–7, 66–72.
2. See above pp. 27–32.
3. The Dutch position can be traced in J. I. Israel, *The Dutch Republic: Its Rise, Greatness, and Fall, 1477–1806* (Oxford, 1997), pp. 524–5, 596–7.
4. R. Bonney, *The King's Debts: Finance and Politics in France, 1589–1661* (Oxford, 1981), pp. 197–8.

Chapter 10: The Frondes

1. A recent exposition of this subject is O. Ranum, *The Fronde: A French Revolution* (New York, 1993), especially chapters 4 and 5.
2. Analyses of the reasons for the Parisian uprising of 1648 are in Ranum, *The Fronde*, chapter 5, and R. and S. Pillorget, *France Baroque, France Classique, 1589–1715* (2 vols, Paris, 1995), pp. 488–96.

3. On the Mazarinades, see C. Jouhaud, *Les Mazarinades: la Fronde des Mots* (Paris, 1985); H. Carrier, *La Presse de la Fronde, 1648–1653. Les Mazarinades*, vol. 1 (Paris, 1989); *La Conquête de l'Opinion*, vol. 2 (Paris, 1991); H. Carrier, *Les Mures Guerrières: les Mazarinades et la Vie Littéraire au Milieu du XVIIe Siècle* (Paris, 1996).

4. *Lettres de cachet* were orders carrying the royal signature and authorising the arrest and imprisonment of a named person, without going through the normal judicial procedures.

5. The course of the Fronde in Bordeaux can be followed in Ranum, *The Fronde*, chaps 7 and 8, and in W. Beik, *Urban Protest in Seventeenth-Century France: The Culture of Retribution* (Cambridge, 1997), chapter 10, and S. Westrich, *The Ormée of Bordeaux* (Baltimore, 1972).

6. D. J. Sturdy, *The d'Aligres de la Rivière: Servants of the Bourbon State in the Seventeenth Century* (Woodbridge, 1986), pp. 124–9.

7. Ibid., p. 135.

8. Its full title was *Jugement de tout ce qui a esté imprimé contre le Cardinal Mazarin, depuis le sixième janvier, jusques à la déclaration du premier avril mil six cens quarante-neuf*.

9. This theme is developed in O. Ranum, *Artisans of Glory: Writers and Historical Thought in Seventeenth-Century France* (Chapel Hill, NC, 1980); see also P. Burke, *The Fabrication of Louis XIV* (London, 1992).

Chapter 11: Mazarin, Foreign Policy and Domestic Tensions

1. R. Jackson, *Vive le Roi! A History of the French Coronation from Charles V to Charles X* (Chapel Hill, NC, 1984), p. 169.

2. For a recent concise account of Jansenism, see W. Doyle, *Jansenism: Catholic Resistance to Authority from the Reformation to the French Revolution* (London, 1999).

3. An outline of policy is in R. Bonney, *The King's Debts: Finance and Politics in France, 1589–1661* (Oxford, 1981), Chapter 6.

4. On this subject, see especially R. Pillorget, *Les Movements Insurrectionnels de Provence entre 1596 et 1715* (Paris, 1975), pp. 751–862, and S. Kettering, *Judicial Politics and Urban Revolt in Seventeenth-Century France* (Princeton, NJ, 1978), Chapter 9.

5. A detailed account of the marriage and its attendant celebrations is in C. Dulong, *Le Mariage du Roi-Soleil* (Paris, 1986).

Chapter 12: Mazarin as Patron and Collector

1. On Sixtus V and the planning of Rome see S. Giedion, *Space, Time and Architecture: The Growth of a New Tradition* (Oxford, 1962), pp. 91–106, and A. G. Dickens, *The Counter-Reformation* (London, 1968), pp. 139–43.
2. Mazarin's championing of the Baroque is discussed in M. Laurain-Portemer, 'Mazarin, Militant de l'Art Baroque au Temps de Richelieu (1634–1642)', in *Société de l'Histoire de l'Art Français* (Paris, 1976), pp. 65–100, and the same, 'La Politique Artistique de Mazarin', in *Il Cardinale Mazzarino in Francia* (Rome, 1977), pp. 41–76.
3. See above, p. 79.
4. Bernini visited France in 1665 and drew up plans for extensions to the Louvre, but the plans were rejected (see Blunt, *Art and Architecture in France*, pp. 194–6, 209–13).
5. The fours nations were Alsace, Pignerol, Artois (with Flanders and Hainault) and Roussillon (with Cerdagne).
6. The careers of the nieces can be followed in J. Hillairet, *Les Mazarinettes, ou les Sept Nièces de Mazarin* (Paris, 1976) and Y. Singer-Lecocq, *La Tribu Mazarin: Un Tourbillon dans le Grand Siècle* (Paris, 1989).
7. They were: 1 (children of Margarita and Martinozzi) Anne-Marie, Princesse de Conti (1637–72) and Laura, Duchess of Modena (1640–87); 2 (children of Girolama and Mancini) Laura, Duchesse de Mercoeur (1636–57); Paolo (1636–52); Olympe, Comtesse de Soissons (1638–1708); Marie, Duchesse de Colonna (1639–1715); Philippe, Duc de Nevers (1641–1707); Hortense, Duchesse de la Meilleraye-Mazarin (1646–99); Marianne, Duchesse de Bouillon (1650–1714).
8. On Mazarin's fortune see D. Dessert, 'La Fortune de Mazarin', in J. Cornette (ed.), *La France de la Monarchie Absolue, 1610–1715* (Paris, 1997), 203–14.
9. On Fouquet see D. Dessert, *Fouquet* (Paris, 1997).

Chapter 13: Conclusion

1. On Sully and his services to Henri IV, see D. Buisseret, *Sully and the Growth of Centralised Government in France, 1598–1610* (London, 1968); B. Barbiche, *Sully* (Paris, 1978); also M. Greengrass, *France in the Age of Henri IV: The Struggle for Stability* (London, 1995).

2. On this subject, see R. Bonney, 'Was there a Bourbon Style of Government?', in K. Cameron (ed.), *From Valois to Bourbon: Dynasty, State and Society in Early Modern France* (Exeter, 1989), pp. 161–77.

3. D. J. Sturdy, *The d'Aligres de la Rivière: Servants of the Bourbon State in the Seventeenth Century* (Woodbridge, 1986), pp. 112–17.

4. A summary of the role of the *intendants* under Louis XIV is in D. J. Sturdy, *Louis XIV* (London, 1998), pp. 46–9, 54–5.

5. The following remarks are based on the works of A. N. Hamscher, *The Parlement of Paris after the Fronde, 1653–1673* (Pittsburgh, 1976), and *The Conseil Privé and the Parlements in the Age of Louis XIV: A Study in French Absolutism* (Philadelphia, 1987).

6. The literature on absolutism is considerable, but a good, recent summary of the debates surrounding absolutism is F. Cosandey and R. Descimon, *L'Absolutisme en France: Histoire et Historiographie* (Paris, 2002).

7. J. Black, *From Louis XIV to Napoleon: The Fate of a Great Power* (London, 1999).

8. See above, pp. 128–30.

Select Bibliography

The following bibliography does not claim to be comprehensive. It limits itself to essential works, many of which (especially those published within the last few years) contain up-to-date bibliographical guides. Most of the entries listed below are in English, but some texts in French are included as a basic guide to readers who wish to consult publications by French scholars.

General

Bercé, Y.-M., *La Naissance Dramatique de l'Absolutisme* (Paris, 1992).
Black, J., *From Louis XIV to Napoleon: The Fate of a Great Power* (London, 1999).
Blunt, A., *Art and Architecture in France, 1500–1700* (London, 1953).
Bonney, R., *Political Change in France under Richelieu and Mazarin, 1624–1661* (Oxford 1978).
Bonney, R., *Society and Government in France under Richelieu and Mazarin, 1624–61* (London, 1988).
Briggs, R., *Early Modern France* (Oxford, 1977).
Briggs, R., *Communities of Belief: Cultural and Social Tensions in Early Modern France* (Oxford, 1989).
Cameron, C. and Woodrough, E. (eds), *Ethics and Politics in Seventeenth-Century France* (Exeter, 1996).
Cornette, J. (ed.), *La France de la Monarchie Absolue, 1610–1715* (Paris, 1997).
Cosandey, F. and Descimon, R., *L'Absolutisme en France: Histoire et Historiographie* (Paris, 2002).

Dickens, A. G., *The Counter-Reformation* (London, 1968).

Giedion, S., *Space, Time and Architecture: The Growth of a New Tradition* (Oxford, 1962).

Hanley, S., *The 'Lit de Justice' of the Kings of France: Constitutional Ideology in Legend, Ritual and Discourse* (Princeton, NJ, 1983).

Holt, M. (ed.), *Society and Institutions in Early Modern France* (Athens, Ga, 1991).

Jackson, R., *Vive le Roi! A History of the French Coronation from Charles V to Charles X* (Chapel Hill, NC, 1984).

Mousnier, R., *The Institutions of France under the Absolute Monarchy, 1598–1789* (Chicago, 1979).

Parker, D., *The Making of French Absolutism* (London, 1983).

Parker, D., *Class and State in Ancien Régime France: The Road to Modernity?* (London, 1996).

Parker, G., *The Thirty Years War* (London, 1984).

Parker, G., *European Crisis, 1598–1648* (2nd edn, Oxford, 2001).

Pillorget, R. and S., *France Baroque, France Classique, 1589–1715*, 2 vols (Paris, 1995).

Russell Major, J., *Representative Government in Early Modern France* (New Haven, CT, 1980).

Russell Major, J., *From Renaissance Monarchy to Absolute Monarchy: French Kings, Nobles and Estates* (Baltimore, MD, 1994).

Shennan, J. H., *Government and Society in France, 1461–1661* (London, 1969).

Sturdy, D. J., *Fractured Europe, 1600–1721* (Oxford, 2002).

Tapié, V.-L., *France in the Age of Louis XIII and Richelieu* (Cambridge, 1984).

Wilkinson, R., *France and the Cardinals* (London, 1995).

Financial Affairs

Bonney, R., *The King's Debts: Finance and Politics in France, 1589–1661* (Oxford, 1981).

Collins, J. B., *Direct Taxation in Seventeenth-Century France* (Berkeley, CA, 1988).

Dent, J., *Crisis in Finance: Crown, Financiers and Society in Seventeenth-Century France* (Newton Abbot, 1973).

Dessert, D., *Argent, Pouvoir et Société au Grand Siècle* (Paris, 1984).

Guéry, A., 'Les Finances de la Monarchie Française sous l'Ancien Régime', in *Annales ESC*, no. 2 (1978), pp. 216–39.

Louis XIII and the Royal Family

Bouyer, C., *Gaston d'Orléans, 1608–1660: Séducteur, Frondeur et Mécène* (Paris, 1999).

Chevallier, P., *Louis XIII* (Paris, 1979).

Dethan, G., *Gaston d'Orléans, Conspirateur et Prince Charmant* (Paris, 1959).

Marvick, E., *Louis XIII: The Making of a King* (New Haven, CT, 1986).

Moote, A. L., *Louis XIII, the Just* (Berkeley, CA, 1989).

Richelieu

Asch, R. G., *The Thirty Years War: The Holy Roman Empire and Europe, 1618–48* (London, 1997).

Bergin, J., *Cardinal Richelieu: Power and the Pursuit of Wealth* (London, 1985).

Bergin, J., *The Making of the French Episcopate, 1589–1661* (London, 1996).

Billacois, F., *The Duel: Its Rise and Fall in Early Modern France* (London, 1990).

Carmona, M., *Richelieu: l'Ambition et le Pouvoir* (Paris, 1983).

Carmona, M., *La France de Richelieu* (Paris, 1984).

Castagnos, P., *Richelieu Face à la Mer* (Rennes, 1989).

Church, W. F., *Richelieu and Reason of State* (Princeton, NJ, 1972).

Duccini, H., *Concini* (Paris, 1991).

Elliott, J. H., *Richelieu and Olivares* (Cambridge, 1984).

Grillon, P. (ed.), *Les Papiers de Richelieu* (Paris, 1975–), vols 1–6.

Harding, R., *Anatomy of a Power Elite: The Provincial Governors of Reformation France, 1542–1635* (New Haven, CT, 1978).

Hayden, J. M., *France and the Estates General of 1614* (Cambridge, 1974).

Hildesheimer, F., *Richelieu: Une Certaine Idée de l'état* (Paris, 1985).

Israel, J. I., *The Dutch Republic: Its Rise, Greatness, and Fall, 1477–1806* (Oxford, 1995).

Klaits, J., *Printed Propaganda under Louis XIV: Absolute Monarchy and Public Opinion* (Princeton, NJ, 1976).

Knecht, R. J., *Richelieu* (London, 1991).

Levi, A., *Cardinal Richelieu and the Making of France* (London, 2001).

Lublinskaya, A. D., *French Absolutism: The Crucial Phase, 1620–29* (Cambridge, 1968).

Lynn, J. A., *Giant of the Grand Siècle: The French Army, 1610–1715* (Cambridge, 1997).

Marvick, E., *The Young Richelieu* (Chicago, 1983).

Mousnier, R. (ed.), *Richelieu et la Culture* (Paris, 1987).

Parrott, D., *Richelieu's Army: War, Government and Society in France, 1624–1642* (Cambridge, 2001).

Ranum, O., *Richelieu and the Councillors of Louis XIII: A Study of the Secretaries of State and Superintendents of Finance in the Ministry of Richelieu, 1635–1642* (Oxford, 1963).

Ranum, O., *Artisans of Glory: Writers and Historical Thought in Seventeenth-Century France* (Chapel Hill, NC, 1980).

Solomon, H. M., *Public Welfare, Science and Propaganda in Seventeenth-Century France* (Princeton, NJ, 1972).

Sturdy, D.-J., 'Tax Evasion, the *Faux Nobles*, and State Fiscalism: The Example of the *Généralité* of Caen, 1634–35', in *French Historical Studies*, IX, no. 4 (1976), pp. 549–72.

Sturdy, D. J., *The d'Aligres de la Rivière: Servants of the Bourbon State in the Seventeenth Century* (Woodbridge, 1986).

Tapié, V.-L., *France in the Age of Louis XIII and Richelieu* (London, 1974).

Thuau, E., *Raison d'état et Pensée Politique à l'Époque de Richelieu* (Paris, 1966).

Treasure, G. R. R., *Cardinal Richelieu and the Development of Absolutism* (London, 1972).

Woodrough, E., 'The Political Testaments of Richelieu and La Rochefoucauld', in C. Cameron and E. Woodrough (eds), *Ethics and Politics in Seventeenth-Century France* (Exeter, 1996), pp. 65–81.

Society and Social Protest

Beik, W. H., *Absolutism and Society in Seventeenth-Century France: State Power and Provincial Aristocracy in Languedoc* (Cambridge, 1985).

Beik, W., *Urban Protest in Seventeenth-Century France: The Culture of Retribution* (Cambridge, 1997).

Bercé, Y.-M., *Croquants et Nu-pieds: Les Soulèvements Paysans en France au XVIIe Siècle* (Paris, 1974).

Bercé, Y.-M., *Histoire des Croquants: Étude des Soulèvements Populaires au XVIIe Siècle dans le Sud-Ouest de la France*, 2 vols (Geneva, 1974).

Coveney, P. J. (ed.), *France in Crisis, 1620–1675* (London, 1977).

Foisil, M., *La Révolte des Nu-Pieds et les Révoltes Normandes de 1639* (Paris, 1970).

Jouanna, A., *Le Devoir de Révolte. La Noblesse Française et la Gestation de l'état Moderne* (Paris, 1989).

Kettering, S., *Judicial Politics and Urban Revolt in Seventeenth-Century France: The Parlement of Aix, 1629–1659* (Princeton, NJ, 1978).

Kettering, S., *Patrons, Brokers and Clients in Seventeenth-Century France* (Oxford, 1986).

Kettering, S., *French Society, 1589–1715* (Harlow, 2001).

Ligou, D., *Le Protestantisme en France de 1598 à 1715* (Paris, 1968).

Mousnier, R., *Peasant Uprisings in Seventeenth-Century France, Russia and China* (London, 1960).

Parker, D., *La Rochelle and the French Monarchy: Conflict and Order in Seventeenth-Century France* (London, 1980).

Pillorget, R., *Les Mouvements Insurrectionnels de Provence entre 1596 et 1715* (Paris, 1975).

Porchnev, B., *Les Soulèvements Populaires en France de 1623 à 1648* (Paris, 1963).

Taveneaux, R., *Le Catholicisme dans la France Classique (1610–1715)*, 2 vols (Paris, 1980).

The Young Louis XIV and the Royal Family

Bluche, F., *Louis XIV* (Oxford, 1990).

Burke, P., *The Fabrication of Louis XIV* (London, 1992).

Dulong, C., *Anne d'Autriche, Mère de Louis XIV* (Paris, 1984).

Dulong, C., *Le Mariage du Roi-Soleil* (Paris, 1986).

Dunlop, I., *Louis XIV* (London, 1999).

Kleinman, R., *Anne of Austria* (Columbus, OH, 1985).

Meyer, J., *La Naissance de Louis XIV* (Brussels, 1989).

Petitfils, J.-C., *Louis XIV* (Paris, 1995).

Sturdy, D. J., *Louis XIV* (London, 1998).

Mazarin

Bertière, A., *Le Cardinal de Retz* (Paris, 1977).

Bordonove, G., *Mazarin: le Pouvoir et l'Argent* (Paris, 1996).

Burke, P., *The Fabrication of Louis XIV* (London, 1992).

Carrier, H., *La Presse de la Fronde, 1648–1653*, vol. 1: *Les Mazarinades* (Paris, 1989); vol. 2: *La Conquête de l'Opinion* (Paris, 1991).

Carrier, H., *Les Mures Guerrières: Les Mazarinades et la Vie Littéraire au Milieu du XVIIe Siècle* (Paris, 1996).

Dessert, D., *Fouquet* (Paris, 1997).

Dethan, G., *Gaston d'Orléans, Conspirateur et Prince Charmant* (Paris, 1959).

Dethan, G., *Mazarin et ses Amis* (Paris, 1968).

Dethan, G., *Mazarin, un Homme de Paix à l'Age Baroque* (Paris, 1981).

Dethan, G., *La Vie de Gaston d'Orléans* (Paris, 1992).

Doyle, W., *Jansenism: Catholic Resistance to Authority from the Reformation to the French Revolution* (London, 1992).

Dulong, C., *La Fortune de Mazarin* (Paris, 1990).

Dulong, C., *Mazarin* (Paris, 1999).

Golden, R., *The Godly Rebellion: Parisian Curés and the Religious Fronde, 1652–1662* (Chapel Hill, NC, 1981).

Hamscher, A. N., *The Parlement of Paris after the Fronde, 1653–1673* (Pittsburgh, PA, 1976).

Hamscher, A. N., *The Conseil Privé and the Parlements in the Age of Louis XIV: A Study in French Absolutism* (Philadelphia, 1987).

Hillairet, J., *Les Mazarinettes, ou les Sept Nièces de Mazarin* (Paris, 1976).

Jansen, P., *Le Cardinal Mazarin et le Mouvement Janséniste Français* (Paris, 1967).

Jouhaud, C., *Les Mazarinades: la Fronde des Mots* (Paris, 1985).

Laurain-Portemer, M., 'Mazarin, Militant de l'Art Baroque au Temps de Richelieu (1634–1642)', in *Société de l'Histoire de l'Art Français* (Paris, 1976), pp. 65–100.

Laurain-Portemer, M., 'La Politique Artistique de Mazarin', in *Il Cardinale Mazzarino in Francia* (Rome, 1977), pp. 41–76.

Michel, P., *Mazarin, Prince des Collectionneurs* (Paris, 1999).

Moote, A. L., *The Revolt of the Judges: The Parlement of Paris and the Fronde, 1643–52* (Princeton, NJ, 1971).

Osiander, A., *The States System of Europe, 1640–1990: Peacemaking and the Conditions of International Stability* (Oxford, 1994).

Pernot, M., *La Fronde* (Paris, 1994).

Pernot, M., 'Le Rôle Politique du cardinal de Retz', in *XVIIe Siècle*, no. 3 (1996), pp. 623–32.

Ranum, O., *The Fronde: A French Revolution* (New York, 1993).

Singer-Lecocq, Y., *La Tribu Mazarin: un Tourbillon dans le Grand Siècle* (Paris, 1989).

Treasure, G. R. R., *Mazarin: The Crisis of Absolutism in France* (London, 1995).

Watts, D. A., *Cardinal de Retz: The Ambiguities of a Seventeenth-Century Mind* (Oxford, 1980).

Westrich, S. A., *The Ormée of Bordeaux: A Revolution during the Fronde* (Baltimore, MD, 1972).

Index